Managing The School Age Child With A Chronic Health Condition

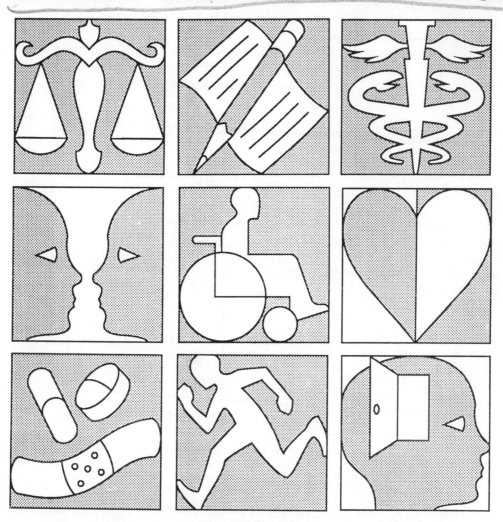

A Practical Guide For Schools, Families And Organizations

Edited By Georgianna Larson, R.N., P.N.P., M.P.H.

A Cooperative Effort Of PATHFINDER° And The School Nurse Organization of Minnesota

DCI Publishing

This manual was developed through grant funding from #MCJ-273206 and 273812, U.S. Department of Health and Human Services, Public Health Service, Health Resource and Services Administration, Bureau of Maternal and Child Health.

Library of Congress Cataloging–in–Publication Data

Managing the school age child with a chronic health condition.
    (DCI Publishing)
    Includes bibliographies and index.
    1. School hygiene—United States—Handbook, manuals, etc. 2. Chronically ill children—Medical care—United States—Handbooks, manuals, etc. I. Larson, Georgianna. II. Series.
LB3416.M36   1988   371.7'12   87-36411
ISBN 0-937721-29-8

Published by DCI Publishing, A division of Diabetes Center, Inc., Box 739, Wayzata, Minnesota 55391

Design and Production: MacLean & Tuminelly

Printed in the United States of America.

10 9 8 7 6 5 4 3 2 1

Table of Contents

PART THREE: BASIC CARE GUIDELINES

Chapter 17
Assessing and Managing Tactile Deficit 187

Chapter 18
The Bowel Training Program..191

Chapter 19
Guidelines for Diapering...195

Chapter 20
Stoma Care for Students with Ostomies..199

Chapter 21
Intermittent Catheterization for Urine...207

Chapter 22
Guidelines for Handling Body Fluids in Schools.................................213

Acknowledgements

This manual represents a joint effort between PATHFINDER, a community network project for children with chronic health conditions, and the School Nurse Organization of Minnesota.

Special thanks go to copy editor Douglas Toft.

PATHFINDER (5000 West 39th Street, Minneapolis, Minnesota, 55416) is a cooperative effort of the MINCEP Epilepsy Centers, Gillette Children's Hospital and the International Diabetes Center of Park Nicollet Medical Foundation. Funding for PATHFINDER has come from the Bureau of Maternal and Child Health, federal Department of Health and Human Services, Special Projects of Regional and National Significance (MCJ-273206-03-0 and 273-812-01-0).

To the contributors—individually acknowledged on the Contributors page—I offer my deepest thanks. They put forth a monumental effort to move this manual from concept to reality. Without their efforts, it would not exist.

Georgianna Larson, R.N., P.N.P., M.P.H.
Executive Director
PATHFINDER

PATHFINDER Sponsoring Organizations:

MINCEP Epilepsy Centers
  2701 University Avenue Southeast
  Minneapolis, Minnesota 55414

Gillette Children's Hospital
  200 East University Avenue
  St. Paul, Minnesota 55101

International Diabetes Center
  Park Nicollet Medical Foundation
  5000 West 39th Street
  Minneapolis, Minnesota 55416

Contributors

Mary Kay Albanese, B.S., Rehabilitation Engineer, Orthotics and Prosthetics Lab, Gillette Children's Hospital, St. Paul, Minnesota

Barbara Balik, R.N., M.S., Vice President for Nursing, Minneapolis Children's Medical Center, Minneapolis, Minnesota

Mary Billington, R.N., School Nurse, Moundsview Public Schools, Moundsview, Minnesota

Elaine Brainerd, M.A., R.N., Connecticut Department of Education, Hartford, Connecticut

Mary Coleman, O.T.R., Occupational Therapist, White Bear Lake Public Schools, White Bear Lake, Minnesota

Clara Gray, R.N., School Nurse, Moundsview Public Schools, Moundsview, Minnesota

Broatch Haig, R.D., C.D.E., Director of Outreach Services, International Diabetes Center, Minneapolis, Minnesota

Patti Jacobson, R.N., M.S., C.P.N.P., Director of Nursing, ATVI, Rice Lake, Wisconsin

Diane Jones, B.S., R.N., Head Nurse, Camp Super Kids, American Lung Association of Hennepin County, Minneapolis, Minnesota

Nancy Kern, R.N., B.S.N., Nursing Consultant, Services for Children with Handicaps, Minnesota Department of Health, Central District, St. Cloud, Minnesota

Susan Lapakko, C.R.T.T., Consultant, Pulmonary Services in the Community, Minneapolis, Minnesota

Georgianna Larson, R.N., P.N.P., M.P.H., Executive Director, PATHFINDER , Minneapolis, Minnesota

Rebecca Lucas, R.P.T., M.S., Physical Therapist, Bridgeview School, St. Paul, Minnesota

Ruth Ellen Luehr, R.N., M.S., Consultant, Health Service/Health Promotion in the School and Community, St. Paul, Minnesota

Kathleen Lytle, R.N., B.A., Head Nurse, Courage Center, Minneapolis, Minnesota

Pam McCullouch, R.N., Head Nurse, Inpatient Care, Shriner's Children's Hospital, Minneapolis, Minnesota

Richard Nelson, M.D., Director, Child Health Specialty Clinics, University

Richard Nelson, M.D., Director, Child Health Specialty Clinics, University of Iowa Hospitals and Clinics, Iowa City, Iowa

Karen Ostenso, R.P.T., B.S., Physical Therapist, Gillette Children's Hospital, St. Paul, Minnesota

Jennifer Phillips, B.S., Speech and Hearing Clinician, Special Education District 916, White Bear Lake, Minnesota

Naomi Quinnell, R.N., B.S.N., Minnesota Department of Health, Public Health Nursing Division (Retired)

Patty Rezabek, R.N., M.A., Coordinator of School Health Services, Minnetonka Public Schools, Minnetonka, Minnesota

Carolyn Jones-Saete, R.N., Gillette Children's Hospital, St. Paul, Minnesota

Cyndy Schuster Silkworth, R.N., M.P.H., C.S.N.P., School Nurse, White Bear Lake Public Schools, White Bear Lake, Minnesota

Marian Sheehan, Ph.D., Speech and Language Pathologist, Seattle Children's Hospital, Seattle, Washington

Eileen Stever, R.N., B.S.N., School Nurse, St. Paul Public Schools, St. Paul, Minnesota

Barbara White, O.T.R., Occupational Therapist, Minneapolis Children's Medical Center, Minneapolis, Minnesota

Introduction

How to Use This Book

Who Should Use This Book

This book is for anyone who works with school age children with chronic health conditions or physical disabilities. Anyone who plans or delivers services to these children can benefit from this book. This includes the people most directly concerned with the child: parents or guardians.

A primary audience for this book is people in schools: teachers, principals, administrators, school nurses, aides, assistants, other health professionals.

However, the ideas in this book still apply to people who work with students outside the formal school setting. Examples are those who work in a YMCA, YWCA, day care, summer camp or any similar organization. For brevity we use the word "student" when referring to the child, but don't let that limit your thinking about our scope.

In any case, this is primarily a manual for "people in the trenches"—those who work directly with students and parents. The language has been simplified so that both health professionals and those without medical training will be able to understand the content. Our goal is a practical book, one that will be referred to often.

What This Book Includes

Again, this book is meant to be practical. You'll find illustrations and step-by-step instructions that tell you what to do when dealing with a chronic health condition or physical disability. We've tried to keep medical jargon at a minimum and include only information that's directly relevant.

Even though the book is written for the "layperson," you'll still find information on a wide range of health conditions and physical disabilities:

- Is there a student with diabetes in your group? You'll find ideas on planning for this student and what to do about low or high blood sugar in Chapter 8.

- Did you feel at a loss when one of your students had an asthma attack? Instructions for managing asthma and avoiding asthma attacks are included in Chapter 7.

- Do you have to give medication to a student? You'll find guidelines for this crucial task in Chapter 12.

These are just a few examples of topics covered. Here are the main sections and what they include:

Part One: Planning School Health Services describes the leading role the school plays in planning services for students with chronic health conditions or physical disabilities. This part of the book explains what's involved in planning these services. You'll also find guidelines for making buildings more accessible for the physically handicapped.

Other chapters in Part One offer ideas for using services in the wider community, considering psychosocial issues, using a case management approach and promoting self care.

Part Two: Selected Health Conditions aims at increased understanding of four health conditions: asthma, diabetes epilepsy (seizure disorder) and AIDS. Here you'll find information on what these conditions are and what you can do to help students manage them.

Part Three: Basic Care Guidelines contains instructions for daily care procedures. Chapters in this section focus on hand washing, medication and feeding through a gastrostomy tube. Also included are chapters on helping students with sensory impairment (vision, hearing, touch) and speech and language difficulties.

Personal care is the main topic in the remainder of this section: procedures for bowel training, diapering, stoma care, catheterization, handling body fluids, respiratory therapy and tracheostomy care.

Part Four: Mobility and the Student with Physical Limitation starts from one basic point: Students with chronic health conditions and physical disabilities differ widely in their mobility. In this section you'll find a framework for dealing with this issue, including how to work with students at five basic levels of mobility.

Closely related are three other topics: sports and extracurricular activities; using equipment commonly known as "aids for daily living"; and adaptive sitting and standing devices. Each subject is addressed in this section.

Part Five: Guidelines for Orthopedic Care includes instructions on how to use orthoses (devices that straighten or correct a body part) and prostheses (devices that replace a missing body part). The final chapter in this section lists guidelines for cast care.

Part Six: Guidelines for Emergency Conditions will help you act effectively when certain health conditions require immediate action. Included here are instructions for dealing with severe allergic reactions, autonomic hyperreflexia, cardiac arrest and obstructed airway. Emergency procedures related to asthma, diabetes and seizure disorder are also included.

The basic message of this section is that you need to know what to do in a health-related emergency. Everyone who works with students should be trained in these procedures--a basic goal for the school nurse or other qualified health professional. Use the instructions in this section to supplement the procedures you already have—or to develop new ones.

How to Use This Book

Certain features of this book are designed to help you find and retain the information you need:

- Each section begins with an overview of topics discussed in the following chapters.

- Each chapter begins with an overview ("In This Chapter You'll Find....") and ends with a summary of the major points.

- The Glossary (before the Index and near the back of the manual) lists definitions for key terms.

- The Index (the last section of the manual) lists page references for major topics.

- The "For Further Reading" sections at the end of many chapters list sources you can turn to for added information.

- Procedures are written in a numbered, step-by-step format, set off from the body of the text. The key action to be performed is explained in the first sentence after each number. Other explanation and illustration follow.

Caution: Work With a Health Professional

One point must be underscored: This manual provides general guidelines and basic overviews of key health topics. *It is not meant to replace instructions from a student's parents or physician. Also, it must not replace instructions from a nurse or other qualified health professional.*

No one can become an expert, for example, in suctioning a tracheostomy tube or handling a seizure simply by reading about these topics. Instead, intensive training and practice are needed.

Use the information in this manual as a starting point, a basic guide and a supplement. Then work closely with students, parents and health care providers to provide the best environment for all students—including those with chronic health conditions or physical disabilities.

A Final Note: The Role of the Schools

The authors of this manual recognize that schools are not in the business of health care delivery. Rather, schools are the place where students with chronic health conditions learn. The basic point is this: To optimize learning, school personnel must, when needed, attend to health needs. This manual aims simply to reinforce that effort.

Part One

Planning School Health Services

Part One

Planning School Health Services

Students with serious chronic health conditions or disabilities are a relatively new presence in many schools. Educators do not have to feel threatened by this development. Instead, they can meet the needs of these students by carefully anticipating those needs. That means planning.

But how is such planning done? Part One of this manual is a response.

Chapter 1 begins with the words, "Community schools will never be the same," setting the tone for the rest of Part One. Students with chronic health conditions are a new presence in the schools, and this chapter sums up the new issues that result.

Chapter 2 focuses on the key role of educators as observers of student behavior—a critical source of information for physicians, therapists and other health professionals who work with students. Here you'll find guidelines on how to refer students for health services, where to get health information and how to incorporate it into an educational plan.

Chapter 3 addresses another critical area of concern: accessibility. Buildings without elevators, doors that cannot be opened with an artificial limb, stairways without handrails—each of these omissions is a real, physical barrier to many students with disabilities or chronic health concerns. In this chapter, you'll find a list of key areas to consider when making schools physically accessible to all students.

Chapter 4 reminds us that educators are not alone in responding to children with special needs. A wealth of outside resources exists in nearly every community to help with this task. They range from children's hospitals and community health services to banks, credit unions and local businesses. Too often, the depth and range of these outside resources is forgotten.

Chapter 5 underscores the importance of looking at all the effects of a chronic health condition—including effects on the student's self concept, family and overall development.

Finally, **Chapter 6** reminds us of a crucial goal for everyone with a chronic health condition: self care and independence.

Chapter 1

Community Health Care For Children With Chronic Illness or Disability: A Role for Schools

Richard P. Nelson, M.D.

Students with Chronic Illness or Disability: A New Presence

Community schools will never be the same. Most adult Americans have difficulty recalling a school classmate with a chronic illness or disability. And for good reasons. Until the mid-1970s most children and youth with serious health conditions were not in our community schools. They were in residential institutions, at special schools or at home.

What happened? There is no single answer. Advances in medical knowledge and technology in preceding decades now enable more children to lead functional and normal daily lives. The child with diabetes can avoid debilitating cycles of ketosis and hypoglycemia. The child with epilepsy can be seizure-free. The orthopedically disabled child is now mobile in physically accessible environments.

There are more examples of the impact of improved health care management on school participation. Yet they provide only a partial explanation for the current presence of children with chronic health conditions in our schools. Larger answers are found in the movement that has fostered greater understanding of the needs and rights of children with special health problems or disability.

Sustained advocacy punctuated by landmark court decisions culminated in the passage of the federal Education for All Handicapped Children Act (PL 94-142) in 1975. Suddenly *every* school-aged child in America was entitled to a free, appropriate public education in the least restrictive setting. Children with special needs were to now learn in schools with other children, often in the same classroom. Today's children are increasingly accustomed to the sight of a classmate with a hearing aid or a wheelchair.

The Issue: Adequate Services

Practical controversies generally revolve around immediate dilemmas. In schools there are special issues. A major issue centers on school health services. Faced with restricted budgets, many districts throughout the county deleted school nurse positions.

The "traditional" school nurse maintained student health records, tended to minor emergency care, and was a caretaker to children and liaison with families when children became acutely ill at school. Few procedures requiring technical expertise were carried out at school. The school nurse was generally minimally involved in classroom health education. Training and experience were highly variable.

School boards noted this situation—an increase in nurse paper work and decrease in "people" work. The boards instructed administrators to replace registered or licensed nurses with less expensive paraprofessional personnel. Boards also have contracted with public health, voluntary or proprietary nursing agencies to provide limited services.

Still, there is a growing realization among health professionals and other providers who care for children with chronic conditions: School health services must be adequate to meet the reasonable care requirements of special-needs children while they are in school. A child with unstable asthma must take medication. A mid-day blood glucose determination may be important to maintain adequate insulin level in a child with diabetes. The child with spina bifida may need several urinary catheterizations. A child in an orthotic device may need a skin check.

Some school districts have protested their responsibility for these services. When the issues have been brought to court for resolution, judges have almost consistently upheld the necessity of the school district to provide a health care procedure when it is vital to assure an appropriate educational program. A homebound program is uniformly viewed as an educationally and socially inferior alternative.

Most schools have been more resilient in their attempt to serve special needs children. Despite considerable obstacles—among them antiquated, inaccessible buildings, lack of trained personnel, inflexible budgets and inexperience—special services administrators seek solutions:

- Classrooms are rearranged to permit wheelchair mobility.

- Students are able to use teacher restrooms when privacy is important.

- Staff members are encouraged to visit health care centers for multidisciplinary staffings and training.

- Community health care professionals are hired as consultants.

- School cafeterias accommodate special diets.

Somehow things are made to work, perhaps but another manifestation of American ingenuity.

Schools and Community Health Care: A Vital Link

Community health care of children and youth with chronic illness or disability can only be accomplished if each aspect of care is workable. What happens at home, at the local doctor's or dentist's office, and at school—each contributes to the totality of health care. Children spend a majority of their waking and learning time in a school during much of the year. If community health care is to be successful, the school must be part of the equation.

Chapter 2

Planning for a Student with a Chronic Health Condition

Ruth Ellen Luehr, R.N., M.S.

In This Chapter You'll Find:

Guidelines for identifying the needs of a student with a physical disability or chronic health condition.

Suggestions for assessing the student's health condition and educational experience.

Ideas for how school personnel can take a team approach to meeting the needs of students with health concerns. The factors discussed include planning, the Individualized Health Plan (IHP) and the Pupil Health Record.

Effective education of the student with a chronic health condition or physical disability takes planning. Planning focuses on a better understanding of the student's health problem. This may lead to changes in the student's medical plan, nutrition or activity. Other results may be increasing the student's self care skills or change in teaching strategies and the educational environment.

Planning means identifying the student's needs, gathering relevant information and devising a concrete plan to meet the student's educational goals. This chapter speaks to each of these concerns.

Meeting the Student's Needs: The Educational Team and the Law

Students with chronic health conditions, physical disabilities, or both, have a complex, interrelated set of needs. Through a deliberate and systematic review of these factors, everyone involved—the student, family and educational team—can work to meet those needs.

Federal and state priority. Efforts to meet the student's needs have the backing of the law. The federal and state mandates for students with chronic health conditions and physical disabilities can be stated as follows: to educate them in the least restrictive environment and provide related services.

In 1983 the 98th Congress confirmed the nation's previous commitment to special education by enacting PL 98-199, a reauthorization of the principles and funding for earlier legislation (the Education for all Handicapped Children Act of 1975, PL 94-142).

The benefit of a team approach. In light of this legislative mandate, how can the schools best respond to the student with a chronic health condition or disability? Many schools have found an answer: a multidisciplinary team approach. That team can include the student's parents and physician, as well as the principal, classroom teachers, the school nurse, social worker and school administrators—and the student. All of these people pool their skills to plan the best possible education for the student.

The team approach has many advantages. It ensures fairer distribution of responsibility. It also provides more information and ideas to draw on for assessing the student's condition. As a result, this approach helps place the student in the least restrictive, most appropriate school setting.

In addition, the team can more effectively draw on resources in the larger community, such as children's hospitals and county health and social services. Using a team approach helps put the student's educational plan into action; it also helps educators make a comprehensive evaluation of the student's progress.

The Individualized Health Plan

The Individualized Health Plan (IHP) is a tool for responding to the needs of student with a chronic illness or physical disability. This document provides a format for summarizing health information; it also includes a problem statement, goals and plan of action. (See the forms at the end of this chapter.)

A health condition may interfere with learning to such an extent that it causes or augments an learning handicap. In that case, some health issues may be addressed by special education and incorporated into another document, the Individualized Education Plan (IEP). However, the student involved may still have additional health goals not included in the IEP. When a health problem is integral to the learning handicap, the entire IHP may be included as the health component of the IEP.

The IHP is also useful when the student's learning is not currently impaired. An example would be the student with diabetes whose condition is stable. This student may have appropriate self-care skills and need only periodic monitoring and guidance. The student's health concerns, however, would fall outside of the special education program. The IHP can respond to those concerns.

In any case, first make a decision about the potential impact of a health problem for the student and peers. This dictates the next step:

- For problems that may result in an emergency or safety concern for the student or others, schedule a health planning conference immediately.

- For problems that interfere with learning, refer the student to the special education team.

- Address other health concerns by scheduling an educational team meeting, a health planning conference, or both.

The results of your decisions will be documented in the IHP.

Three Ground Rules for Gathering Information

The work of the educational team depends on accurate information. To be useful in planning services for the student with a chronic health condition or physical disability, that information must fulfill at least three conditions: It must be based on daily observation. It must be documented in writing. And it must must take health factors into account. Each condition is discussed below.

Teachers are primary observers. All members of the team will depend on one person as a primary observer of the student's daily behavior at school: the classroom teacher. This teacher is in an excellent position to note changes in the student's health, behavior and overall school performance.

Specialists in education and health need to recognize and reinforce the pivotal role of classroom teachers. These specialists can provide inservices and consultation to sharpen classroom teachers' observation skills. They can develop teachers' abilities to name behaviors of concern and to resist premature labeling or diagnosis of underlying problems. The better the observation, the speedier and more efficient the assessment, diagnosis and intervention.

Put relevant information in writing. Health information should be communicated in writing. For example, when a student is identified for special education services, the school nurse is notified within 24 hours. The educational team does not meet until the school nurse has had time to assess the student. When that assessment is done, it should be shared in writing.

Besides the advantages for the student, there are advantages for those who follow this practice. Teachers and other staff members who use a system that provides accurate and timely feedback are positively reinforced. They will continue to depend on the system and the other members of the team.

Your school may already have in place a written procedure for sharing information on a student. To it you can add the forms discussed in this chapter: the Individualized Health Plan and the Pupil Health Record.

Take health factors into account. Physical and emotional health are central to any student's development and educational success. This points to a logical guideline: Review the health status and current health practices of a student whenever a behavioral, educational or health problem is noted. Through this process, the impact of a physiological or psychological problem can be "ruled in" or "ruled out."

The school nurse is best equipped to determine if health is a factor in planning for the special needs of children. Thus, the school nurse plays an essential role as a member of the educational team—as team leader or case manager.

Sources of Health Information

Listed below are sources of essential baseline information for determining two things: whether or not health is a factor interfering with a student's educational experience, and the extent and nature of the interference.

It may not be realistic, given staff shortages, to collect all the baseline information outlined here. In that case, the school nurse should choose the most appropriate sources for a particular student.

Sources of health information include:

• Discussions with the student and family.

• The Pupil Health Record. (See the forms at the end of this chapter.)

• Other developmental, psychological, special learning and behavior assessments.

- A complete health history (if not present in the Pupil Health Record). This should include information provided by the student, parents and health care provider.

- Physical assessment or examination, including neurological review.

- Assessment of sensory functions, including vision and hearing.

- Developmental assessment.

- Family assessment.

- Teacher observation.

- Observations by the school nurse and other child study team members.

Some of the sources on this list are discussed in more detail below.

As in assessments for special education or other special needs, it's appropriate to obtain written permission from parents for health assessment.

Health history and current health status. The health history and current health status provide essential baseline data. This is the place to start. Because it usually involves interviewing the student and a parent, the health history also provides a vehicle to explore student and parent perceptions of a problem.

Sources for this information include the student, parents and other family members, the classroom teacher, the Pupil Health Record and the attendance record. Other school personnel such as bus drivers, teaching assistants and school secretaries may have pertinent information about the student's behavior, health status and needs.

Physical assessment and measurements. The need for further assessment depends on findings from the health history and observation of current health status. At a minimum, current assessment of vision and hearing is essential. Next comes information about the student's regular source of health care and most recent visit to a physician or nurse practitioner.

A sample health profile and current health status review form is included in the forms at the end of this chapter. It includes a brief review of the student's school experience, development and family relationships.

Developmental assessment. Developmental assessment is a key component. Findings from this assessment must be combined with other data: historical information from the parent, observation of the student in several settings, health histories, physical assessment findings and information from the classroom teacher.

Several factors make up a developmental assessment (Robinson, 1983):

- Physical growth, including height and weight, nutrition and sexual maturity.

- Motor development.

- Cognitive growth, including learning styles and abilities.

- Language development, including receptive and expressive language.

- Psychosocial development.

- Psychosexual development.

- Moral and spiritual development.

- Affective development including self concept, fears and anxiety.

Family assessment. An important relationship exists between the health status of individual family members and the family as a whole. The success or failure of a student is influenced by the student's family. Focusing on the student in the home environment adds a significant dimension to the evaluation. Furthermore, it allows the family to take part in the evaluation.

The Pupil Health Record

The Pupil Health Record (PHR) establishes a consistent format for documenting and communicating about the student's health—a positive health status as well as health concerns. (See the end of this chapter for a sample form.)

You can make the IHP part of the Pupil Health Record. To do this, cite the health condition on the problem list of the Pupil Health Record. Record a brief summary statement in the narrative notes section in the record. Then mark the IHP as a permanent part of the record. If the student is being served through special education, a summary of essential concerns and a reference to the student's special education file may be sufficient.

Summary

Students with chronic health conditions or physical disabilities have a complex set of needs.

School personnel—especially classroom teachers—are a primary source of information about a student's health and the way it affects classroom performance.

School personnel need a formal written procedure for referring students with special needs for the appropriate help.

The school health professional plays an essential role as team leader for students with chronic illness or disability.

Review the health status of a student whenever a behavioral, educational or health problem is noted.

Sources of information on the student's health include: the health history, current health status, vision and hearing screening, developmental assessment, family assessment and observations by school personnel.

The Individualized Health Plan (IHP) is a tool for responding to student needs. It summarizes key health information, goals and a plan of action.

The Pupil Health Record provides a consistent format for documenting the student's health status.

On the following pages are these attachments (sample forms):

- Profile of the School-Aged Child for Health and Educational Planning by Cyndy Schuster, M.P.H., R.N., C.S.N.P. and Ruth Ellen Luehr

- Individualized Health Plan

- Authorization for Release of Information

- Pupil Health Record

- Pupil Health Record—Immunization Record

- Authorization for Administration of Specialized Health Care Procedures

- Specialized Health Care Procedure Record

References

Robinson, Thelma. "Concepts and Tools in Health, Development and Family Assessment," in Iverson, Carol, Ed. *Health and Developmental History Assessment Skills Manual.* 2nd ed. Englewood, Colorado: National Association of School Nurses, Inc., 1983.

For Further Reading

American Nurses' Association. *Nursing, A Social Policy Statement (Publication Number NP-63).* Kansas City, Missouri, 1980. (2420 Pershing Road, Kansas City, MO 64108)

ANA, APHA, ASHA, NAPNAP, NASN, NASSNC. *Standards of School Nursing Practice.* Kansas City, Missouri, 1983.

Iverson, Carol, Ed. *Health and Developmental History Assessment Skills Manual,* 2nd ed. Englewood, Colorado: National Association of School Nurses, Inc., 1983.

Sahler O. and E. McAnarney. *The Child from Three to Eighteen.* St. Louis: C.V. Mosby Company, 1981.

Wold, S. *School Nursing: A Framework for Practice.* St. Louis: C.V. Mosby Company, 1981.

Profile of the School-Aged Child
for Health and Educational Planning

Name: _____ Date of Birth: _____

Parents/Guardians: _____ Date of Assessment: _____

Address: _____ Chronological Age: _____

Phone: _____

Sex:

Regular source of health care:
            last visit:
Regular source of dental care:
            last visit:

Present Concerns:

Expectations of the visit:

Child Health Profile

Prenatal: Pregnancy number -   number of living children -
           medical care initiated -   (month)
           maternal health during pregnancy -
           illnesses or infections -
           complications -
           treatments or procedures done -
           smoking -   frequency -
           alcohol use -   frequency -
           medications -
           diet and nutrition -

Natal: length of gestation -   (weeks)
           labor - spontaneous/induced/augmented:
           length: (hours)
           delivery - type:
                 anesthesia or medications used:
                 problems
           birth weight -
           APGAR score - (1 minute),   (5 minutes)

Neonatal: health problems -
           feeding problems -
           day of discharge -   (postnatal)

Illnesses: infections   (type, age of child, medical care, treatment,
                      severity, duration, sequelae)

            chronic illnesses or health problems (type, age of onset,
               medical care, treatment, severity, complications,
               reevaluation schedule)

Immunizations:

TYPE OF VACCINE	1ST DOSE MONTH-YEAR	2ND DOSE MONTH-YEAR	3RD DOSE MONTH-YEAR	4TH DOSE MONTH-YEAR	5TH DOSE MONTH-YEAR	6TH DOSE MONTH-YEAR
DTP (Diphtheria, Tetanus and Pertussis)						
POLIO						
MEASLES						
RUBELLA						
MUMPS						

HIB -
T.B. - date: type:

Hospitalizations/Surgery: (reason for hospitalization or surgery, age of the child,
                      response of the child, problems, outcome)

Summary of Data

Accidents/Injuries:	(age of the child, nature of the accident/injury, precipitating factors, medical care, treatment, sequelae)

Health Behaviors: hygiene - bath or shower
                                wash hair
                                brush teeth
                    sleep - hours/night
                            nap
                            disturbances
                    exercise and play - how often
                                        types of activities
                                        favorite sports
                    elimination - bowel movement frequency
                                    urinary frequency
                                    changed in regular pattern
                    chemical use - smoking
                                    alcohol
                                    other
                    T.V. watching - hours/day
                                    favorite programs
                    safety practices - seatbelt use
                                        bike safety
                                        water safety

Review of Systems: general - last physical exam
                                last dental exam
                                allergies
                    head -

                    EENT -

                    cardio-resp -

                    GI -

                    GU -

                    musculo-skeletal -

                    neurological -

                    skin -

Nutritional Profile

Infant: breast or formula -
             vitamin supplement -
             solid foods introduced -   type -
             food intolerance -
Current: 24 hour food recall - breakfast:
                                    lunch:
                                    dinner:
                                    snacks:
             vitamin supplements -
             appetite -
             favorite foods -   dislikes -
             food allergies -
             meals with the family -

Family Profile
Genogram:

Family roles and responsibilities:

Family decision making:

Extended family relationships and support:
Marital relationship:
Parents/Guardians occupations:　father -　　　　hours -
　　　　　　　　　　　　　　　　mother -　　　　hours -
　　　　　　　　　　　　　　　　other -　　　　　hours -

Home environment:

Family financial status:

Family health history:　asthma　　　　　　kidney disease
　　　　　　　　　　　　tuberculosis　　　　ulcers
　　　　　　　　　　　　rheumatic fever　　cancer
　　　　　　　　　　　　arthritis　　　　　　obesity
　　　　　　　　　　　　seizures　　　　　　smoking
　　　　　　　　　　　　heart disease　　　chemical dependency
　　　　　　　　　　　　hypertension　　　　mental health
　　　　　　　　　　　　allergies　　　　　　　problems
　　　　　　　　　　　　congenital
　　　　　　　　　　　　　abnormalities

Childcare/daycare:
Discipline:
Family activities:

Cultural influences:

Developmental Profile

Achievement of developmental milestones:　sat alone -
　　　　　　　　　　　　　　　　　　　　　crawled -
　　　　　　　　　　　　　　　　　　　　　stood alone -
　　　　　　　　　　　　　　　　　　　　　walked -
　　　　　　　　　　　　　　　　　　　　　first word -
　　　　　　　　　　　　　　　　　　　　　sentences -
　　　　　　　　　　　　　　　　　　　　　toilet trained - day:
　　　　　　　　　　　　　　　　　　　　　　　　　　　night:

Growth:　　　　height -
　　　　　　　　weight -
　　　　　　　　sexual -
　　　　　　　　period of failure to grow or unusual growth -
Comparison of development with peers:
　　　　　　　　　　　　with siblings:

Psycho-sexual:　dating
　　　　　　　　sexual activity

Personality Profile
Self concept:
Parent/Guardian description of the child:

Relationships with adults:
　　　　　　with peers:
Child's locus of control:
Child's strengths:
Child's weaknesses:
Child's fears:
Child's ability to cope and ways of coping with stress:

Summary of Data

37

School Profile

Child's attitude toward school and learning:

Parent/Guardian attitude toward school and learning:

Learning style:

Classes: favorite -
            dislikes -
            problems -

Attendance: patterns of attendance -
              reasons for absences-

Academic performance:
Perception of academic performance:

Special education services:

Schools attended: 1.
                    2.
                    3.
                    4.

Extracurricular activities:
     school -
     non-school -

SCHEDULE OF DAILY ACTIVITIES

On this chart, record the activities of a student's typical day. Review for factors such as safety, activity and support. Have a member of the educational team physically walk through the activities of the day with the student. This may be collapsed by the student as he/she gives a "guided tour" of his/her schedule - walking to and from places on the schedule so the environment can be assessed for each activity, energy expenditure can be measured, and support needs identified.

TIME	ACTIVITY	SAFETY/ COMFORT/ ACCESS/	ACTIVITY/ ENERGY/ REST	ASSISTANCE/ SUPPORT
Early A.M.				
En route to school				
Arrival				
Homeroom				
1st hour				
2nd hour				
3rd hour				
4th hour				
5th hour				
6th hour				
7th hour				
After school				
En route home				
Evening				

Developed by Cyndy Schuster and Ruth Ellen Luehr

Summary of Data

INDIVIDUALIZED HEALTH PLAN

INDENTIFYING INFORMATION

Student I. D. # _____

IHP initiation date _____

Name _____

Birthdate _____

Address _____

Grade _____ Teacher _____

School _____

Parent/Guardian _____

Telephone (home) _____

(work) _____

Health Care Provider(s) _____

Telephone _____

Special Health Need(s) [Presenting Problem(s)] _____

May result in an emergency   NO _____ YES _____ ➤ HEALTH PLANNING CONFERENCE _____ date

May interfere with learning   NO _____ YES _____ ➤ Refer to CHILD STUDY TEAM _____ date

Other health impairment   NO _____ YES _____ ➤ HEALTH PLANNING CONFERENCE _____ date

➤ Refer to CHILD STUDY TEAM _____ date

ASSESSMENT

Health History/Present Status/

Health Practices [interviewer] _____ [interviewee] _____ date

Sensory assessment [assessor] _____ _____ date

Physical Assessment [assessor] _____ _____ date

Developmental Assessment [assessor] _____ _____ date

Findings: _____

Nursing Diagnosis _____

39

HEALTH PLANNING CONFERENCE

[for health needs that may result in an emergency, and/or require management and monitoring]

date ―――――――

Participants ――――――― Roles ―――――――

Goals

Objectives

Timeline

Plan implemented by ―――――――

Monitored by ―――――――

Evaluation/Follow-up Plan ―――――――

date ―――――――

Parental Approval ―――――――

Case Manager ―――――――

40

Authorization for Release of Information

_____ _____ _____
Student's Name   Student I.D. No.   Date of Birth

_____ _____ _____
Parent's/Guardian's Name   Telephone   School

Information obtained on individual students is classified as private by Minnesota's Data Privacy Act and is available only to the student or the student's parent or guardian. Private information cannot be discussed with or released to anyone outside the School District except as authorized by the parent(s) or guardian.

The undersigned hereby authorizes _____

to release to_____
information from his/her health record.

The following information is requested:

_____ Health History

_____ Physical Examination Report

_____ Immunization Records

_____ Other (specify) _____

_____

Information received on your child will be used for one or more of the following:

1.   To facilitate evaluation of your child's individual educational program.

2.   To determine health needs of you child which may require special services during school.

3.   To facilitate health counseling or school health services which you may wish for your child.

4.   To provide school district personnel with a better understanding of your child's health needs.

This authorization may be revoked by you at any time in writing and automatically expires on June 30th at the end of the school fiscal year.

_____ _____ _____
Date   Signature of Parent/Guardian   Relationship to child

We are not authorized or funded to pay for this information.

PUPIL HEALTH RECORD

NAME _____

PARENTS' OR GUARDIAN(S) NAME _____

ADDRESS _____ PHONE _____

PHYSICIAN _____ PHONE _____

DENTIST _____ PHONE _____

STUDENT NO. _____ SEX _____ BIRTHDATE _____

HEALTH CLASSIFICATION *

	PS	K	1	2	3	4	5	6	7	8	9	10	11	12

PROBLEM 1/HEALTH MAINT.
—MED. EXAM
—HEALTH SCREENING
—IMMUNIZATIONS
—DENTAL EXAM/RX
—OTHER

* HEALTH CLASSIFICATION I = FULL ACTIVITY

HEALTH CLASSIFICATION II = RESTRICTED ACTIVITY

PROBLEM LIST	DATE IDENTIFIED	DATE RESOLVED
2		
3		
4		
5		
6		
7		
8		
9		
10		
11		
12		
13		

PROBLEM LIST	DATE IDENTIFIED	DATE RESOLVED
14		
15		
16		
17		
18		
19		
20		
21		
22		
23		
24		
25		

Walter S. Booth Co.—St. Paul
W1F Pupil Health/Rev. 1980

43

NAME _____   STUDENT NO. _____

SCHOOL HEALTH SCREENING AND FOLLOW - UP RECORD

GRADE	DATE	ACUITY		WITH GLASSES	TEST	VISION						HEARING			SCOLIOSIS			OTHER
						M/B*		COLOR										
		R	L			P	R	P	F		COMMENTS	R	L	COMMENTS	P	R	COMMENTS	

M/B — Muscle Balance

44

NARRATIVE NOTES

DATE	PROBLEM NUMBER & PROBLEM	FINDINGS (SUBJECTIVE & OBJECTIVE)	ASSESSMENT & PLAN (SIGN EACH ENTRY)

Name _____

Student No. _____

Pupil Health Record
Immunization Record

Minnesota Statutes 1980, Section 123.70, requires that all children who are enrolled in a Minnesota school be immunized against diphtheria, tetanus, pertussis, polio, measles, mumps, and rubella, allowing for certain specified exemptions*. This form is designed to provide the school with information required by the law and will be available for review by the Minnesota Department of Health and the local board of health.

Enter the MONTH and YEAR in which the pupil received each of the following vaccines. DO NOT USE (✓) or (X).

TYPE OF VACCINE	1ST DOSE MONTH - YEAR	2ND DOSE MONTH - YEAR	3RD DOSE MONTH - YEAR	4TH DOSE MONTH - YEAR	5TH DOSE MONTH - YEAR	6TH DOSE MONTH - YEAR
DTP (Diptheria, Tetanus and Pertussis)						
POLIO						
MEASLES						
RUBELLA						
MUMPS						

Shading indicates the minimum number of doses which are recommended.

Indicate immunization status and source of above information by choosing one of the following alternatives.

1. ☐ I certify that the above named child is *completely* immunized according to Minnesota state law for school enrollment.

_____
Signature of physician or public clinic   Date

2. ☐ The above information has been transferred from records maintained by the child's parent/guardian and indicates that the minimum recommended number of doses of vaccine have been received.

_____
Signature of parent or legal guardian   Date

3. ☐ I certify that the above child has received at least one dose of each vaccine and is *in the process of completing* the DTP/ Td and/or polio vaccine series. The dates for which the remaining doses are to be given are

_____
Signature of physician or public clinic   Date

(Note: If information submitted for the above three alternatives has been received verbally or from pre-existing records, the school should indicate the source of the original information and include initials of the recorder.)

*See reverse side

47

Legal Exemptions to Minnesota Statutes 1980, Section 123.70

1. No student 7 years of age or older shall be required to be immunized against pertussis.

2. No student 7 years of age or older shall be required to be immunized against mumps, although such immunization is highly desirable.

3. No female student 12 years of age or older shall be required to be immunized against rubella, although such immunization is highly desirable.

4. No student shall be required to receive an immunization for which laboratory evidence of immunity exists or for which there is a medical contraindication. The following (or similar) statement must be signed by a physician in order for the student to receive a medical exemption.

   I hereby certify that immunization is contraindicated for medical reasons or that laboratory confirmation of the presence of adequate immunity exists for the following immunizations: _____

   _____   _____
   Signature of Physician   Date

5. No student shall be required to receive an immunization which is contrary to the conscientiously held beliefs of the parent or guardian. The following (or similar) statement must be signed and notarized in order for the student to receive an exemption.

   I hereby certify by notarization that immunization for my child is contrary to my conscientiously held beliefs. Indicate vaccine(s) _____

   _____   _____
   Signature of Parent or Legal Guardian   Date

   Subscribed and sworn to before me this _____ day of _____ 19 _____.

   _____
   Signature of notary

Authorization for Administration
of Specialized Health Care Procedures

Students who need specialized health care procedures provided during the school day must have, in writing, a physician's prescription and parental authorization.

Name of Student:_____ Student No.:_____

Birthdate:_____ Grade:_____

Diagnosis:_____

Name of Procedure:_____

_____

Treatment Prescription:_____

Description of the Procedure:_____

_____

_____

_____

Time/Interval Procedure is to be Done:_____

_____

Amount - (If Applicable):_____

Precautions and/or possible adverse reactions:_____

_____

_____

_____

Discontinuation Date:_____

Authorization for this procedure is required annually.

Physician: Name (Signature):_____ Date:_____

                    (Type or Print):_____

★★

I hereby give my permission for my child to receive the specialized procedure named above as prescribed by my child's physician.

Date:_____ Signature:_____
                                                Parent/Guardian

49

Specialized Health Care Procedure Record

Name: _____

Procedure: _____

Grade: _____ Homeroom Teacher: _____

Physician: _____ Phone #: _____

Date	Time	Comments (Include absenses, problems, modifications made, etc.)	Initials

Signatures	Initials	Titles

Chapter 3

A Barrier-Free School Environment

Mary Kay Albanese, B.S.

In This Chapter You'll Find: Specific guidelines for making school facilities accessible to all students—including those with physical disabilities.

The Goal: Accessibility for Everyone

When students with a physical disability share educational facilities with other students, we must give special attention to building structure and program activities. This chapter provides a basic overview of this issue. You can use it to identify areas of concern. For more information, go to the references cited at the end of this chapter.

The equal rights of students with a physical disability are often denied by inaccessible facilities. The Education for All Handicapped Children Act, PL 94-142) should make funds available to school districts for renovation or construction of barrier-free facilities.

The people who plan renovation should represent a variety of interests and responsibilities. All of them can benefit from the guidelines given here.

Removing physical barriers brings an added advantage: safety. In fact, a barrier-free environment is safer for everyone.

Many physical barriers—often subtle—need to be identified. The goal is helping students function safely and with maximum mobility. Among the factors to consider are those listed in the following sections.

Getting to School

Transportation. Consider the specific needs of each student when you designate daily transportation plans. Both school buses and private vehicles need to adhere to public laws regarding secure positioning for safety. Students should use seat belts.

Check with your State Department of Transportation for requirements that apply to passengers using wheelchairs or adaptive seating devices.

Parking lots. Set aside parking spaces that are accessible (12 feet wide) and close to the facility. Identify these for use by people with physical disabilities. A parking space open on one side—with room for wheeling and walking—is adequate. This space should allow people in wheelchairs and people with braces or crutches to get in and out of an automobile onto a level surface.

Walks and curbs. Curbing should not create any barriers to students with a physical handicap. Where barriers have been created, remove or ramp previously laid curbs. Other guidelines are these:

- Public walks should be at least 48 inches wide and should have a gradient (angle of incline) not greater than 5 percent.

- Such walks should be of a continuing common surface, not interrupted by steps or abrupt changes in level.

Building Access

Entrances, doors and windows. People in wheelchairs should be able to use at least one primary entrance to each building.

Exterior doors should be sliding rather than swinging.

Doors, both exterior and interior, should be operable by a single effort.

Use safety glass for doors and accessible windows.

Hallways and floors. Use carpeting or other non-slip surface on all floors to reduce slipping and to cushion falls.

Avoid sharp corners, surfaces and projections.

Elevators. Unless ramps meeting the accessibility requirements of students exist on each floor level of a building, provide at least one elevator for:

- All buildings over two stories high, with occupancy of 100 or more persons above or below the main entrance floor.

- All publicly-owned school buildings and other privately-owned buildings of similar occupancy over one story (such as full-time, privately-owned schools, colleges and universities).

- All non-publicly owned school buildings over three stories with over 200 persons above or below the main entrance floor level. Basements with over 100 persons are counted as a story.

- Elevators should be accessible to the physically disabled at all levels normally used by the general public. Elevator operation buttons should be at a level accessible to someone seated in a wheelchair.

Ramps. Ramps should be used where steps and curbs create inaccessible barriers.

All ramps, indoor or outdoor, should have a slope no greater than 1 foot rise in 12 feet, or 8.33 percent.

A ramp should have hand rails on at least one side, preferably two. These should be smooth and extend one foot beyond the bottom of the ramp—except in places where the extension itself presents a hazard.

Ramp surfaces should be non-slip.

The minimum ramp width should be 36 inches.

A ramp should have a level platform at the top.

- This platform should be at least 5 feet deep if a door swings out onto the platform or toward the ramp. The platform should also extend at least 1 foot beyond each side of the doorway.

- If the door does not swing onto the platform and toward the ramp, the platform should be at least 3 feet deep and 5 feet wide. The platform should extend at least 1 foot on each side.

Each ramp should have at least 6 feet of straight clearance at the bottom.

Ramps should have level platforms at 30-foot intervals for purposes of rest and safety. The ramps should also have level platforms wherever they turn.

Stairs. Steps in stairs that might require use by people with disabilities should not have abrupt (square) nosing.

Handrails should be placed on each side of a stairway and should measure 2 feet, 9 inches vertically from the stair tread to the top of the handrail.

Handrails should be continuous across landings, where possible.

Handrails should be designed to support 250 pounds and should be kept securely fastened at all times.

Use non-slip grips on concrete stairwells.

Assistance. Provide help to students with disabilities: Have aides or staff members assist these students as they enter and leave school. If needed, also provide help during the day for the classroom and for toileting.

Inside the Classroom

Entrance. Use wide classroom entry ways without doors to permit free access.

Doors to outside hallways should have glass areas arranged so that students clearly see the other side.

Use minimal door thresholds—or none at all.

For fire safety, there should be two doors: one near the front and one near the back of the classroom.

Avoid sharp corners, surfaces and projections.

Floor. Floors should have a non-skid surface. Rubber tile is satisfactory.

A warm floor is essential.

Furniture. Furniture that can be adjusted vertically and horizontally is helpful.

Chalkboards should be low, with a bottom edge 24 inches from the floor. Chalkboards should be adjustable for raising and lowering.

Bed or resting area. Any bed or resting surface should be the same height as a wheelchair seat; this helps transfers. An adjustable height feature is desirable.

Sink. Each classroom should have a sink accessible from three sides.

Storage. Specially designed storage space helps to accommodate wheelchairs, walkers, standing tables or other large equipment.

Sanitary Facilities

Toilets/stalls. Install convenient toilets—those with space and hardware to permit independence.

On each floor, at least one toilet for each sex should be accessible to the physically disabled.

The stall door to the accessible toilet should have a 2- foot, 8-inch opening clearance; the door should swing out.

The stall should be 3 feet wide, and 4 feet 10 inches to 5 feet 6 inches deep.

The toilet, preferably wall-mounted, should have a seat 19 inches above the floor.

Grab bars should be 1-1/2 inches in diameter and 1-1/2 inches from the wall, fastened securely at ends and center. Place grab bars on both walls, 33 inches above floor.

Sinks. Clear space below a sink for the physically disabled should be at least 26 inches above floor level.

All faucet handles should be easy to operate—for example, with level handles.

Hot water lines and drains under sinks should be shielded to protect the wheelchair user's legs.

Mirrors. Mirrors should be placed so that the bottom edge is not more than 3 feet above floor level.

Showers. Two stalls should be accessible to the physically disabled and should measure 3 feet by 3 feet.

The floor surface should be non-slip, with a curb no more than 2 inches above floor levels.

A seat should be positioned 19 inches above the floor. Seats should be hung to fold against the wall.

A grab rail should be attached to the stall wall opposite the seat and extend around the back wall.

Water control, shower spray, and soap tray should all be placed 3 feet, 6 inches above the floor.

Other School Areas

Assembly seating/auditorium. Seating space for the physically disabled must be an integral part of the seating plan, not a segregated section.

Laboratory. At least one student lab station should be accessible, with a 30-inch clearance beneath the work surface.

Library. At least 1 percent of study carrels and tables should be accessible, with 30 inches clear space beneath work surfaces.

Controls and Fixtures

Hardware/switches. Install hardware on all doors, sinks, and cabinets that can be used by any student with a disability and quickly identified by the blind. This includes elevator controls.

Switches, controls, fire alarms and the like should be within reach of students in wheelchairs.

Drinking fountains. Drinking fountains should be accessible for those in wheelchairs.

Telephone. Each telephone area should have one telephone accessible to the physically disabled.

All operating mechanisms (dial, coin slot) should be 4 feet above the floor or lower.

Emergency Systems

Install superior emergency and fire protection systems, with easily operated emergency doors and barrier-free corridors.

Make sure all students can comprehend warning signals. For example, use fire alarms with tactile signals for the blind and visual signals for the deaf.

Develop an emergency plan for transporting all students with limited mobility out of the school building in case of fire or other school emergency. Review and update the emergency plan at the beginning of each school term.

Summary

A barrier-free school environment is safer for everyone.

When planning to remove physical barriers, consider all logical areas:

- Transportation plans.

- Parking lots.

- Walks and curbs.

- Building entrances, doors and windows.

- Hallways and floors.

- Elevators, ramps and stairs.

- Assistance for students with handicaps.

- Factors inside the classroom: entrance, floor, furniture, resting area, sink and storage.

- Seating in the auditorium, library and laboratory.

- Controls and fixtures such as drinking fountains and telephones.

- Emergency and fire protection systems.

For Further Reading

Educational Research Service. *Barrier-Free School Facilities for Handicapped Students.* Arlington, VA, 1977. (Price: $7.00. Available from Educational Research Service, Inc., 1880 N. Kent Street, Arlington, VA 22209 703-243-2100)

Aicello, Barbara, ed. *Places and Spaces: Facilities Planning for Handicapped Students.* (Available from: The Council for Exceptional Children, 1920 Associated Drive, Reston, VA 22091-1589.)

Chapter 4

Using Community Resources

Nancy Kern, R.N., B.S.N.

In This Chapter You'll Find:

A way to classify the needs of students with chronic illnesses or physical disabilities.

Resources to consider when meeting those needs.

Guidelines for referring a student to an outside resource.

Working With Three Types of Need

When the need for outside resources to assist the student with a chronic health condition has been identified, the school health professional must: 1) identify available resources, 2) assess their appropriateness and 3) evaluate the family's readiness and ability to use these resources.

We can group identified needs into three general categories: financial, medical and social support. Examples in each of these categories are:

- Financial   Cost of treatment.
  Cost of transportation and lodging.
  Cost of equipment.

- Medical care   Specialist diagnostic evaluation.
  Health care maintenance.
  Health education.

- Social support systems   Support groups.
  Respite care.
  Counseling.
  Recreation.

When trying to meet each kind of need, consider local, regional and state or national resources. Those resources can vary widely—from the March of Dimes to a children's hospital.

You should ask two questions when selecting a resource. First, is the resource appropriate for the identified need? Second, are the student and family willing and able to use its benefits? When answering this question, consider these aspects of the student and family:

- Their perception of the need.

- Their past history of using such resources.

- Their receptiveness to local, regional and state assistance.

- Their transportation capabilities.

- Their financial resources.

Resources for Meeting Needs

Listed here are resources for you to consider. These are not meant to be all-inclusive lists; rather, they are examples of the services and agencies at various levels.

Financial resources.

Local

Clubs (Lions, Eagles, VFW, etc.)
Church groups
Banks and credit unions
Employers
Fund drives for special needs

County and Regional

County financial services
Farm bureaus
Clubs (Masons, etc.)
Foundation grants

State and National

Shriners hospitals
Services for Children with Handicaps (Crippled Children's Services)
Specific associations, (for example, Muscular Dystrophy, Arthritis, March of Dimes, etc.)

Resources for medical care.

Local

Physicians
Nurses
Hospitals
Other licensed health care professionals
School health services

County and Regional

Specialists
County community health services
Clinics

State and National

Children's hospitals
Specialty clinics
University hospitals

Social and emotional support systems.

Local

Counselors
Church groups
Ministers
Social groups (Boy Scouts, Girl Scouts, etc.)
Clubs

County and Regional

Mental health centers
County social services
County community health agencies
Specialty camps for children with disabilities

State and National

Specific associations, (United Cerebral Palsy, Association for
    Retarded Citizens, etc.)
PACER (Parent Advocacy Coalition for Educational Rights)

Referring to an Outside Resource

When referring a student or family to an outside resource, make sure the following information is at hand:

- Student's name and address.

- Birthdate.

- Parent's name.

- Address.

- Phone number.

- Name of referring person.

- Address and phone number for resource.

- Brief description of reasons for referral.

Keep a reference file of specific resources. For each resource, list the name, address, phone number, and contact person. Also make notes about their services and your previous experience with them.

It is important to find someone who can help you identify resources beyond those in your file. This person might be a school nurse, a county public health nurse, a regional or state consultant or a referral service.

Summary

The needs of a student with a chronic illness or physical disability fall into three groups: financial, health care and social support.

To meet each category of need, consider resources at the local, regional, state and national level.

Have the necessary information on hand when referring a student to an outside resource.

Keep a file on specific resources you use. Find someone who can help you identify additional resources.

Chapter 5

Psychosocial Issues: Looking at the Whole Person

Patty Rezabek, M.S., R.N.
Pam McCullouch, R.N.

In This Chapter You'll Find:

A definition of psychosocial issues.

Why these issues are important for students with chronic health conditions or disabilities.

The key questions you should ask about the student's self-concept, family, education and development.

Why Deal with Psychosocial Issues?

Chronic health conditions or disabilities in students are as varied and unique as every human being. And they affect many aspects of the student's life—self-concept, relationships with family and friends, performance at school and emotional development. These are psychosocial issues.

If we believe that all students should have an optimum level of wellness—and that our long-range goal for all students is the most normal, healthy lifestyle, or the highest degree of independent functioning—then we can well defend an important idea: Students with chronic health conditions or disabilities are more like other students than different. Subsequently, if we look at psychosocial development and adaptation, we have a common base for making assessments.

Our mission here is not to detail lengthy theoretical materials already well researched, documented and widely published. Instead, we provide a framework for careful understanding when developing individual plans to care for students in your school.

With this in mind, let us consider the key questions.

Ask About Self Concept

How does the student feel about him or herself as a worthwhile person?

What is the impact of the chronic health condition or disability on the student?

What are the student's strengths and weaknesses? What is compromised?

Is the student encouraged to develop independently?

Ask About the Family

How is the diagnosis perceived by the student, parents, school and community?

What are the relationships between student, family, peers, school and community?

What have levels of coping been for the student and parent?

How is love, warmth and caring expressed in the family?

Is there accepting and uncritical love with appropriate demands and expectations?

What are the reactions of the student, parents, siblings, peers and other family members to the chronic condition or disability?

Where are the support systems for student and family? (Support systems include friends, relatives, clergy, etc.)

Where are the student's and parent's advocates?

Where are the financial supports?

Ask About the Student's Education

What have earlier learning experiences been?

What is the developmental stage of the student—at the condition's onset? At its diagnosis? Currently?

What is the student's level of self-care skill?

What is the student's learning pattern and school attendance pattern?

What are the student's educational goals?

What adaptations need to be made to assist the student's learning process?

Ask About Social and Emotional

Are there limitations to the student's ability to socialize?

Where are the power struggles in the student's life?

Are there control issues such as treatment compliance, school attendance, disruptive behavior or acting-out behaviors of concern?

Are sexuality issues recognized and dealt with openly?

Are chemical use issues recognized and dealt with openly?

Dealing with Psychosocial Issues: The Benefits

It's important to consider how students with chronic health conditions or disabilities obtain and analyze experience. With increased awareness of the student's life system, more time will be applied to developing a new and multidimensional vision of psychosocial issues.

School personnel can help students develop abilities that give an optimum level of wellness: The ability to recognize joy, sorrow, pain; to give, love and relate to others; to assertively make decisions; to experience consequences; to explore new boundaries and challenges.

Summary

Psychosocial issues involve the effects of a disability or chronic health condition on all aspects of the student's life.

The long range goal is wellness for *all* students. Looking at psychosocial issues is a means to that goal.

When assessing students, ask key questions in several areas: self concept, the family system, the educational system and the student's emotional and social development.

For Further Reading

Bleck, Eugene E. and Donald A. Nagel. *Physically Handicapped Children: A Medical Atlas for Teachers*, 2nd ed., New York: Grune and Stratton, 1982.

Fithian, Janet. *Understanding the Child with a Chronic Illness in the Classroom.* Phoenix, Az: The Oryz Press, 1984.

National Association of School Nurses, Inc. *HADHAS Manual.* Denver, CO: NASN, Inc., 1983.

Siantz, Mary Lou deLeon. *The Nurse and the Developmentally Disabled Adolescent*, Baltimore, MD: University Park Press, 1977.

Chapter 6

Self Care: Fostering Student Independence

Naomi Quinnell, R.N., M.P.H.

In This Chapter You'll Find:

An explanation of the concept of self care.

Guidelines for developing a self care plan.

Overview: What is Self Care?

With skillful training and observation, most students can take part in all steps of their care, thereby encouraging self care. With self care, an important shift takes place: less emphasis on the caregiver telling, advising and directing; more emphasis on talking, questioning, considering alternatives and sharing the decision-making with the student.

The basic components of self care have been described this way:

- Self care is making decisions and taking actions that improve personal, physical and emotional health and reduce risk factors.

- Self care is two-dimensional. It involves both decision making and action taking by the student who is learning to cope with a disease or disability.

Understanding development. This process can guide students to make reasonable decisions about their health care. Self care skills hinge on the student's development, however, and the caregiver must understand where the student "is at."

In order to understand the readiness of an individual student to learn self-care, the school nurse or other qualified professional must have a working knowledge of the various cognitive stages as students develop. The decision-making process begins with values clarification. Students at different ages or those with health impairments may have immature values that lead to unhealthy decisions if the choices were left solely to them. Just how much input a person should have in the care process should be based on that person's cognitive level of maturity and life experiences.

Health education is essential. If we are to realize the goals for self care, students must have two kinds of reinforcement: a formal health education curriculum, and a team approach in a participatory health care program.

To the extent of their ability and potential, students with disabilities should have the same opportunity as others to benefit from a health education program. The curriculum should include decision making, self reliance, and responsibility for ones's own body.

Developing a Plan for Self Care

How do we apply the self care model in everyday practice? What follows is one approach. The strategy is to elicit information or opinions from the student by asking leading questions or making leading statements in certain areas.

Procedure:

1. *Prior experience with a problem:*

   What do you usually do when this happens?

   How well does that work?

   Tell me what happened.

2. *Deriving options or considering alternatives:*

   What would you like to do?

   What do you think would help?

   What do you remember about clean technique (or cleaning your skin, etc.)?

   Which of these ways works the best?

Soap and water are the best cleansers. How will you manage this in school?

How will you know when your bladder is empty?

Now you know what can help. What do you plan to do?

Now that you've seen how I do it, you can do it while I watch.

How do you want me to help?

Let's write this down together.

3. *Guiding students to make reasonable decisions:*

Your idea about keeping a record of the amount of water you drink is good.

Would you be willing to try sitting up a little longer each day and let me know how it feels?

You were correct in calling me when you noticed that. This way you will learn when to call for help.

You did that really well.

How will you know when it's time to turn over (or loosen the brace, etc.)?

Throughout Part Three of this manual you'll find recommendations for self-care or steps in a care procedure that might appropriately be carried out by the student. As you apply these procedures, be alert for the opportunities to promote self care.

Summary

With appropriate help, students with chronic health conditions can take an active role in their own care.

Guiding students to self care requires an understanding of child development. Appropriate health education is also essential.

Follow systematic procedures when developing a self care plan.

For Further Reading

Groninga, Sheryl and Ojala, Elizabeth. "Participatory Health Care for Children: The Pros and Cons." *Journal of School Health*, (March 1981).

Jenkins, Ruth L., "New School Nurse Role: Facilitator to Learning," *School Nurse*, (Fall 1982).

Jones, E. H. "P.L. 94-142 and the Role of School Nurses in Caring for Handicapped Children." *Journal of School Health*, (March 1979) 147-56.

Lewis, C.E. and Lewis, M.A., "Child Initiated Health Care." *Journal of School Health*, (March 1980) 144-48.

Orem, D.E., *Nursing Concepts of Practice*. New York: McGraw-Hill, 1971.

Schoenhofer, Savina O. "Support as Legitimate Nursing Actions." *Nursing Outlook*, (July-Aug 1984) 218-19.

Verzmnieks, Inese L. and Nash, Debra, "Ethical Issues Related to Pediatric Care." *The Nursing Clinics of North America*, (June 1984).

Part Two

Selected Health Conditions

Part Two

Selected Health Conditions

To many of us, the term "illness" connotes something temporary, something that troubles us only temporarily until we "recover" or are "cured." To many students, these concepts need refining. These students live instead with a daily health concern—one that may last a lifetime. For them, to be as healthy as possible means not recovery or cure, but management and control. These are the students with chronic health conditions.

There were several reasons for choosing to cover asthma, diabetes and epilepsy in Part Two. Each of them may be "invisible" to the eye. Students with these chronic health conditions will show few visible signs of illness, and most often they will not be in a special education program. Finally, each of these chronic conditions can be managed—if appropriate planning and prevention takes place.

Chapter 7 gives essential information about asthma, including specific suggestions for helping a student manage the condition.

Chapter 8 takes a similar approach to diabetes. Included is information on what diabetes is; how to respond to hypoglycemia, hyperglycemia and other related conditions; and actions you can take daily to help students control diabetes.

Chapter 9 is about epilepsy (seizure disorder). Here you'll find basic information on seizures, the medications used to control them and how you can effectively contribute to a student's overall management of epilepsy.

Chapter 10 reviews our current understanding of AIDS—including how it is spread and what is symptoms are. Most importantly, it outlines the issues that organizations face when they respond to a child with AIDS—and the actions they can take.

Chapter 7

Helping the Student with Asthma

Cyndy Schuster Silkworth, M.P.H., R.N., C.S.N.P.
Diane Jones, B.S., R.N.

In This Chapter You'll Find:

A definition of asthma and information on why asthma episodes occur.

Actions you can take to help the student with asthma.

Guidelines for managing students with asthma during physical education.

Procedures to follow when a student has an asthma episode.

Overview

Childhood asthma is a chronic disease that affects about 6 percent of the children in the United States. It causes more hospital admissions, visits to emergency rooms and more school absences than any other chronic disease of childhood.

What is asthma? Asthma is a chronic disease in which the air passages (bronchioles) overreact. During an asthma "attack" or episode, the air passages become temporarily narrowed or blocked.

The bronchioles become narrow or blocked in three different ways in asthma attack: (See Figure 7-1.)

Figure 7-1: Small airway and alveoli: normal (left) and during asthma attack.

- The muscles encircling the bronchioles tighten, causing narrowing of the air passage.

- The cells lining the bronchioles swell and narrow the air passage even further.

- The cells lining the bronchioles secrete mucus which can plug the remaining opening in the air passage.

Why asthma episodes occur. Five basic things may trigger asthma attacks:

- Colds and other viral infections are the most common triggers of asthma. Because of asthma, a small cold can sometimes lead to a bigger infection.

- Allergens are tiny particles that people can breathe in, drink, eat or get on their skin. They cause specific reactions only in people sensitive to them. Common allergens that can lead to asthma attacks include tree and grass pollens, house dust, feathers, animal dander, molds, medications and foods.

- Exercise or overexertion can trigger an attack, especially in cold weather.

- Irritation from air pollution, such as cigarette, cigar or pipe smoke, perfumes, dust chemicals, strong odors and smog.

- Emotions may trigger asthma if they lead to an outburst of yelling, crying, screaming or laughing. This is rare, however.

What School Personnel Can Do

School personnel can take specific actions to help the student with asthma.

Provide the student with a normal classroom experience. Treat the student with asthma as you would a student without it. Accept the student and understand the condition. Do not label the child as "sick" or isolate the child.

Initiate a conference with the parents, child, school nurse, and teachers. Discuss the student's asthma, school and home management and medication.

Establish a plan to manage asthma at school. This record needs to include a variety of information: a description of student's asthma; known triggers of asthma episodes; medications used in asthma management (name, dose, how often they are taken, when should they be given, how they are administered, and under what circumstances should additional doses be given); and steps to take and persons to be notified in case of severe breathing difficulty.

Update this plan, particularly as it relates to medications and dosages, every six months.

Make sure medication is taken. Medications may be needed during the school day for managing asthma. Medication should be given by or under the direct supervision of the school nurse.

Encourage the student to be as active as possible and take part in physical education. Students with asthma will learn their limitations and can stop exercise if wheezing or coughing begins. Some medications can be taken prior to physical activity to prevent an attack—if they have been prescribed they should be given. Warm-up exercises also help.

Encourage the student to drink plenty of fluids. This helps thin the mucus in the lungs.

Watch for medication effects. Some asthma medications can cause side effects that, in turn, cause behavior changes such as tiredness, inattention and hyperactivity. Therefore, if a student known to have asthma suddenly exhibits behavior problems, check with the student, school nurse or parents. Adjustments in medications may be needed.

Encourage a good attendance pattern. With good asthma management, most students with asthma can attend school regularly. However, students with severe asthma may miss school. Help these students by providing encouragement and time to keep up with assignments and course requirements.

Consider classroom adjustments. Whenever possible, make sure the student doesn't sit next to someone with a respiratory infection. Any student allergic to pollen should not sit by an open window during allergy season. On very cold days, it may be best to have the student with asthma recess indoors.

Watch for dust and molds. Gym mats, lockers and library books are often loaded with dust and molds. Regular cleaning and airing are important.

Physical Education: Managing Students with Asthma

Some special considerations apply when the student with asthma is involved in physical education or sports. Here are some points to remember, as suggested by the American Lung Association:

- Use warm-up exercises. They may help ward off episodes caused by athletics.

- Find out if the school nurse has information on the student's asthma.

- Schedule a conference with the parent, student, classroom teacher, physical education teacher and nurse.

- Discuss feelings about exercise and establish physical education goals for the student.

- Establish emergency procedures for assisting a student who is having an asthma episode.

- Do not have a student participate in physical education activities if there are noticeable symptoms of asthma at that time.

- Discontinue the student's physical education activities for the day if an asthma episode develops.

- Help the student learn the joy of physical activity and how to pace him or herself.

(American Lung Association, 1983)

Judging the Severity of an Episode

When dealing with an asthma episode, you will have to judge its severity. Three indicators are used in making this judgement: the intake and output (I:O) ratio, the presence of wheezing and signs of retraction.

The I:O ratio is the best way to tell how the student is doing. This is a measure of how long an inhalation lasts, as compared to an exhalation. To get the feel of the I:O ratio, breathe in and out with the student. In a normal breathing pattern, inhalation lasts 50 percent longer than exhalation—an I:O ratio of 1.5:1.

When an asthma episode occurs, it takes longer to exhale. With a mild episode, this increase is hardly noticeable. In a moderate episode, inhalation and exhalation become about equal, an I:O ratio of 1:1. However, in a severe asthma episode the exhalation takes longer than the inhalation (Plaut, 1983).

Retractions are the sucking-in of the soft tissues in the chest; they occur with breathing difficulty. These are first seen below the rib cage, in the soft part of the neck above the breast bone, in the soft tissue over the collarbone and in the area at the bottom of the breastbone. In more severe episodes, the tissue between the ribs may be sucked in. These changes are a measure of the difficulty of breathing—a good guide to the severity of the attack (Plaut, 1983).

Wheezing is the high-pitched whistling sound that occurs when air flows through the narrowed bronchial tubes. When an episode starts, the wheezing only occurs on exhalation. In mild episodes, wheezing occurs at the end of the exhalation phase. As the episode gets worse, wheezing lasts through all of the exhalation; finally it occurs with inhalation.

Wheezing does not take place in a bronchial tube that is totally blocked. The absence of wheezing in a student who has severe retractions and a reversed I:O ratio (1:2) is a sign of serious trouble. When this student improves through the reopening of some windpipes, the wheezing will reappear (Plaut, 1983).

The following table summarizes these signs as they relate to the severity of an asthma episode.

Table 7-1

	Mild	Moderate	Severe
I:O Ratio	About 1.5:1	About 1:1	Less that 1:1
Wheezing	Mild, on inhalation	Full	On inhalation and marked on exhalation
Retractions	None	Mild	Marked

What to Do When an Asthma Episode Occurs

Make sure your school, working with a health professional, establishes a standard procedure to follow in dealing with an asthma episode. Then encourage all staff members to be trained in that procedure. The instructions in this section are general guidelines for such a procedure.

Keep the information in Table 7-1 in mind for step 2 of managing an asthma episode, described in the procedure that follows.

What to Do When an Asthma Episode Occurs

Procedure:

1. *Determine if the student is having an asthma episode.* Watch for these symptoms:

   - Wheezing.

   - Coughing.

   - Difficulty in breathing or breathlessness.

   - A feeling of tightness in the student's chest.

   - A bluish color in the lips and nail beds.

   - A decrease in peak flow. See "Use of the Peak Flow Meter," page 90.

2. *Judge the severity of the episode.* Take into account wheezing, retractions and the I:O ratio. (See Table 7-1.)

3. *Find out if the student has been exposed to any asthma triggers.*

   The most common triggers are: colds and other viral infections, irritants, exercise and over-exertion, air pollution and strong emotion.

4. *Help the student sit up, with shoulders relaxed.*

   As you speak, be calm and reassuring. The student's anxiety can be lessened if you show you understand and know how to help.

5. *Encourage the student to drink fluids.* This helps to thin mucus.

6. *Help the student take the prescribed amount of the prescribed medicine.*

   Medications should be given or directed by the school nurse or other qualified health professional. For help on using inhaled medication, see "How to Use Your Inhaler," page 91.

7. *If the medication doesn't seem to work, notify the student's parents and health care provider.*

   Only in rare cases do students with asthma need emergency medical care.

8. *Document the asthma episode.*

   Note it in the the daily log and student health record.

9. *Follow up.* Let the student's parents know about any medical intervention. Try to identify what triggered the episode. Remove it or plan to help the student avoid it.

   Check the supply of prescribed medication, and notify the student and parent if more is needed.

10. *Help other staff members and students understand what asthma is and why it occurs.*

    Explore their attitudes and feelings about asthma, and explain what to do if a student has an asthma episode. This can be done through health education, counseling and small group discussion.

Summary

Asthma is a chronic disease in which the air passages become temporarily narrowed or blocked.

Asthma episode can be triggered by a variety of causes, including colds and other viral infections, common irritants, physical activity and strong emotions.

Help the student avoid allergies that may trigger an asthma episode.

Try to provide a normal classroom experience for the student with asthma. Encourage the student to be as active as possible.

Schedule a conference with the key people involved in managing the student's asthma.

For every student with asthma, establish and maintain a plan to manage asthma at school.

Make sure medication is taken, and watch for side effects. Encourage the student to drink plenty of fluids.

Encourage a pattern of good attendance.

Encourage students with asthma to take part as fully as possible in physical education and athletic programs.

Follow logical, pre-planned procedures when an asthma episode occurs.

The following pages include these sample forms and educational materials:

- Sample Letter to Parents of the Child with Asthma

- Questionnaire for Parents of the Child with Asthma

- Asessing the Student's Knowledge of and Responsibility for Control of His/Her Asthma

- Goals of Asthma Management

- School Attendance

- Common Asthma Medications

- Using the Mini-Wright Peak Flow Meter or Pulmonary Monitor

- How to Use Your Inhaler

- Common Problems with Inhalers

References

American Lung Association. *Asthma Alert Series* (For Administrators, Teachers, School Nurses and Physical Education Teachers), 1983.

Plaut, Thomas F. *Children with Asthma.* Amherst, MA: Pedipress, 1983.

For Further Reading

Pfuetze, Bruce L. *Asthma: A Matter of Control.* American Lung Association of Kansas, 1983.

Sample Letter to Parents of the Child with Asthma

Dear Parent:

You have told us that your child has asthma.

Please fill out the attached school asthma record and return it. I will share the information with appropriate personnel, such as your child's classroom teacher(s) and physical education teacher. This information will help them work with your child to minimize unnecessary restriction, feeling of being treated differently, and possible absence from school.

To help your child, please let us know of changes in your child's asthma or medication schedules.

Sincerely,

School Nurse
(Courtesy of American Lung Association)

Common Asthma Medications

Oral Theophylline Medications	Theodur®
	Slobid®
	Somophyllin®
	Slophyllin®
	Quibron®
	Aminophyllin®
Oral Beta-adenergic Medications	Albuterol – Ventolin®, Proventil®
	Terbutaline – Brethine®
	Metaproterenol – Alupent®
Inhaled Beta-adrenergic Medications	Albuterol – Ventolin®, Proventil®
	Terbutaline – Brethine®
	Metaproterenol – Alupent®
	Isoproterenol – Isuprel®
	Isoetharine – Brokosol®
Injectable Beta-adenergic Medications	Epinephrine – Adrenalin®
	Terbutaline®
Oral Steroid Medication	Prednisone – Delasone®, Pediapred®
Inhaled Steroid Medication	Vanceril®
	Beclovent®
	Azmacort®
	Aerobid®
Cromolyn	Intal®
Anticholinergic Medication	Atropine – Atrovent®

Questionnaire For Parents of Child With Asthma

PARENT INTERVIEW

Student's Name _____ School Year _____

School _____ Grade _____ Classroom _____

Parent's Name(s) _____ Telephone (home) _____ (work) _____

The following information is helpful to your child's school nurse and school staff in determining any special needs for your child. Please answer the questions to the best of your ability. If you desire a conference with the school nurse, please call for an appointment.

Nurse's Name _____ Telephone Number _____

1. How long has your child has asthma? _____

2. Please rate the severity of his/her asthma. (circle)

   (Not Severe)   0   1   2   3   4   5   6   7   8   9   10   (Severe)

3. How many days would you estimate he/she missed school last year due to asthma? _____

4. What triggers your child's asthma attacks? (Please check any that apply.)

   ☐ Illness   ☐ Emotions   ☐ Medications   ☐ Foods
   ☐ Weather   ☐ Exercise   ☐ Cigarette or other smoke   ☐ Chemical odors
   ☐ Allergies (please list) _____   ☐ Fatigue
   ☐ Other (please list) _____

5. What does your child do at home to relieve wheezing during an asthma attack? (please check any that apply.)

   ☐ Breathing exercises   Takes medication: ☐ Inhaler
   ☐ Rest/relaxation   ☐ Nebulizer
   ☐ Drinks liquids   ☐ Oral medication
                                  Other (please describe) _____

6. What medications does your child take and how often?

   Every day _____

   Just for wheezing/attacks _____

   Before exercise _____

   Just certain times of the year or when ill _____

7. What medications will your child need to take in school? (Please list name of medication and when it is to be taken.)

   _____

   _____

   _____

   Who is responsible for remembering to take the medication at home?

   ☐ Parent   ☐ Child   ☐ Both

8. What if any, side effects does your child have from his/her medication?

   _____

9. Has your child been taught how to use an extension tube, pulmonary aid, Inspirease kit or other device with his/her inhaler? ☐ Yes   ☐ No

10. How many times has your child been hospitalized overnight or longer for asthma in the past year?

_____

11. How many times has your child been treated in the emergency room for asthma in the past year?_____

12. How often does your child see his/her doctor for routine asthma evaluations?_____

13. Name of child's doctor (for asthma) _____

    Address _____

14. Does your child also have allergies?   ☐ Yes   ☐ No

    If yes, please describe: _____

    _____

15. What reactions does child have with above allergies?

    _____

    _____

16. Does your child need any special considerations related to his/her asthma while at school? (Check any that apply and describe briefly.)
    ☐ Modified gym class _____
    ☐ Modified recess outside _____
    ☐ No animal pets in classroom _____
    ☐ Avoiding certain foods _____
    ☐ Emotional or behavior concerns _____
    ☐ Special consideration while on field trips _____
    ☐ Special transportation to and from school _____
    ☐ Observation for side effects from medication _____
    ☐ Need to take medication during school day (described in question 7) _____
    ☐ Other_____

17. If your child suffers a severe attack in school (not relieved by medication or rest), what plan of action would you prefer school personnel to take?

    _____

    _____

18. Do you know what your child's baseline peak flow rate is?   ☐ Yes   ☐ No   Rate _____

19. Do you think your child holds him/herself back from participating in all activities at school because of his/her asthma? If so, please describe.

    _____

20. Have you ever attended an asthma education class?   ☐ Yes   ☐ No
    Has child had asthma education?   ☐ Yes   ☐ No

21. Has child attended Camp Superkids (a special camp sponsered by the American Lung Association at YMCA's Camp Iduhapi)?   ☐ Yes   ☐ No

22. Would you be interested in receiving information on asthma education programs?   ☐ Yes   ☐ No
    Receiving a free monthly newsletter from the American Lung Association called Asthma Update?   ☐ Yes   ☐ No

Thank you for your time and assistance in assessing your special child's very special needs in school.

Developed by:
Donna Amidon, RN, PNP, SN, MPH Candidate

ASSESSING THE STUDENT'S KNOWLEDGE OF AND
RESPONSIBILITY FOR CONTROL OF HIS/HER ASTHMA

STUDENT INTERVIEW

Student's Name _____ Grade _____

School _____ Classroom _____

SUBJECTIVE ASSESSMENT

1. What medications do you take? Name, dose, how often and what does it do?

   _____

   _____

   ☐ Knows well   ☐ Knows some   ☐ Knows nothing

2. Who is responsible for your medications at home? (Do you remember on your own or does someone need to remind you or actually give it to you?)

   _____

   _____

   ☐ Totally self-responsible   ☐ Needs reminding   ☐ Not responsible

3. How do you feel when your asthma is acting up? (Include symptoms just before and during an attack.)

   _____

   _____

4. What are your triggers - things that make you wheeze? (list)

   _____

   _____

5. What, besides taking medication, do you do to help control your asthma?

   _____

   _____

6 What do you think is happening inside your lungs during a wheezing episode (asthma attack)?

   _____

   _____

   ☐ Understands physiology well   ☐ Understands physiology some   ☐ Doesn't understand physiology

7. Can you demonstrate breathing exercises? ☐ Yes   ☐ No

8. What, if any, special problems do you have in school that are related to your asthma? (gym, recess, foods, teasing, etc.)

   _____

   _____

Goals of Asthma Management

1. Prevention of asthma episode that needs a doctor's visit or a trip to the emergency room.

2. Prevention of asthma symptoms such as chronic cough, difficulty of breathing, easy fatigability from normal activities.

3. Reduction in the number of hospitalizations.

4. Control of asthma symptoms with the least amount and side effects of medications.

5. Participation in sports and other normal activities without many restrictions.

6. Education of the family and the patient about the important aspects of asthma so everybody can help cope and improve their lifestyle.

7. Attain a normal pulmonary function at all times.

8. Attain normal growth and development both physically and mentally.

9. Reduce school and work absenteeism.

10. Prolong life span.

11. Attain self-confidence and self-esteem.

Leo Leonidas, M.D.
Editor
Asthma Today

School Attendance

Asthma and School Attendance: Checklist For Deciding About School Attendance

Clues for Sending Child to School:

1. Stuffy nose but no wheezing

2. Mild wheezing which clears after medicine

3. Good exercise tolerance (able to participate in usual daily activities)

4. No extra effort needed with breathing pattern.

Clues for Keeping Child at Home:

1. Evidence of infection-red/sore throat, or swollen glands;

2. Fever over 100 degrees (hot and flushed);

3. Wheezing which continues to increase one hour after medicine is taken;

4. Child is too weak or tired to take part in routine daily activities;

5. Breathing pattern is labored, irregular, rapid (more than 25 breaths per minute at rest).

Each child is different and follows his/her own special pattern during an asthma episode. Therefore, it is best to observe your child closely and learn his/her particular body signs which serve as a guide to his/her state of health.

From: "The Impact of Bronchial Asthma On School Attendance and Performance," *Journal of School Health*, Nov., 1980.

Using the Mini-Wright Peak Flow Meter or Pulmonary Monitor

Peak flow meters can detect early changes in the bronchioles—before the wheezing or tightness in the chest that signals an asthma attack.

Two peak meters, both inexpensive, are useful in managing asthma: the Mini-Wright Peak Flow Meter and Pulmonary Monitor. What follows are general instructions applying to both. Remember: You must use any peak flow meter under guidance from your physician.

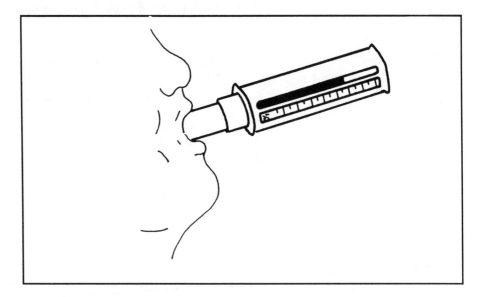

Figure 7-2: The Mini-Wright Peak Flow Meter.

1. Stand up.

2. Make sure the pointer is at zero.

3. Hold the meter with the vent free.

4. Take in all the air you can.

5. Put the mouthpiece on your tongue and your lips around the mouthpiece.

6. Blow out forcefully and quickly. Note the measurement on the side of the meter.

7. Do this three times—but wait 15 seconds between tries.

8. Record your best measurement from each session (once in the morning and once at night). For best results, do this at the same time each day.

(Plaut, 1983)

How to Use Your Inhaler

Medication helps to open or dilate the bronchial tubes. When treating asthma, it is often best to deliver the medication directly to the lungs via the inhaler. This makes it very important that your technique with the inhaler is correct.

You can help the student cooperate by:

- Explaining in advance.

- Describing as you demonstrate.

- Keeping a calm voice.

- Reassuring and praising when you're through.

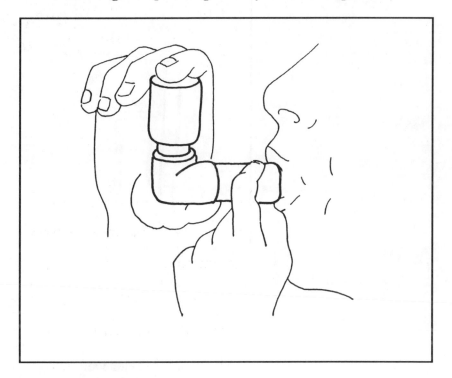

Figure 7-3: Use of the inhaler—tube.

Summary of directions for tube:

1. Shake the inhaler well.

2. Breathe out to the end of a normal breath.

3. Hold the inhaler in the upright position in one hand. Hold the tube attached to the inhaler in the other hand.

4. Place the tube in your mouth.

5. Tilt your head slightly and start to breathe in slowly.

6. Spray the inhaler at the start of a normal breath.

7. Breathe in as deeply as possible over a period of 2 to 3 seconds.

8. Take the inhaler out of your mouth and hold your breath for the count of 10.

9. If another puff is needed, wait for 5 minutes and repeat.

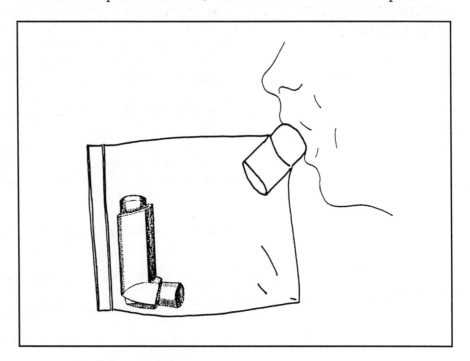

Figure 7-4: Use of the inhaler—bag.

Summary of directions for bag:

1. Shake the inhaler well.

2. Place the inhaler in the bag (a one quart zip lock plastic freezer bag).

3. Snip off one corner of the bag to make a hole just large enough to insert a cardboard tube.

4. Blow up the bag using the cardboard tube.

5. Spray the inhaler inside the bag.

6. Breathe in slowly to collapse the bag (or empty it).

7. Slowly breathe out into the bag (to blow it up).

8. Breathe in and out of the bag a total of three times.

9. After taking your last breath from the bag, hold your breath for the count of 10, if you can.

10. If another puff is required, wait 5 to 10 minutes and repeat steps 1 through 9.

Common Problems with Inhalers

1. **Not taking the medication as directed.** Do not take more puffs than the directions tell you to without talking to your doctor. When you are told to take more than one puff at a time, your medicine will work better if you wait several minutes between puffs.

2. **Not shaking the inhaler.** If you don't shake the inhaler, the right amount of medicine may not spray out.

3. **Breathing in too fast.** Breathing in too fast makes most of the medicine stick in your mouth and throat instead of getting to your lungs.

4. **Holding the inhaler upside down.** If you hold the inhaler upside down, it will stop spraying.

5. **Spraying the inhaler at the wrong time.** If you spray at the end of your breath instead of at the start, the medicine won't work as well.

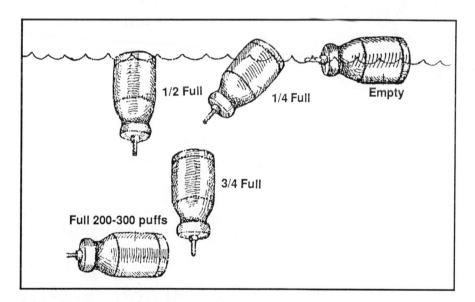

Figure 7-5: To tell if your inhaler is empty, put it in some water in a clear glass or plastic container.

(Materials on inhaler courtesy: Pharmacy, Minneapolis Children's Medical Center, Minneapolis, Minnesota.)

Chapter 8

The Student with Diabetes

Barbara Balik, R.N., M.S.
Broatch Haig, R.D., C.D.E.

In This Chapter You'll Find:

A definition of diabetes.

Information about the symptoms, causes and treatment of hypoglycemia.

Information on the symptoms and causes of hyperglycemia.

Suggestions for managing nutrition for the student with diabetes.

A description of blood glucose monitoring (BGM).

Guidelines on extracurricular activities for the student with diabetes.

Suggestions for communicating with parents of a student with diabetes.

Diabetes is a chronic condition that affects nearly one in every 600 school-aged children. It is similar to other non-visible health conditions (for example, epilepsy and asthma) in that it requires close daily attention to ensure wellness. Diabetes also requires that school personnel cooperate in helping the student attain long-term physical and emotional health.

What is Diabetes?

Diabetes is a chronic health condition that results in a lack of insulin—or the inability of the body to use insulin. Today we identify two types of diabetes.

Diabetes in children used to be called juvenile diabetes. The condition has been reclassified as insulin-dependent diabetes mellitus, or Type I diabetes. Type I diabetes refers to complete or near-complete lack of insulin production from certain cells in the pancreas.

People with Type I diabetes require daily insulin injections. Insulin, a protein, is broken down by the digestive system if taken orally. Thus, it must be taken by injection.

When insulin levels are deficient, the body is unable to appropriately use and store glucose, a form of sugar. Protein and fat must then be used as energy sources. One of the outcomes of the use of fat as an energy source is the production of acids called ketones. An excess of ketone bodies in the blood is called diabetic ketoacidosis, and it can result in diabetic coma and death.

In children, insulin also acts as a growth hormone. Children who have an inappropriate balance of food and insulin do not grow adequately because of decreased utilization of the food consumed.

Most older adults who develop diabetes have normal or higher than normal amounts of insulin in their blood; however, their use of insulin at the cellular level is impaired. This is known as Type II diabetes. People with this kind if diabetes may or may not inject insulin.

Dealing With Hypoglycemia

What is hypoglycemia? Insulin reaction, insulin shock and hypoglycemia are different names for the same thing—low blood glucose. The symptoms are the body's way of telling a person that the amount of glucose in the blood is dropping or has dropped. Reactions usually come quickly. They occur most frequently before meals, during or after exercise and at peak action time of the insulin.

Table 8-1

Symptoms of Hypoglycemia

When the blood glucose drops, the brain does not receive enough glucose and sends out warning signals. These signals may include:

- Shaking
- Sweating
- Hunger
- Dizziness

- Paleness
- Numbness or tingling of the lips
- Irritability

- Poor coordination
- Confusion
- Headaches
- Double or blurred vision

Causes of hypoglycemia. Hypoglycemia can result from too much insulin, too little food or strenuous unplanned exercise. The signals of hypoglycemia may vary from one episode to another with the same student. Parents or students are usually able to identify two to three consistent signals. (See Table 8-1.)

Students are able to recognize their own signals and treat their reactions at different ages. Lower elementary grade school students will usually need help in recognizing the signals and treatment. Older students may not be able to handle their own reactions when signals such as confusion, irritability and poor coordination are present.

Table 8-2

Treating Hypoglycemia

Any student having a signal of a reaction should eat a food containing 10 to 15 grams of fast-acting glucose. Some suitable foods and amounts are:

    1 small box (2 Tbsp.) raisins
    1 Fruit Roll-up®
    1/2 cup regular pop or soda (not diet)
    6 or 7 Lifesavers®
    4 or 5 dried fruit pieces
    1/2 cup of any fruit juice
    5 small sugar cubes or 2 large sugar cubes
    1/3 bottle Glutose®
    2 or 3 BD Glucose Tablets®
    Monoject® Insulin Reaction Gel

Gym teachers and coaches need to recognize signals of an insulin reaction and carry a source of glucose. Lifesavers, Glucose Tablets® , Monojel® (in single dose form) and Glutose are non-prescription, stable, portable forms of glucose.

Treating hypoglycemia. Foods for treating hypoglycemia (see Table 8-2) need to be suitable for the classroom. They should be portable and "quiet"—no crackly wrapping. The student does not need to leave the classroom for a mild reaction. You may need to coax the student to eat during a reaction. Avoid using foods not usually in the student's meal plan, such as malts and candy bars.

If a meal or snack time is not due for one hour or more, follow up the reaction treatment with a class of milk or three or four crackers. The reaction should begin to resolve in ten to fifteen minutes. If the student doesn't feel better, he or she should go to the health office, check blood glucose and again eat the same amount of food. (See page 111 for a description of blood glucose monitoring.)

If after another ten to fifteen minutes there is little response, the school nurse or other qualified health professional should check the student's blood glucose. When symptoms persist, call the parent or health care provider.

Following these guidelines will avoid over-treating a reaction—something that can result in elevated blood glucoses.

Some students use a "buddy system" with vigorous sports or activities. A friend who recognizes early signals can help the young person treat the reaction promptly by reminding the partner to eat a snack, or by alerting a coach.

In any case, report severe or repeated reactions to parents.

Dealing With Hyperglycemia

Hyperglycemia is another word for high blood sugar, which is present in undetected, untreated or poorly regulated diabetes.

Physical and emotional stress will usually raise blood sugar. Physical stress can include infection (such as cold or flu) or trauma. Emotional stress can stem from all the things that influence feelings, either positive or negative. Students with or without diabetes face stress: school performance, family conflicts, the excitement of a holiday or athletic event, or the concerns of dating and other peer relationships. The school setting cannot be free from stress, but we can work toward positive ways to deal with stress.

Some students with diabetes occasionally omit insulin—accidentally or deliberately. Deliberate mismanagement signals emotional stress.

Hyperglycemia and ketoacidosis. High blood glucose can lead to ketoacidosis. Ketoacidosis develops when there is not enough insulin in the blood to allow glucose to be used for energy. The body then must rely on fat for energy. When the body uses too much fat for energy, that fat can't be broken down completely by the liver. Acids called ketones are then formed. At the same time, the high blood glucose leads to high urine glucose and loss of large amounts of body fluid and minerals.

Table 8-3

Medical Emergency: The Signs of Ketoacidosis.

Ketoacidosis is dangerous. It can cause unconsciousness (diabetic coma) and death if not treated immediately. Call the student's parents and health care provider if any of the following signs are present:

- Moderate to large ketones in the urine along with high blood glucose levels.

- Severe nausea.

- Vomiting.

- Abdominal pain.

- Rapid breathing.

High blood sugar levels for several days can produce the following symptoms:

- Nausea.

- Thirst and dry mouth.

- Frequent urination.

- Weight loss.

- Tiredness.

Symptoms of hyperglycemia. If high blood sugar levels persist and the urine tests positive for ketones, the student may experience abdominal pain, nausea, vomiting and blurred vision. (See Table 8-3.)

Hyperglycemia can cause other symptoms. Students with moderately elevated blood glucose levels may not develop ketoacidosis but may complain of difficulty reading or seeing the board. Corrective lenses should not be prescribed or changed until blood glucoses are brought into a normal range. An increased number of infections and delayed healing can occur with hyperglycemia.

Insulin and Pattern Control

Students will probably not need to take their insulin while at school. However, school personnel need to recognize one fact: Insulin doses given before school will continue to act during the day and will influence the student's needs for regular food intake. Bus drivers need to be aware of riders who have diabetes and of the signs of hypoglycemia, in case a student decides to skip or share an afternoon snack. If necessary, the bus driver should allow children with diabetes to eat a snack.

Nutritional Management

The student with diabetes does not require supervision while eating in school. Eating should be a nonintrusive part of the day. The student does, however, need a school environment that supports the variations needed for an individualized meal plan.

A diabetes meal plan may be described in terms of exchanges, points, low sugar or other terms. But these plans generally follow guidelines recommended by the American Diabetes Association, American Heart Association and the American Cancer Society. Consistency in amounts and timing of meals is crucial: Insulin dosages are based on the meal plan and the student's individual needs.

You do not need extensive knowledge of or experience with diabetes meal plans to help students with diabetes in the school setting. Some of the major points include:

Minimize restrictions. Stress the student's ability to function independently and support it. Help the student and family coordinate meals and snacks with the school schedule, and plan for a consistent lunch and gym time. This is especially important in schools with a rotating lunch and class schedule.

Seek out information. Not all students can articulate their needs to other school personnel. Follow-up with the family to find out if the student needs help in communicating with coaches, bus drivers and others.

Suggest healthy snacks. Without singling out the student with diabetes, you can send suggestions for healthy snacks and treats to all parents. Some nutritious snack ideas include: fruit, pretzels, popcorn, cheese, some homemade cookies (for example, oatmeal cookies with raisins), angel food cake with fruit topping and homemade granola.

Make lunch part of the plan. School lunch can be worked into the diabetes meal plan, and it is important for the student to take part in this if he or she chooses. This can be done in a variety of ways. For example, fresh fruit or fruit in its own juice should be available to substitute for fruit in heavy syrup and desserts. Students learn to substitute such foods on their own as they grow older.

Promote "low noise" foods. These are foods that students can unwrap quietly. With them, students can avoid disrupting the classroom when eating a scheduled snack or treating hypoglycemia. Such snacks might include raisins or other dried fruits, fruit juice, Fruit Roll-ups and cheese.

Keep snacks handy. Avoid storing snacks outside the classroom—for example, in the health office. Instead, keep the snack in the classroom. Help the teacher recognize the need for the student to have the snack at the appropriate time and not to single out a student with diabetes. The student can treat hypoglycemia without leaving the classroom.

Help overcome resistance. If a student resists snacks—something often seen in the upper grades—the parent may hope to enlist you as an enforcer. ("Make her go to the office so I know she's eating her snack.") Instead, suggest consulting with the health care provider. It may be possible to rearrange insulin doses and meals to eliminate snacks. In short, avoid supporting battles between parents and student.

Remember snack times. Key timing for snacks is before gym period and other high activity times such as recess—unless the activities follow a meal. Students with diabetes, gym teachers and coaches should carry a glucose source.

Support smart diets. Weight gain is often a concern for adolescent females with diabetes. They aren't able to use some of the dieting measures their peers employ: skipping meals, starvation diets, etc. These students may need support to watch calories reasonably. Even better, the school can offer education for all adolescents in "eating smart."

Blood Glucose Monitoring: A New Tool

Blood glucose monitoring (BGM) has gained remarkable acceptance within the past few years. This procedure allows the student to check and record blood glucose levels several times a day. If they choose, students can check their blood glucoses at noon, before major exercise or when they think they're having a reaction. Either a visually-read strip or a meter can be used.

Figure 8-1: Blood Glucose Monitoring device (reflectance meter).

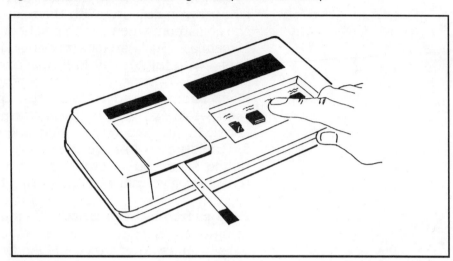

BGM is a practical, reliable method of measuring blood glucose levels. It also provides more information for self-management of diabetes than urine testing. Diabetes control requires primary management by the parents and student with supervision from the heath professional. As an aid to immediate decision making and long term diabetes management, BGM offers a useful tool to all these people.

Students' attitudes toward BGM vary widely. Some students with diabetes have used blood glucose monitoring as a science project. Others want no additional attention focused on their diabetes and refuse to test at school. Testing is the student's choice.

In response, you can be sensitive to the student's wishes and offer support and encouragement. Don't treat blood glucose readings as "good" or "bad"; see them as useful pieces of information. Offer students praise for completing the task, not for the outcome. Don't withhold food for elevated blood glucose readings. Don't give advice on insulin or meal plans; leave these to the family physician or primary care provider.

Reliable use of BGM depends on consistent and accurate technique. Students must follow step-by-step instructions for timing, testing and accuracy. Contact a local diabetes center, state office of the American Diabetes Association (ADA) or pharmaceutical company—all excellent sources of information and training for use of specific testing equipment.

Diabetes and Extracurricular Activities

Students with diabetes are encouraged to participate in as many school activities as they choose. Extracurricular activities often promote self-esteem and a sense of well-being—important factors for all students but especially for those with a chronic health condition.

Here are the major points for parents and school personnel to remember when planning sports and other vigorous activities:

- Be sure the student's diabetes is under control. This information should be entered on the annual pre-participation physical examination and shared with teachers and coaches.

- Start the activity slowly and gradually increase it. Actually, this is important for all students involved with vigorous activities.

- When beginning a new activity or sport, the student may need to check blood glucose before, during and after exercise. This provides information when planning for food and insulin needs.

Communicate with Parents Early On

Talk to the family of a student with diabetes before school begins in the fall. This aids in planning and promotes full participation by school personnel. Moreover, early communication clarifies the parents' main concerns.

Early planning also prevents a minor problem (for example, mild hypoglycemia) from becoming a major problem (convulsion resulting from lack of early treatment). Through planning, school personnel can learn specific ways to help the student with diabetes—behaviors that are supportive, nonrestrictive and nonintrusive.

As you do this, keep the following points in mind.

Recognize the parents—and upper-grade student—as the experts. These people live with diabetes 100 percent of the time. Their management skills may not be excellent, but the first step is to recognize their present ability.

Demonstrate a willingness to work with the family. Parents of younger students may face school personnel who are uninformed or not helpful. This can be stressful. Emphasize to the parents and student your interest in promoting the student's independence as he or she is able to assume responsibilities.

Ask about specifics. Find out the details about diabetes management:

- The times for snacks and what teachers need to know about food in classroom.

- Early symptoms of hypoglycemia. Is student able to recognize and treat these, or does a teacher need to intervene? What are the usual signals of hypoglycemia?

- How exercise is managed. Is a snack required before gym or recess?

- When parents want to be called.

- Who the primary diabetes health care provider is, and when parents want them contacted.

- Whether or not blood glucose or urine testing should be done at school.

- How much assistance the student needs.

Avoid "collecting" information and keeping it within the school file. Communicate, both in written and verbal form, the specifics to the appropriate teachers, coaches and other school personnel.

You can help achieve the goal: full school participation for helping any student with a chronic illness. Diabetes requires a balance of food, time, activity—all things students usually take for granted. The school system can develop its role as a supportive part of a student's life by informing key personnel of what they need to know about diabetes.

Families and health care providers don't expect school personnel to assume medical management. However, informed and concerned school personnel can act in the best interest of a student with diabetes.

Summary

Diabetes is a chronic health condition resulting from the body's decreased ability to use insulin.

Hypoglycemia refers to low blood sugar levels. It can result from a variety of factors, including too much insulin, too little food or strenuous, unplanned exercise.

The student with symptoms of an insulin reaction should eat a food containing 10 grams to 15 grams of fast-acting glucose.

Hyperglycemia is another word for high blood sugar, which is present in poorly regulated diabetes. It can lead to ketoacidosis, a dangerous condition that can result in diabetic coma or death if not treated promptly.

Some students will manage diabetes by taking insulin injections two or more times per day. This does not mean the student's condition is worse; it merely reflects individual needs.

The student with diabetes does not require special supervision while eating at school. The school, however, does need to allow for an individualized meal plan—for example, extra bread, peanut butter or cheese if necessary.

You can help by making sure the school lunch fits in with the student's meal plan, keeping appropriate snacks handy and supporting wise dieting.

Blood glucose monitoring (BGM) is a relatively new method for keeping track of blood glucose levels.

Encourage students with diabetes to take part in extracurricular activities. Make sure the student's diabetes is under control, and start activities slowly.

Communicate with the student's family before school begins. Find out the specifics of diabetes management.

For Further Reading

Balik, B., Haig, B., Moynihan, P. "Diabetes and the School-Aged Child." *American Journal of Maternal Child Nursing*, Vol. 2, No.5 (September-October 1986) 324-330.

Bowlin, H., Joynes, J., Sandell, J., Strock, E.: *Recognizing and Treating Insulin Reactions.* Minneapolis, MN: International Diabetes Center.

Franz, M., Joynes, J.: *Diabetes and Brief Illness.* Minneapolis, MN: International Diabetes Center.

Franz, M.: *Diabetes and Exercise: How to Get Started.* Minneapolis, MN: International Diabetes Center.

Loman, D. and Galgani, C. "Monitoring Diabetic Children's Blood Glucose Levels at Home." *MCN*, Vol. 9 (May-June 1984) 192-196.

McNeil, L. "Self Blood Glucose Monitoring: An Update." *The Diabetes Educator*, (Winter 1983) 15-18.

Stein, R.: "Growing Up With a Physical Difference." *Children's Health Care*, Vol. 12 (Fall 1983) 53-61.

Stein, R. and Jessop, D.: "Relationships Between Health Status and Psychological Adjustment Among Children with Chronic Conditions." *Pediatrics*, Vol. 73, (February 1984) 169-74.

Following are two tables: Characteristics of Type I Insulin-Dependent Diabetes Mellitus, and Guidelines for Sports and Other Vigorous Activity.

Also included are several educational materials:

- Blood Glucose Monitoring Precautions
- Blood Glucose Monitoring in Schools—Guidelines
- Sample Consent Form

All are courtesy of the International Diabetes Center, Minneapolis, Minnesota.

Characteristics Of Type I Insulin-Dependent
Diabetes Mellitus

ONSET: Rapid, sudden. Usually within days or weeks. May be confused with flu-like illness.

SYMPTOMS: Increased thirst (polydipsia). Frequent urination (polyurial). Increased appetite (polyphagia). Weight loss. Tiredness. Dehydration.

KETOACIDOSIS: Common

PREVALENCE: 0.3% of general population. 15% of all cases of diabetes.

TREATMENT: A balance of: insulin, diet, exercise, stress management.

CAUSE: Some genetic relationship but not clearly identified. Some theories relating viral illness and genetic predisposition. Some auto immune response noted.

COURSE: Sudden changes can result.

COMPLICATIONS:

Short term: Hypoglycemia

Intermediate: Hyperglycemia episodes. Inadequate growth.

Long term: Small blood vessel damage, especially in the in the retina and kidneys.

Guidelines For Sports And Other Vigorous Activities

Type of Exercise And Examples:	If Blood Sugar Is:	Increase Food Intake By:	Suggestions of Food To Use:
Exercise of short duration and of low to moderate intensity	less than 80 mg	10 - 15 gms of carbohydrates per hour	1 fruit or 1 starch/bread exchange
	100 mg or above	not necessary to increase food	
Examples: Walking a half mile or leisurely bicycling for less than 30 minutes			
Exercise of moderate intensity	less than 100 mg	25 - 50 gms of carbohydrate before exercise then 10 - 15 gms per hour of exercise	1/2 meat sandwich with a milk or fruit exchange
Examples:	100 - 180 mg	10 - 15 gms of carbohydrates per hour of exercise	1 fruit or 1 starch/bread exchange
Tennis, swimming, jogging, leisurely bicycling, gardening, golfing or vacuuming for one hour	180 - 300 mg	Not necessary to increase food	
	300 mg or greater	Don't begin exercise until blood glucose is under better control	
Strenuous activity or exercise	less than 100	50 gms of carbohydrate, monitor blood glucose carefully	1 meat sandwich (2) slices of bread with fruit and milk exchange
Examples:	100 - 180 mg	25 - 50 mg of carbohydrate depending on intensity and duration	1/2 meat sandwich with a milk or fruit exchange
Football, hockey, racquetball, or basketball games Strenuous bicycling or swimming, shoveling heavy snow	180 - 300 mg	10 - 15 gms of carbohydrate per hour of exercise	1 fruit or 1 starch/bread

Blood Glucose Monitoring Precautions

Recent concerns about certain infectious diseases—hepatitis, AIDS—has raised several questions regarding exposure of school personnel and children to potentially infectious body fluids from students with communicable diseases. The International Diabetes Center (IDC) in its work with schools and the Masons throughout Minnesota recognizes its responsibility to acknowledge this concern and would like to offer the following guidelines for all personnel who work with students who are doing Blood Glucose Monitoring (BGM). These guidelines are meant to provide simple and effective precautions against transmission of disease by BGM.

1. The BGM school supervisor should always wash hands with warm water and soap before working with each student.

2. A BGM supervisor should avoid self demonstration of finger poking.

3. Change both the lancet (needle) and the platform of the Autolet between students.

4. Penlet, Autoclix or Monojector platforms need to be soaked in a disinfectant* for 15 minutes before reusing. Autolet platforms may also be reused if soaked in this manner.

5. Demonstrate the "milking the finger" procedure to the student *prior* to puncturing the student's finger. Avoid touching the student's blood whenever possible. If the student actually has AIDS, or hepatitis virus, wear disposable gloves.

6. Wipe blood off on a disposable paper towel rather than directly on a hard surface.

7. The *student* should dispose of the lancet in safety container.

8. The student should dispose of soiled paper towels and cotton balls in double lined wastebaskets. Double bag any trash exposed to blood.

9. Clean and wash off working area daily with disinfectant*.

It is important to know that the likelihood of *any* school aged child, which includes those students with diabetes, to have a communicable disease such as AIDS or hepatitis is **Very Low**. Diabetes and/or BGM does not increase the likelihood that a child has or will get AIDS or hepatitis.

Blood Glucose Monitoring (BGM) Precautions

*Disinfectants

An intermediate level disinfectant should be used to clean surfaces contaminated with body fluids. Such disinfectants will kill vegetative bacteria, fungi, tubercle bacillus and viruses. The disinfectant should be registered by the U.S. Environmental Protection Agency (EPA) for use as a disinfectant in medical facilities and hospitals.

Various classes of disinfectants are listed below. Hypocholorite solution (bleach) is preferred for objects that may be put in the mouth.

1. Sodium Hypochlorite (household bleach) freshly prepared 1:10 dilution of 5.25% household bleach in water.

2. Ethyl or isoprophyl alcohol (70%).

3. Phenolic germicidal detergent in a 1% aqueous solution (e.g., Lysol).

4. Quaternary ammonium germicidal detergent in 2% aqueous solution (e.g., Tri-quat, Mytar or Sage).

5. Iodophor germicidal detergent with 500 ppm available iodine (e.g., Wescodyne).

In summary, there is not a problem with the transfer of any infectious disease by BGM as long as you follow these simple and usual precautions.

Blood Glucose Monitoring In Schools Guidelines

The Identified School Person IS Responsible for:

1. Obtaining parental consent and notifying parents of testing results according to mutually agreed upon instructions.

2. Supervising use of the meter and ensuring accurate testing and recording.

3. Being sensitive to the issue that it is the child's choice to test.

4. Dealing with the manufacturer in regard to any meter malfunction. (The warranty is made out to the school.)

5. Maintaining proficiency in performing blood glucose monitoring.

The Identified School Person IS NOT Expected to:

1. Be an expert on diabetes.

2. Advise changes in food, insulin, exercise or other areas of diabetes management. This is up to the physician, the child, and the parents.

3. React to high test numbers as "bad" or *necessarily* something the child could control or to low numbers as "good." Young people need praise for completing the task, not for the outcome. The meter gives information to be used in context with many other parameters.

Meter accuracy should be checked regularly every three months with another meter, and daily with "normal control solution." Options: 1) Verify meter reading per visual reading; 2) Take meter to doctor appointment and test school meter reading against lab fasting blood glucose; 3) Buy control solution (costly option); 4) Test your meter against another school meter.

If you have any questions or concerns in regard to these guidelines, please feel free to call the International Diabetes Center at 612/927-3830.

Chapter 9

The Student with Epilepsy

Carolyn Jones-Saete, R.N.

In This Chapter You'll Find:

A definition of epilepsy and different types of seizures.

Guidelines for communicating with parents and physicians about the student with epilepsy.

Information on medications for epilepsy.

Information about what seizures are and what causes them.

How to plan school-wide for effectively managing seizures.

What to do when a student has a seizure.

What is Epilepsy?

Epilepsy is a chronic disorder of the brain characterized by a tendency for recurrent seizures. A person has epilepsy if he or she has had more than two seizures unaccompanied by fever or illness. A seizure is a sudden, uncontrolled episode of excessive electric discharge of brain cells; this is accompanied by sensory, motor or behavioral changes.

In this chapter we use the term epilepsy rather than seizure disorder. The two terms mean the same thing.

Seizures are called by various names, including fits, spells, convulsions, and attacks. A seizure is a symptom of the disorder, just as a fever is a symptom of an infection. There are several types of seizures, and some of the most common are described on page 000.

Not all seizures indicate that a person has epilepsy. For example, a single seizure would not be classified as epilepsy. Specific seizures not classified as epilepsy are those resulting from:

- Fever (febrile convulsions).

- Alcohol and drug withdrawal.

- An imbalance of body fluids or chemicals.

- Severe allergic (anaphylactic) reactions.

- Lack of oxygen to the brain

Seizures may occur at long or short intervals: as frequently as several times per day or as infrequently as once every so many years. Some patients have seizures only in the night, some only in the day, and some both day and night. Seizures are more common in periods of relaxation than during activity. In women they may occur only, or more frequently, at menstrual periods.

Epilepsy has many different causes. In addition, the cause is unknown for 70 percent of the people with epilepsy. Known causes include prenatal influences, birth trauma, head trauma, toxic disorders, hemorrhage, cerebral vascular thrombosis, tumors and electrolyte imbalance.

As we begin our discussion about types of seizures, remember one crucial point: each student's seizure pattern is different. Moreover, a student may have more than one type of seizure, and the seizure pattern has the potential to change at any time.

It's important for school personnel and parents to use the same methods of managing seizures. Parents and school personnel have a joint responsibility to develop a plan for handling in-school seizures.

Types of Seizures

Seizures can be classified as partial or generalized. A very small number of seizures may be termed "unclassified." Partial seizures arise from a specific part of the brain. In contrast, generalized seizures do not have an identifiable focus in the brain and seem to arise from areas over the entire brain. Some seizures arise from a specific focus but then generalize to affect the entire brain. Although more than 30 types of seizures exist, the four types of seizures included here comprise the majority seen in people who have epilepsy:

- Absence

- Generalized tonic-clonic

- Simple partial

- Complex partial

Generalized seizures. This category includes absence and generalized tonic-clonic seizures.

Absence seizures were formerly called petit mal seizures. They consist of a sudden, brief loss of consciousness (one to ten seconds), and it is possible for a person to experience several hundred in a day. Absence seizures generally last less than ten seconds. They may be called generalized because they involve large areas of the brain.

Absence seizures are most common in children. And if they occur frequently during the school day, the child's learning may be severely affected. Seizure activity—often mistaken for daydreaming in children—may include staring spells, eye blinking and mild facial twitching.

In *generalized tonic-clonic* seizures there is a loss of consciousness, followed by stiffening for a few seconds (tonic phase), followed by a period of jerking (clonic phase). Usually these seizures last from less than a minute to three minutes. Then the person regains consciousness but is often confused or sleepy. In fact, some people may sleep for several hours.

This type of seizure affects the entire body. The person, usually with no warning, abruptly loses consciousness and may fall. You may hear the person make sounds—not from pain, but from air rushing out of the lungs as part of the seizure. Tongue biting, drooling and incontinence (loss of bladder or bowel control) often accompany the seizure. Breathing may be irregular, leading to a pale or blue complexion.

Partial seizures. This second major group of seizures is called partial because only one side or one part of the brain is involved.

The *simple partial* seizure was formerly known as a focal motor, focal sensory, or Jacksonian seizure. Here the person is aware that the seizure is occurring; consciousness is not impaired. These seizures are characterized by several types of symptoms:

- Motor—hand or mouth movement.

- Focal motor—head and eyes deviated to one side.

- Focal sensory—a "pins and needles" sensation or feelings of numbness.

- Auditory—a loud, rushing noise heard by the person having a seizure.

In some cases, this seizure activity may spread to a generalized tonic-clonic seizure.

A *complex partial* seizure impairs consciousness: The person may be partially aware or have distortion of consciousness. From person to person, what occurs during the seizures may vary greatly; however, for each person the occurrences seem consistent.

Complex partial seizures are characterized by purposeless activity—for example, a glassy stare or random movement of the arms or legs. People undergoing such a seizure appear to be in a dreamlike state and don't respond when you talk to them. They may walk about aimlessly, pick at their clothes or move their lips.

This seizure may also progress to a generalized tonic-clonic seizure.

Communicating about the Student with Epilepsy

It's rare for a physician to see a patient have a seizure. For this reason, a record of all seizures is essential.

Develop a plan to ensure that information gathered at school is communicated to parents. What school personnel observe about a student's seizures provides important information. These observations can:

- Assist in accurate diagnosis.

- Note changes in the character of seizures.

- Help the physician evaluate seizure control.

- Alert the family to events that may precipitate seizures.

- Alert medical staff to problems.

For students with frequent seizures, you may want to start a notebook to record seizure activity. Send this notebook back and forth between school and home. You may decide to use the notebook prior to the doctor's appointment or only when the student has a seizure.

At the student's appointment with the physician, a physical examination will be done. Blood levels of anticonvulsant medications will also be measured and information on seizures recorded.

A brief note that summarizes seizure activity and behavior will help the physician evaluate the student's current status. Generally, it's best to send these notes with parents. Often times, notes sent directly to the physician get misplaced or left in the office. After they receive notes from the parents, physicians will generally send the information back to school if requested.

What questions to ask. As you can see, it's important for parent, teacher and other school personnel to stay in close contact with each other. The following questions suggest what information parents need to share with school personnel:

Does the student have more than one kind of seizure? Describe what usually occurs before, during, and after each type of seizure.

How long has the child had seizures? Parents of a child with long-standing seizure problems may be able to give you more information.

What about prolonged seizures? Ask parents if their child has ever had a prolonged seizure requiring transportation to an emergency room for treatment.

Does the student have any allergies to medication? If so, what medications are involved?

Does the student have special needs for first aid? For example, a student that falls frequently may need to wear a helmet, with or without a face mask. A student who suddenly drops with a seizure may need to be watched closely during some activities—on stairs, climbing or swimming.

Medications and Anticonvulsants

It's important to learn specific information about medication:

- What medications are to be taken, along with their names and color.

- How much medication to take.

- When to take medication (how many times a day).

- What to do if there is a missed dose.

Refer to Chapter 12 for more help with administering medication at school. Also see the chart at the end of this chapter for a list of common anticonvulsive medications.

Planning for Effective Seizure Management

The first step in seizure management is training. That training should cover the appropriate procedures for helping a student having a seizure. It should also help staff members become aware of their attitudes toward people with seizure disorders.

The next steps are:

- Identify students with a history of seizures. Obtain information from them, their parents and physicians about: the type of seizures the student has, including a description of the seizure; medications the student is receiving (drug, dose, time and side effects); the most recent assessment by the physician; and past and current seizure patterns.

- Tell appropriate staff members about students with known seizure disorders.

- Encourage students with known seizure disorders to wear identification (a medical alert bracelet or necklace).

Managing a Seizure

Work with the health professional. School staff members need to cooperate with designated health personnel in performing the appropriate emergency procedures. Moreover, medications need to be administered or directly supervised by the school nurse or other qualified health professional.

Table 9-1

Act Immediately for Prolonged Seizures (Status Epilepticus)

Status Epilepticus is characterized by prolonged seizures during which the person does not regain consciousness.

If a student's seizure lasts longer than 5 minutes, call the student's physician and parents. Generally, seizures lasting longer than 5 minutes are cause for concern. However, refer to the individual seizure guidelines to determine if this is longer than usual.

If you can't reach the physician at once, take the student to the nearest emergency room. *This is a medical emergency.*

Procedures to follow. Develop a standard procedure for responding to a student experiencing a seizure. These are the essential points to include:

Managing a Seizure

Procedure:

1. *Determine if the student is having a seizure.* Seizures may be expressed as any one or combination of the following:

   - An abrupt change in consciousness or responsiveness, including no response or inappropriate response.

   - An alteration in perception of the environment. Any of the senses may be altered.

   - An involuntary alteration of the individual's movement, such as rigidity or loss of muscle control.

2. *Try to remain calm.* This will help others around you remain calm.

3. *Gently protect the student from injury.* If there is a possibility of the student falling, help him or her to a lying position. This is especially important if altered movements are present. Clear the area of hard or sharp objects.

   Do not try to stop or restrain the student or insert anything into the student's mouth. Likewise, do not offer food or drink until the student is fully awake. Never agitate the student. Stay with the student until he or she is fully alert and aware.

4. *Remember that it is rarely necessary to call for emergency help—unless:*

   - The student has one seizure immediately after another (status epilepticus).

   - The student does not start breathing after the seizure. When this occurs, begin mouth-to-mouth resuscitation and activate your school's system for handling a medical emergency.

   - The student's seizure lasts longer than five minutes.

   - The student has been injured seriously.

5. *After the seizure is over, stay with the student until full recovery has occurred.* Allow the student to rest if he or she chooses or needs to.

   Offer reassurance and reorient the student, providing any needed information about what happened. Disorientation can last for several minutes following a seizure.

6. *Document the seizure*, making notes in three areas: what happened before, during and after the seizure.

7. *Establish guidelines for reporting the seizure* to the student's parent or guardian, teacher and physician. If it is the student's first seizure, or if there has been a change in the type of seizure, send a copy of the seizure record home. Or send a copy to the student's physician.

8. *Help staff members and other students deal with the seizure.* Talk about what seizures are and why they happen. Explain what to do if a seizure occurs. Beyond this, explore attitudes and feelings about the seizure. Methods for doing this include health education, health counseling small group discussion.

9. *Follow up.* Talk with parents to learn about any medication changes or activity restrictions after the student visits the doctor. If necessary, schedule a conference with the student, parents and any teachers who work with the student. At this time share new information, concerns, questions, reactions and attitudes.

Summary

Epilepsy is a disorder of the brain characterized by a tendency for recurrent seizures. We don't know the cause for most of these seizures.

Seizures are sudden, brief attacks of altered consciousness, motor activity, sensory phenomena or inappropriate behavior. They are associated with abnormal electrical discharges within the brain.

Seizures fall into two broad groups: partial and generalized. Some seizures remain unclassified.

Keep a detailed record about the student's seizures. This greatly enhances communication with the physician and parents.

For each student with epilepsy, learn the specifics about required medications and how to use them.

Methods of managing seizures should be consistent between home and school.

Plan ahead for effective seizure management. Train staff members in appropriate procedures. Get a medical history from each student with a seizure disorder. Tell appropriate staff members about these students, and encourage the students to wear some form of identification.

Working with a health professional, develop a clear and consistent procedure for managing seizures. Use the instructions in this chapter as a guide.

For Further Reading

Commission on Classification and Terminology of the International League Against Epilepsy. "Proposal for Revised Clinical and Electroencephalographic Classification of Epileptic Seizures." *Epilepsia* 22 (1981) 4829.

Dreifuss, F.E.: *Pediatric Epileptology.* Classification and Management of Seizures in the Child. Littleton, Mass. 1983, Wright, J. Publisher.

Gillette Children's Hospital. Publications of the Epilepsy Program for Children. St. Paul, MN.

Gumnit, Robert J.: *The Epilepsy Handbook: The Practical Management of Seizures.* New York: Raven Press, 1983.

Lagos, J.C. *Seizures, Epilepsy, and Your Child.* New York: Harper and Row, 1974.

Nogen, A.G. *Epilepsy: A Medical Handbook.* Dallas, Texas: Taylor, 1982.

Medical Economics Co. *Physicians Desk Reference.* Orandell, New Jersey: Augel, 1984.

Swaiman, K.S., Wright, F.S.: "Seizure Disorders," Harshberger, S.E., Gunter, A. ed. *The Practice of Pediatric Neurology.* St. Louis: Mosby, 1982.

Symonds, C. "Classification of Epilepsies." *British Medical Journal,* 1 (1985) 1235-38.

Trauner, D.A. *Childhood Neurological Problems.* Chicago: Year Book Medical Publishers, 1979.

The following table, "Most Common Antiepileptic Drugs," is used courtesy of MINCEP Epilepsy Centers, Minneapolis, Minnesota, from *Medical Aspects of Epilepsy.*

Most Common Antiepileptic Drugs

TRADE NAME (name used by the company to market the drug)	GENERIC NAME (name based on the chemical composition of the drug)	COMMON USE (types of seizures the drug is most commonly used to control)	POSSIBLE SIDE EFFECTS (These may require adjustment of the drug dosage)	UNACCEPTABLE SIDE EFFECTS (These usually require discontinuation of the drug)
Klonopin®	clonazepam	absense (petit mal), atonic, myoclonic	lethargy, dizziness, nausea/vomiting, increase in salivation, increase in bronchial secretions	hypersensitivity, allergic reaction
Depakene®	valproic acid	absence (petit mal) generalized tonic-clonic (grand mal)	nausea/vomiting, indigestion, sedation, dizziness, hair loss, tremor	hypersensitivity, allergic reaction, impaired liver function
Depakote®	divalproex sodium	absence (petit mal), generalized tonic-clonic (grand mal)	nausea/vomiting, indigestion, sedation, hair loss, tremor, changes in liver function	hypersensitivity, allergic reaction, impaired liver function
Dilantin®	phenytoin	any seizure except absence (petit mal)	body hair increase, gum overgrowth, tremor, anamia, loss of coordinatiion, double vision, nausea/vomiting, confusion, slurred speech	hypersensitivity, allergic reaction
Mysoline®	primidone	complex partial (psychomotor, temporal lobe), generalized tonic-clonic (grand mal), simple partial	drowsiness, appetite loss, irritability, nausea/vomiting, dizziness, loss of coordination	hypersensitivity, allergic reaction
no trade name commonly used	phenobarbital	most types of seizures	drowsiness, lethargy, hyperactivity	hypersensitivity, allergic reaction
Tegretol®	carbamazepine	complex partial psychomotor, temporal lobe), generalized tonic-clonic (grand mal), simple partial	drowsiness, dizziness, blurred vision, double vision, lethargy, nausea/vomiting	hypersensitivity, allergic reaction
Tranxenel®	clorazepate dipotassium	complex partial (psychomotor, temporal lobe)	drowsiness, dizziness, irratability	hypersensitivity, allergic reaction
Tranxenel®	ethosuximide	absence (petit mal)	drowsiness, hyperactivity nausea/vomiting, sleep disturbance	hypersensitivity, allergic reaction

Reprinted from Epilepsy: Medical Aspects. Minicep Epilepsy Centers, 1984

Chapter 10

Helping the Student with AIDS Virus Infection

Ruth Ellen Luehr, R.N., M.S.

In This Chapter You'll Find:

Information on the AIDS virus infection, including its symptoms and how the infection is spread.

Guidelines on school district policies for children and adolescents infected with the AIDS virus.

A model for developing an Individualized Health Plan for the person with AIDS.

Facts About the AIDS Virus Infection

AIDS (Acquired Immune Deficiency Syndrome) is a blood-borne disease. The Human Immunodeficiency Virus (HIV), or AIDS virus, infects certain cells in the immune system, causing a defect in the natural immunity against disease.

People who have AIDS are vulnerable to serious illnesses that would not threaten anyone whose immune system is functioning normally. For that reason, these illnesses are called "opportunistic" infections or diseases. The AIDS virus also infects other body cells, including brain cells, causing neurological disorders.

The virus is transmitted by sexual contact, sharing hypodermic needles and, prior to March 1985, through transfused blood or its components. The virus may also be transmitted from infected mother to infant during pregnancy or birth.

Sharing needles for intravenous drug use is a high-risk behavior related to AIDS; so is unprotected anal, vaginal or, possibly, oral intercourse—particularly with multiple partners. A person infected with the AIDS virus may be free from symptoms after exposure but can still transmit the virus through high risk behaviors.

Along the spectrum of infection—when the immune system is impaired—we can say a person has ARC (AIDS Related Complex). That condition may then progress to AIDS. This is a characteristic of AIDS determined by the Centers for Disease Control, based on clinical and laboratory confirmation of the syndrome.

To date, 50 percent or more of those with AIDS virus infection progress to end-stage AIDS. This illness is eventually fatal.

As the epidemic continues, there will be children, adolescents and adults with AIDS in our schools and communities. They may have acquired the virus from a blood or blood products transfusion before March 1985—though it may be years before there is evidence of resulting AIDS virus infection. Others may acquire the virus through maternal-child transfer, in utero or during birth. (Many mothers acquire the virus through intravenous drug use.) Other sources of infection are sexual contact, including sexual abuse, and contaminated needles.

Symptoms of AIDS

Most people with the AIDS virus have no symptoms and feel well. Some develop symptoms that may include tiredness, fever, loss of appetite and weight, diarrhea, night sweats, and swollen glands (lymph nodes)—usually in the neck, armpits, or groin. Anyone who has symptoms continuing for more than two weeks should see a doctor.

How Contagious Is AIDS?

Casual contact with AIDS patients or infected persons does *not* place others at risk for getting the illness. No cases have been found where the virus has been transmitted by casual household contact with AIDS patients or infected people. Infants with AIDS or HTLV-III infection have not transmitted the infection to family members living in the same household.

Emergency medical personnel, police and firefighters who have assisted AIDS patients have not become ill. Nurses, doctors and health care personnel have not developed AIDS from caring for AIDS patients. Two health care workers in the United States have developed antibodies to the AIDS virus following needlestick injuries.

Health care and laboratory workers should follow standard safety procedures carefully when handling any blood and tissue samples from patients with potentially transmissible diseases, including AIDS. Special care should be taken to avoid needlestick injuries.

Providing Support and Understanding

Although expected only in small numbers, the cases of AIDS virus infection in children and youth pose many challenges—legal, educational and developmental. They also challenge our capacity for supportive response.

Educators, parents and community members need to be ready to provide support, teaching and counseling on AIDS for all students. Consider these questions:

- What is your knowledge of AIDS virus infection?

- What are your feelings about AIDS virus infection?

- What do you know and what are your attitudes about adolescent sexual activity? About homosexuality? About intravenous drug use?

- How comfortable are you with talking about sexuality?

- What resources are available for people who need help dealing with issues related to sexuality, chemical use and AIDS issues?

Establishing a Local District Policy

The first cases of AIDS in schools will raise concern among community members, students and the school staff. Preparation is essential; without it, regular education for the student with AIDS may be interrupted at a critical time. Undue attention to AIDS may also interrupt education for other students.

Components of a local school district policy should include these topics:

- Students with AIDS attending school.

- Employing staff members infected with the AIDS virus.

- Communicable disease control.

- Planning for students with special health needs.

- Planning for curriculum and instruction.

Your state may already have policies on educating students with AIDS. As an example, this chapter includes guidelines established by the Minnesota Department of Health, based on recommendation from the U.S. Public Health Service Centers for Disease Control; see page 132.

Developing the Individualized Health Plan

With permission to disclose information, a team of people can develop an Individualized Health Plan. The crucial steps are assessment, identifying areas of concern and goal setting, intervention and evaluation.

Assessment. Assessment should include the following steps:

- Identify which data are essential for meeting the educational and health needs of the student. (See Chapter 2 for a complete description of health and developmental profiles.) Include a:

  - Health profile.

  - Development and personality profile.

  - Profile of family structure, function and health.

  - School profile.

- Gather data from appropriate and relevant sources.

Identifying Areas of Concern and Setting Goals. To complete this step:

- Compare the data you've gathered to norms and standards for growth and development.

- Identify the student and family strengths and weaknesses.

- Take a comprehensive approach, integrating each finding with all others.

- Summarize the concern into a nursing diagnosis, including problem, causes, symptoms and student and family response.

- Rank the conditions or problems.

- Set positive goals.

To provide a framework for developing the Individualized Health Plan, related nursing diagnoses and potential goals are listed on page 39.

Intervention. Intervention includes these actions:

- Formulate objectives and action plans related to the goals.

- Determine specific services needed.

- Determine who is accountable for each plan of action.

- List the evaluation criteria and set a timeline for periodic review.

- Put the plan into action.

The intervention for a particular child or adolescent will be based on the identified needs and capabilities of the school and community. The following are areas most likely to require specific planning and action—both from the view of the student and family and the view of the school and community:

- Building a supportive environment. Here the relevant concerns are:

  - Education and counseling for the individual and the community.

  - Community network for education and to provide support.

  - Parental skills in communicating with children and youth.

- Health and hygiene practices in schools. This includes:

  - A review of precautions for handling all bodily fluids. (See Chapter 22.)

  - Special precautions, if any, based on the student's needs.

  - Protection of the student with AIDS from disease.

- Special health care procedures for the individual.

- Coping with the future for individual, family and peers.

- Ongoing assessment. Remember to consider:

  - Physical and neurological status.

  - Immune system status.

- Coping skills.

- Educational needs.

- Knowledge, attitudes and behavior related to AIDS.

Evaluation. This includes two main steps:

- At predetermined times, review the objectives, looking at how many are attained.

- Modify the plan based on new information or inability reach objectives.

Summary

The AIDS virus undermines the body's immunity to disease. It can be transmitted through sexual contact and sharing hypodermic needles. Mothers can also infect their babies with the AIDS virus in utero or during birth.

Before they can help students with AIDS, educators, parents and community members need to explore their attitudes toward the disease. They also need to consider feelings about adolescent sexual activity, homosexuality and sexuality in general.

Educators should establish a comprehensive policy on educating students with AIDS.

To work effectively with the student with AIDS, develop an Individualized Health Plan; follow the steps listed in this chapter.

On the following pages are these related materials:

- Responding with Support, An Individualized Health Plan for a Student with AIDS or AIDS-Related Conditions

- Minnesota Department of Health Guidelines for the Placement in Schools of Children and Adolescents Infected with the Human Immunodeficiency Virus (an example of state policies for students with AIDS)

Note: Material in this chapter ("Symptoms of AIDS" and "How Contagious Is Aids?") was adapted from *Facts About AIDS*, a publication of the U.S. Department of Health and Human Services.

Resonding With Support
An Individualized Heath Plan for a Student with AIDS or AIDS-Related Conditions
by C. Schuster, M.K. Haas, M. Villars and R.E. Luehr

Nursing Diagnosis (Problem Statement)	Goal
Knowledge deficit related to existing/new health condition (condition, transmission, prevention, care)	Increases knowledge of his/her health condition
Knowledge deficit related to misinterpretation of information	
Potential for *alteration in nutrition* less than body requirements related to debilitation from re-current infections	Achieves optimal nutrition
Potential for *fluid volume deficit* related to repeated infections resulting in physiological instability	
Potential for *alteration in activity* tolerance related to active infectious process/fatigue/chronic health condition	Achieves optimal activity level
Potential for *self management deficit*	Develops self-directed management of a lifestyle that will promote health
Potential for *growth in health decision making*	
Potential for alteration in health maintenance related to ineffective family coping	
Potential for *alteration in health management* related to change in health status	Participates in health management
Potential for *self-care deficit* related to treatment regimen (complex, frequent changes)	
Potential for *non-compliance* related to inability to perform task/nontherapeutic environment/poor self concept/complex regimen	

Nursing Diagnosis (Problem Statement)	Goal
Potential for infection related to alteration in immune response	Knows and follows procedures for prevention of transmission of infectious diseases
Potential for *transmission of infection to others* related to infectious agent (AIDS virus)	
Potential for *disturbance in self-concept* related to having a terminal/infectious disease	Develops age-appropriate psychosocial skills
Potential for *role changes* related to varying physical capacity	
Potential for *alteration in self identity* related to perception of self as different than before acquiring AIDS virus infection	
Potential for *impaired social interactions* related to infection with the AIDS virus resulting in experiencing negative or unsatisfactory responses from others	
Potential for *ineffective individual coping* related to inability to manage internal/external stressors (physical/psychological/behavioral)	Develops coping skills that will assist in dealing with self, family, peer, and social reactions to his/her physical health condition
Potential for *alteration in family process* related to illness of family member	
Potential for *social isolation* related to altered state of health/inability to engage in satisfying peer relationships/hospitalization	
Potential for *disturbance in body image* related to physical changes/symptoms	

Nursing Diagnosis (Problem Statement)	Goal
Potential for *powerlessness* related to incurable nature of health condition (AIDS)	
Potential for *powerlessness* related to inability to control situation (physical/psychosocial)	
Anxiety related to threat to or change in health status	
Fear related to having a terminal illness	
Fear related to knowledge deficit	
Grieving related to perceived loss of physical/psychosocial well-being	
Knowledge deficit related to risk of transmission of AIDS virus to others	Develops sexual health attitudes and behaviors and chemical health attitudes and behaviors that will prevent transmission of AIDS virus to others
Alteration in sexual patterns related to physical condition and/or risk of transmission of the AIDS virus to others	

Minnesota Department of Health Guidelines for the Placement in Schools of Children and Adolescents Infected with the Human Immunodeficiency Virus Revised September 1987

Statement of the Problem

As of September 7, 1987, no known cases of acquired immunodeficiency syndrome (AIDS) among school-age children or adolescents in Minnesota have been documented. Two cases have occurred in children less than four years of age. However, school-age children and adolescents currently reside in Minnesota who are infected with human immunodeficiency virus (HIV), the virus that causes AIDS, and the Minnesota Department of Health (MDH) anticipates that additional children and adolescents will become infected in the future. Thus, a statewide policy on the placement in school of children and adolescents infected with HIV is needed. To avoid unwarranted fear and confusion by students, parents, teachers, and school administrators, the following guidelines have been developed. These recommendations are based on scientific data currently available on the transmission of HIV and apply to all school-age children and adolescents from kindergarten through grade twelve. Separate guidelines have been developed for the placement of HIV infected children in preschool and child day care settings.

Background

Children and adolescents who are infected with HIV, but are currently asymptomatic or who have mild illness, may go on to develop more severe illnesses including opportunistic infections or cancers and be diagnosed as having AIDS. Therefore, more pediatric AIDS cases are expected to occur in Minnesota in the near future.

Many infected children acquire the virus from their infected mothers in the perinatal period. In utero or intrapartum transmission is likely, and one child in Australia apparently acquired the virus postnatally, possibly from ingestion of breast milk. Children and adolescents may also become infected through transfusion of blood or blood components that contain the virus. This risk, although small, was significantly reduced in Minnesota in June 1985 with the advent of routine screening of donors of blood and blood components for HIV antibody; however, the number of children and adolescents infected before that time is not currently known. As evidence of how transmission occurs, 77% of the pediatric cases reported to the Centers for Disease Control (CDC) have occurred among children whose parent had AIDS or was a member of a group at increased risk of acquiring HIV infection; 14% of the cases have occurred among children or adolescents who had received blood or blood components; and for 8%, investigations are incomplete.

In adults HIV is transmitted primarily through sexual contact (homosexual or heterosexual) and by injection through the skin of infected blood or blood components. Such modes of transmission may also be important in school-age adolescents. HIV has been isolated from blood, semen, saliva, breast milk, tears, vaginal and cervical secretions, and other body fluids and tissues, but transmission has been shown epidemiologically to occur from contact with semen, blood, vaginal and cervical secretions, and rarely breast milk.

None of the identified cases of HIV infection in the United States are known to have been transmitted in the school setting or through other casual person-to-person contact. Other than the sexual partners of HIV infected patients and infants born to infected mothers, none of the family members of the over 41,000 AIDS patients identified to date have been reported to have AIDS. Over ten different studies of family members of patients with HIV infection have failed to demonstrate HIV transmission to adults who were not sexual contacts of the infected patients or to older children who were not at risk from perinatal transmission. Based on current evidence, nonsexual person-to-person contact, as would occur among school children, appears to pose negligible risk.

The guidelines below are based on recommendations developed by the CDC and published in the August 30, 1985 Morbidity and Mortality Weekly Report (1). Representatives from the following governmental agencies and professional and social organizations from Minnesota reviewed the guidelines in September 1985 and provided comments:

> Minnesota Department of Education
> Minnesota Department of Labor and Industry
> Minnesota Congress of Parents, Teachers, Students, Inc.
> Minnesota Association of School Administrators
> Minnesota Education Association
> Minnesota Federation of Teachers
> School Nurse Organization of Minnesota
> Archdiocesan School System
> University of Minnesota Comprehensive Hemophilia Clinic
> Mayo Clinic
> Minnesota AIDS Project
> Memorial Blood Center of Minneapolis
> American Red Cross Blood Services, Saint Paul Region
> Hennepin County Health Department
> Saint Paul Division of Public Health

These guidelines are the official policy of the MDH and do not necessarily reflect the specific views of the above agencies and organizations.

School-age children and adolescents will be referred to as "students" in the recommendations.

Recommendations   A. Most students infected with HIV should be allowed to attend school and before- and after-school care in an unrestricted manner because of the apparent negligible risk of transmission of HIV in this setting. The presence of HIV-infected students in school does not constitute a significant threat to other students. In addition, for most HIV-infected students, the benefits of their unrestricted school attendance outweigh the risks of *their acquiring* potentially serious infections in that setting.

B. Some infected students may potentially pose more of a risk to others. Students who lack control of their body secretions or who display behavior such as biting and those students who have other medical conditions, such as uncoverable oozing lesions, require a more restricted environment until more is known about transmission of the virus under these conditions.

For infected students with questionable behavior or other medical conditions, individual judgments need to be made regarding placing those students in an unrestricted school setting. The Minnesota Commissioner of Health will convene an Advisory Committee to evaluate each of these students on an on-going basis. The Committee will consist of four permanent members and will include the State Epidemiologist, a representative from the Minnesota Department of Education, a pediatrician with expertise in infectious diseases, and a physician with expertise in the care of AIDS patients. Other members of the Committee will be specifically assigned for each student and will include the student's personal physician, and the Superintendent of Schools, the primary teacher for the student and the designated school nurse for the school in which the student is to be enrolled. The State Epidemiologist will chair the Committee and will be responsible for convening the Committee as necessary. The Committee's recommendation to the Commissioner on each student's placement will be based on the student's behavior, neurologic development, physical condition, and the expected type of interaction with others in the school setting. The Committee will weigh the risks and benefits to both the infected student and to others. The hygienic practices of a student with HIV infection may improve as the child matures; conversely, the hygienic practices may deteriorate if the student's condition worsens. The Committee will reevaluate students periodically as deemed necessary by the State Epidemiologist.

C. Some students may be unknowingly infected with HIV or other infectious agents, such as hepatitis B virus; these agents may be present in blood or body fluids. Thus, all schools, regardless of whether students with HIV infection are known to be in attendance, should adopt routine procedures for handling blood or body fluids in the school setting. School health care workers, teachers and other employees should be educated about these procedures. For example, soiled surfaces should be promptly cleaned with disinfectants, such as household bleach (diluted 1 ounce of bleach to 1 gallon of water). Disposable towels or tissues should be used whenever possible and disposed of properly, and mops should be rinsed in the disinfectant. Those who are cleaning should avoid exposure of their mucous membranes or any open skin lesions to blood or body fluids.

D. Students infected with HIV may experience immunodeficiency. Immunosuppressed persons are at increased risk of experiencing severe complications from such infections as chicken pox, cytomegalovirus, tuberculosis, herpes simplex, and measles. Students may have a greater risk of encountering these infectious agents in school than at home. Thus, assessment of the risk to the immunosuppressed student of attending school in an unrestricted setting is best made by the student's physician who is aware of his/her immune status.

E. Persons involved in the care and education of HIV infected students should respect their right to privacy, and private records should be maintained as specified by state law.

F. Based on available data, mandatory screening of students, as a condition for school entry is not warranted.

Reference

1. CDC. Education and Foster Care of Children Infected with Human T-Lymphotropic Virus Type III/Lymphadenopathy-Associated Virus. MMWR 1985; 34:517-521.

For Further Reading

Benenson, A. S., Ed. *Communicable Diseases in Man*, 14th Edition. Washington, D.C.: American Public Health Association, 1985.

Centers for Disease Control. *Educational and Foster Care of Children Infected with HTLV-III/LAV. Morbidity and Mortality Weekly Report (MMWR), 34* (34) (August 30, 1985) 517-21.

Minnesota Department of Health. *Guidelines for the Placement in Day Care Settings of Children Infected with the Human T-Lymphotropic Virus Type III*, January 1986.

Minnesota Department of Health. "Summary of Nine Studies that Demonstrate Lack of Human T-Lymphotropic Virus-Type III (HTLV-III/LAV) Transmission Among Family Member Contacts of HTLV-III Infected Persons". *MDH Disease Control Newsletter, Vol. 12* (7) (October 1985) 7-8.

Minnesota Department of Education. *Sample Policies Regarding Educational Implications of Health Needs of Students including AIDS (Acquired Immune Deficiency Syndrome)*, October 30, 1985.

Northeast Metropolitan Intermediate District. *The First 24 Hours.* January 1988 (3300 Century Avenue, White Bear Lake, Minnesota 55110).

Rogers, M. F. "Aids in Children: A Review of the Clinical Epidemiologic and Public Health Aspects." *Pediatric Infectious Disease*, Vol. 4 (3) (May 1985) 230-236.

School Nurse Organization of Minnesota and Minnesota Department of Education. *Responding with Support: An Individualized Health Plan for a Student with AIDS Virus Infection* by C. Schuster, M. K. Haas, M. Villars, R. E. Luehr, January 1988.

Schuster, Cynthia, Sue Will, Ruth Ellen Luehr and Mary Jo Erickson-Connor. "AIDS in Children and Adolescents—Learning to Cope with a Harsh Reality." *School Nurse Journal*, (November/December 1986) 14-25.

U. S. Department of Health and Human Services. *Surgeon General's Report on AIDS*, 1986.

U. S. Public Health Service. *Facts about AIDS*, Spring 1987.

U. S. Public Health Service. *Report of the Surgeon General's Workshop on Children with HIV Infection and Their Families*, April 1987. (DHHS Publication No. HRS-D-MC 87-1)

Part Three

Basic Care
Guidelines

Part Three

Basic Care Guidelines

Part One addressed the broad issue of planning for students with disabilities or chronic health concerns. Part Two provided an introduction to the needs of students with certain chronic health conditions.

In the remainder of this manual, we shift gears to a "how to" orientation. Much of this material provides instructions for procedures you may use in working with students—such as giving medication, changing a diaper or caring for student with a tracheostomy.

Chapter 11 is an essential review of hand washing. This everyday task is one of the most important tools for halting the spread of infection—but only if done properly.

Chapter 12 focuses on students who will need medication during the school day. Here the main concerns are careful documentation, administration and communication between parents, physicians and educators.

Chapter 13 is a guide to working with students who have special feeding needs. Into this group, for example, falls a student with a gastrostomy.

The rest of Part Three deals with two areas. First is helping students with a sensory impairment.

Chapter 14 provides guidelines to help you communicate with students who have a speech or language difficulty.

Chapters 15, 16 and **17** take a corresponding approach, focusing on impairments to other senses: vision, hearing and touch.

The second area is personal care. Here a variety of procedures and programs are covered:

Bowel programs **(Chapter 18)**, diapering **(Chapter 19)**, stoma care **(Chapter 20)**, catheterization **(Chapter 21)**, guidelines for handling body fluids **(Chapter 22)**, respiratory therapy **(Chapter 23)** and tracheostomy care **(Chapter 24)**.

Chapter 11

Hand Washing Techniques

Cyndy Schuster Silkworth, M.P.H., R.N., C.S.N.P.

In This Chapter You'll Find: A step-by-step procedure for effective hand washing.

Hand Washing: An Essential Measure

Studies on hand washing report that good hand washing technique is the single most important factor in preventing cross-infection. Good hand washing accomplishes three main objectives:

- Removing disease-causing organisms from the hands.

- Preventing the spread of micro-organisms to students and school personnel.

- Preventing the spread of micro-organisms into the caregiver's body—for example, through a break in the skin or through food.

Staff members and volunteers may have direct contact with students or contaminated clothing, equipment, supplies and surfaces; these people should follow procedures for hand washing. In general, specialized health care procedures need to be administered or done under the supervision of the school nurse, public health nurse or physician.

When caregivers should wash hands. Those who provide direct care to students should always wash hands at certain times:

- Before and after caring for any student.

- After contact with any contaminated (dirty) equipment: urine collection bags, toilets, dressings and sinks.

- After contact with any bodily fluid: blood, drainage from wounds, vomitus, feces, urine, respiratory or nasal secretions, saliva and so on.

- Before and after assisting with a special procedure, such as tracheostomy suctioning or catheterization.

- Before eating, drinking or smoking.

- Before administering medication.

- Before handling any clean or sterile equipment or utensils.

- Before and after handling student's food or dishes.

- After handling soiled diapers, garments or equipment.

- Before and after going to the bathroom.

When students should wash hands. Students should also be sure to wash hands at the following times:

- Before eating.

- After going to the bathroom.

- After the hands have come in contact with any infected material: bandages, respiratory or nasal secretions, or body fluids from their own or others' bodies.

- Before and after a self-care procedure, such as catheterization.

How To Wash Hands Properly

Get the right equipment. Equipment you'll need includes:

- Liquid soap in a dispenser.

- Paper towels.

- Hand lotion.

- A covered waste receptacle with disposable plastic liner.

- A disposable or soakable scrub brush.

How To Wash Hands Using the Clean Technique

Procedure:

Remove all your jewelry.

Jewelry should not be worn when working with students who require repeated physical contact and care. Micro-organisms can become lodged in settings or stones of rings.

Wet your hands with warm, running water.

Warm water, combined with soap, makes better suds than does cold water. Hot water removes protective oils and will dry skin. Running water is necessary to carry away dirt and debris.

Apply liquid soap and water well.

Liquid soap is preferred to bar soap. Bacteria can grow on bar soap and in soap dishes.

Wash your hands, using a circular motion and friction, for 15 to 30 seconds.

Include front and back surfaces of hands, between fingers and knuckles, around nails, and the entire wrist area. To prevent skin breaks, avoid harsh scrubbing.

Rinse your hands well under warm, running water.

Hold hands under the water so that water drains from wrist area to fingertip.

Repeat steps 3 through 5.

All remaining bacteria and soil should now be removed.

Wipe surfaces surrounding sink with clean paper towel and discard the towel.

Damp surfaces promote the growth of bacteria.

Dry hands well with paper towels and discard towels immediately.

With frequent hand washing, it is important to dry gently and thoroughly to avoid chapping. Chapped skin breaks open, thus permitting bacteria to enter the body.

Apply lotion as desired.

Lotions help keep skin soft and reduce chapping. They may also serve as barriers to infection.

Summary

Good hand washing is essential to preventing the spread of infection.

Both care providers and students should wash their hands at crucial times—such as after coming into contact with body fluids, before eating or before administering medication.

Follow the procedure for hand washing described in this chapter.

A chart with a visual summary of the steps in proper hand washing technique follows the "For Further Reading Section."

References

California State Department of Education. *Techniques for Preventing the Spread of Infectious Disease.* Sacramento, CA: California State Department of Education, 1983.

For Further Reading

Kolzer, Barbara and Glenora Erb. *Techniques in Clinical Nursing.* Reading, MA: Addison-Wesley, 1982.

Figure 11-1: Proper Hand Washing Technique

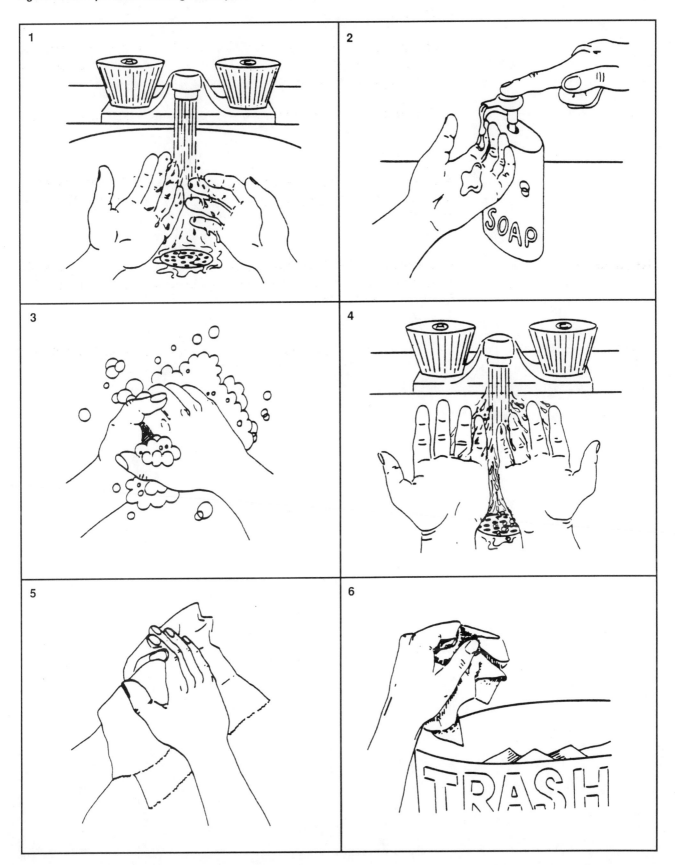

Chapter 12

Administering Medication

Cyndy Schuster Silkworth, M.P.H., R.N., C.S.N.P.

In This Chapter You'll Find: Guidelines for properly administering medication to students during school hours.

Whenever possible, the parent or guardian should make arrangements so that medication can be administered at home, before and after school. However, there are cases when a student's health could be compromised by not getting medication during school hours.

In response, school districts need written policies and procedures for administering prescribed medications. These help to ensure that the student—who must use medication to treat a disability or illness—will attend school.

Take Care of Preliminaries

Before actually administering any medication, make sure certain preparatory steps have been completed.

Identify students who require medication. The school nurse, principal, teacher and other school personnel should know which students require medications during the day. If the school does not have a school nurse, the principal should assume responsibility, with the parents.

Get a written prescription. Require this from the physician. The prescription should indicate:

- The name of the child.

- The name of the medication.

- The reasons for the medication (diagnosis).

- That it's required to administer medication during school hours.

- The dosage, route, and times it is to be given.

- Any special directions for administering the medication.

- Possible side effects.

- The date medication should be stopped.

Get a written statement from the parents or guardian. This should give permission for the student to receive the medication in school, as prescribed by the physician.

Get a duplicate bottle. Parents should ask the pharmacist for duplicate bottles of the medication. One bottle should be kept at home, the other at school. Both bottles should contain the name and telephone number of the pharmacy, the student's identification, name of the physician, name of the medication, dosage and times to be given and the route.

Keep a list of students on medication during school hours. This list should be kept in a central place. For each student, include the name of the medication, the medication dosage and times medication should be given. Also include information on why the student is taking medication and the route medication is to be given. ("Route" refers to how the medication is taken: by mouth, by injection, on the skin, etc.)

Let the school nurse supervise medication administration. Medications should be administered by or under the supervision of the school nurse, public health nurse or physician. The person administering medications must have:

- Knowledge about the effective use of medications and their side effects.

- Knowledge of the condition for which the medications were prescribed.

- Ability to understand the range of coping mechanisms used by students who must take medication more than once a day.

- Ability to properly administer and record medications given in school.

- Ability to observe, evaluate and report the student's reaction to the medication in school—including expected or adverse reactions.

Administering the Medication

To properly administer prescribed medication, the school nurse—or staff member directly supervised by the school nurse—must follow these steps:

Procedure:

1. *Check the label on the medication bottle* to assure the correct medication is given to the student.

2. *Check the prescription* to assure the proper dosage is given in the prescribed way.

3. *Record the medication* given on the medication record.

4. *Make sure the school nurse, public health nurse or physician:*

   - Informs the appropriate school staff of the potential benefits and side effects of the medication being taken by the student.

   - Observes, evaluates, and reports the student's health status and reaction to the medication at school. Give this information to the student's parents or guardians—and the student's physician if necessary.

5. *Store medication in a locked cabinet or drawer.* Only designated personnel should have access to the medication.

6. *Watch out for any student self-administering medication* for which the school has no authorization. Report this to the student's parents.

Table 12-1

**Safety Precaution:
The Five "R's" of Administering Medication**

The five "R's" point to factors you should remember when administering medication to a student:

- Right name (of student)

- Right drug

- Right dose

- Right time

- Right route (by mouth, injection, on the skin, etc.)

Summary

School personnel should have written policies and procedures to follow when administering medication.

Identify the students who need medication during school hours.

Make sure that anyone administering medication is supervised by the school nurse, public health nurse or physician.

Get a written prescription for the medication from the student's physician.

Get written authorization to administer medication from the student's parents.

Ask the pharmacist for duplicate bottles of medication—one for home and one for school.

Keep a list of the students who require medication during the school day.

When administering medication, follow the five "R's" and keep a record of the medication.

Tell appropriate staff members about the effects of any medication. Report the student's reactions and health status to parents.

Store the medication in a locked cabinet or drawer.

References

Loebl, Suzanne and George Spratto. *The Nurse's Drug Handbook.* New York: Wiley, 1984.

The following pages include a sample form for Medication Authorization and a sample Medication Record.

Medication Authorization

_____
DATE

Dear Dr._____

    The policy of the_____regarding the matter of dispensing medication in school is that medications shall be administered only when the student's health requires that they be given during school hours. Medications that are administered at school must be in a properly labeled container or prescription bottle. Written authorization from the student's parents and physician is required. Medications will be kept in a locked cabinet in the school health office and be administered by or under supervision of the school nurse.

                                    Sincerely,

                                      NURSE_____
                                      SCHOOL _____ PHONE_____

The following form should be completed by the physician and returned to the school nurse by the parent:

_____ is to receive _____
              PATIENT'S NAME   MEDICATION AND DOSAGE

at _____ for the treatment of _____
                 TIME

POSSIBLE SIDE EFFECTS:_____

_____

ESTIMATED TERMINATION DATE:_____

DATE_____ SIGNATURE _____ M.D.

                                   ADDRESS: _____

                                   _____

                                   TELEPHONE NUMBER: _____

    I hereby give my permission for my child to receive medication at school as prescribed by my child's physician.

DATE_____ SIGNATURE _____
                                           PARENT'S/GUARDIAN'S

NOTE: Medication to be supplied in original prescription bottle. Ask your pharmacist for the medication to be divided into two bottles completely labeled; one for home and one for school.

Medication Record

School: _____

Month/Year: _____

Key: ✓ - medication taken (initialed)
A - student absent
X - school not in session

Name	GR	Medication: reason, doseage, time	1	2	3	4	5	6	7	8	9	10	11	12	13	14	15	16	17	18	19	20	21	22	23	24	25	26	27	28	29	30	31

Persons Administering Medications

Signature	Initials	Title	Date

152

Chapter 13

Care for the Student with a Gastrostomy

Georgianna Larson, R.N., P.N.P., M.P.H.

In This Chapter You'll Find:

Information on what a gastrostomy is and why it is performed.

Guidelines for feeding through a gastrostomy tube.

Guidelines for using the gastrostomy feeding button.

Students with some chronic health conditions or disabilities may use alternative methods of eating. One of these methods involves a surgical procedure known as a gastrostomy.

With the gastrostomy, a small opening is made in the wall of the abdomen. Into this opening, called a stoma, a small tube is inserted. One end of this tube, known as the gastrostomy tube, opens into the stomach; the other end can be attached to a feeding device.

When is a Gastrostomy Performed?

The search for an alternative feeding method such as a gastrostomy often starts with students who have a disorder of the central nervous system. One example is cerebral palsy. Other conditions may be involved too: muscle and nerve disorders in the face or cranium (the part of the skull that surrounds the brain); reflex problems; and malfunction or malformation of the stomach and intestines.

When observing such students with these conditions, you may notice some of the following:

• A hypersensitive mouth, tongue and throat.

• Chronic gagging or vomiting.

- Refusal to eat certain foods or tantrums about eating.

- Refusal to eat solid foods.

- Refusal to take liquid from a cup.

- Poor control of the jaw during eating and drinking.

- Difficulty in chewing.

- Tongue thrusting that results in pushing out foods.

- Inability to close lips around a spoon, cup or nipple.

- Profuse drooling.

- Physical tightness in the mouth and throat, making it difficult to suck, swallow or chew.

Certain health professionals are trained to work with such symptoms and behaviors. They include occupational therapists, nutritionists and speech pathologists. Along with the student's physician, these people should be your first contacts in dealing with feeding problems.

Besides the gastrostomy, another alternative is tube feeding. Often this is a temporary measure, used in case of medical complications or an emergency. Still, to do tube feeding safely, you will need special training. (This chapter focuses on gastrostomies. For more information on tube feeding, consult this excellent source: *Home Care for the Chronically Ill or Disabled Child* by Monica Loose Jones (Philadelphia: Harper and Row, 1985).

With either the gastrostomy or tube feeding, it's always desirable to maintain the student's ability to eat through the mouth, and this should be done as soon as possible. Some students may continue using a combination of mouth and tube feeding or gastrostomy feeding.

Feeding Through a Gastrostomy

What follows are guidelines for feeding the student with a gastrostomy. They are not meant to replace directions from the student's physician. Use the instructions in this chapter as guidelines, and add to them any specific directions you receive.

The basic procedures involved are these:

- Checking the placement of the tube.

- Positioning the student.

- Administering the feeding.

- Instilling water.

- Caring for the gastrostomy site.

- Taping the gastrostomy tube.

Instructions for each of these procedures are presented here.

What you'll need to get started. Before you feed a student through a gastrostomy tube, you'll need instructions from the student's parents or physician. Those instructions should include the specific equipment and supplies you'll need. Most often, this includes:

- Feeding bag (for the bag feeding method).

- 60 cc syringe (or smaller, if the feeding amount is smaller).

- Tape for securing the gastrostomy tube.

- Gauze or sterile dressing.

- Feeding fluid.

- Water.

- Solution for cleaning the ostomy site.

- Nipple (baby bottle style).

Checking the placement of the gastrostomy tube. The gastrostomy tube is kept clamped between feedings to prevent loss of feeding fluid and to keep air from entering the stomach. Proper placement of the gastrostomy tube is crucial, so check it before each feeding.

Feeding Through a Gastrostomy Tube

Procedure:

1. *Unclamp the tube and attach the syringe,* following directions from the student's physician.

2. *Draw back on the syringe.*

   If you feel resistance, or if you retain residual fluid, the tube is probably in place.

3. *If the residual fluid is more than the amount specified by the student's physician, push the fluid back into the stomach.* Delay the feeding and check again in 30 minutes.

4. *Pull back on the gastrostomy tube gently* to make sure it's tight against the stomach wall.

5. *If, for some reason, the tube comes out, tape several pieces of gauze over the stoma.* Notify the student's parents and physician. Then call the the designated hospital.

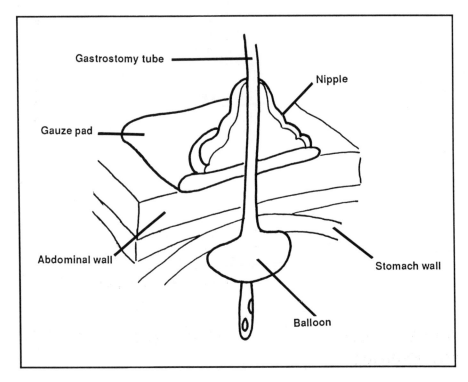

Figure 13-1: Proper placement of the gastrostomy tube, with balloon tight against stomach wall.

Positioning the student. Again, follow any specific directions you receive for positioning the student. Aim for a comfortable position, with the student's head at about a 45-degree angle. To do this, you can hold the student, prop the student on pillows or use a wheelchair.

Administering the feeding. Feeding can be accomplished in two ways: the gravity method or pump method. The latter involves using a feeding bag, sometimes called a "kangaroo bag."

Any medications to be given through the gastrostomy tube should be administered by the gravity method. This medication can be given in liquid form, or it can be crushed finely and dissolved in a liquid solution.

Note: All medications should be administered under the direct supervision of the school nurse or other qualified health professional.

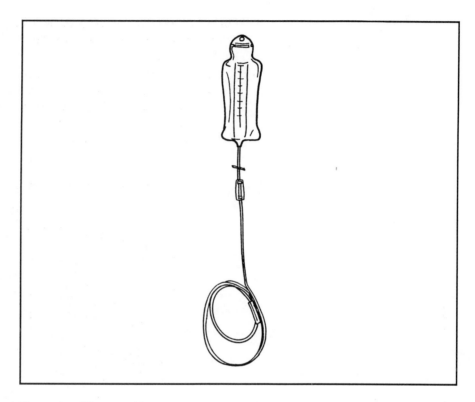

Figure 13-2: "Kangaroo" bag and tube.

Administering the Feeding

Procedure for the gravity method:

1. *Fill the kangaroo bag or similar feeding bag* with the prescribed amount of fluid.

2. *Drain the fluid to the end of the tube* on the feeding bag. This removes any excess air.

3. *Connect the tubing* from the feeding bag to the gastrostomy tube.

4. *Elevate the tube* and syringe to about 4 and 3/4 inches above the student's abdomen.

   This will start the feeding; you will not have to apply any pressure.

5. *Feed slowly for 20 to 45 minutes.* To avoid instilling air, refill the syringe before it is empty.

6. *Observe the student's reaction* during the feeding. If he or she becomes agitated, this could indicate that the gastrostomy tube is not in the stomach.

   If this happens, gently apply pressure on the tube, pushing toward the stomach. If the student continues to be agitated, stop the feeding. Gently tug on the tube. If the inside balloon has broken, the tube will slide out.

7. *After you administer the feeding fluid, instill the prescribed amount of water.* Use the same method to do this that you used to do the feeding. Avoid instilling any air.

8. *When the feeding is done, clamp the gastrostomy tube.* Do not clamp above the "Y" in the tube: This may cause the balloon to break.

9. *Disconnect the syringe.*

10. *Keep the student elevated* for the prescribed number of minutes after the feeding.

11. *Clean the kangaroo bag and tubing* according to the manufacturer's directions.

12. *Disconnect the tube* from the feeding bag.

13. *Clean the bag* according to the manufacturer's directions.

14. *Keep the student elevated* for the prescribed number of minutes after the feeding.

Administering the Feeding

Procedure for the pump method:

Note: The types of pumps and bags used for this method will vary. Before you begin this procedure, get specific instructions from the student's physician on how to attach the gastrostomy tube to the feeding bag, and the feeding bag to the pump.

Administering the Feeding-Pump Method

1. *Before unclamping the gastrostomy tube, fill a 60 cc syringe with feeding fluid.*

2. *Connect the tubing* from the syringe to the gastrostomy tube.

3. *Unclamp the gastrostomy tube and attach the syringe to it.*

4. *Begin the pump* at the prescribed rate—the number of cubic centimeters (cc) per hour.

5. *Observe the student's reaction* during the feeding. If he or she becomes agitated, this could indicate that the gastrostomy tube is not in the stomach.

   If this happens, gently apply pressure on the tube, pushing toward the stomach. If the student continues to be agitated, stop the feeding. Gently tug on the tube. If the inside balloon has broken, the tube will slide out.

6. *After you administer the feeding fluid, instill the prescribed amount of water.* Use the same method to do this that you used to do the feeding. Avoid instilling any air.

7. *When the feeding is done, clamp the gastrostomy tube.* Do not clamp above the "Y" in the tube: This may cause the balloon to break.

8. *Dispose of the syringe and tubing or clean them* according to the manufacturer's directions.

9. *Keep the student elevated* for the prescribed number of minutes after the feeding.

Caring for the gastrostomy site. To prevent skin irritation, you must give attention to gastrostomy site.

Caring for the Gastrostomy Site

Procedure:

1. *Change the site dressing* at the prescribed intervals.

2. *Cleanse the area around the gastrostomy tube* whenever you change the dressing. Follow the specific directions you receive from the student's physician.

3. *Immediatly clean off any formula or milk* spilled on the stoma site.

4. *If mild soap and water does not prevent irritation, clean the stoma site* with half-strength hydrogen peroxide followed by betadine. Use a stomahesive powder and clean the site more often.

5. *Dry the stoma site and leave it exposed to air* for 30 minutes.

Taping the gastrostomy tube. It's essential to keep the tube in the proper place between feedings. Tape is used to do this—and to keep the tube in an unobtrusive position under the student's clothes.

Taping the Gastrostomy Tube

Procedure:

1. *If you are so directed, slit a nipple* and place it over the ostomy site to secure the tube in place.

2. *Whether or not you use a nipple, you should tape the tube securely in place.* Follow directions from the student's physician.

   Taping prevents the possibility of the tube making its way to the pyloric sphincter and blocking the stomach outlet. If this happens, vomiting and abdominal distension could occur.

3. *Prevent excessive pulling on the tube.* This might widen the opening and cause irritating gastric juices to leak.

4. *Re-insert the gastrostomy tube if it comes out—but only if you've been instructed on how to do this.*

   If you don't know how to insert the tube, cover the ostomy site with a sterile dressing and tape. Then call the designated physician or hospital.

Using the Gastrostomy Feeding Button™

Another method of feeding through a gastrostomy uses a more recent device—the feeding button™. Some people find the sight of the tube distressing; others experience the problems that may be associated with feeding through a tube. For both groups, the button can be an attractive alternative.

Instructions for using the feeding button follow. Also included are guidelines for troubleshooting—how to deal with difficulties you may encounter. If you lose feeding equipment or find defective parts, contact the manufacturer.

Note: only a physician, nurse or other trained health professional should insert the feeding button. This person should also provide training and emotional support to anyone using this feeding method.

Any medication you administer through the button should be liquid—or well-ground and diluted. This helps prevent clogging of the button.

Feeding Through the Gastrostomy Button

Procedure:

1. *Attach the adapter and tubing to the syringe.*

2. *Clamp off the lower part of the tube.* Use a clamp or your fingers to do so.

3. *Fill the syringe (or bag) and catheter with the feeding.*

4. *Open the safety plug.* Then attach the adapter and tube to the feeding button.

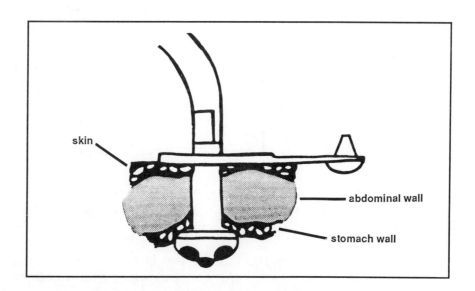

Figure 13-3: Attaching the feeding tube to the feeding button

5. *Begin the feeding by using gravity:* keep the syringe or feeding bag above stomach level. Continue feeding for 15 to 30 minutes.

   Troubleshooting tips: Watch the tubing; it may become dislodged if the student coughs or moves too much. If this happens, estimate how much feeding has been lost. Then attach the tubing again and resume feeding. If the button does become dislodged, save it to be inserted again.

   If the button becomes plugged, attach a 10 cc syringe with 2 to 3 cc of air or water to it. Then carefully dislodge the plug.

6. *Refill the syringe before it empties.* Doing so helps keep air out of the stomach.

7. *When you are done with the feeding, flush the button* with 10 cc of tap water or amount recommended by child's physician.

8. *After flushing, lower the syringe.* Keeping it below stomach level will help the student burp.

9. *Take out the adapter and tubing. Then snap the safety plug.*

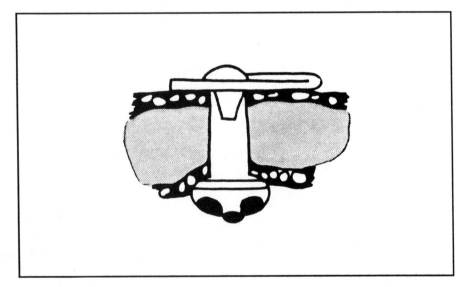

Figure 13-4: Snapping the safety plug

10. *Prevent the button from getting plugged.* You can clean it out with tap water and a cotton-tipped applicator after the feeding is done.

11. *Care for the stoma site.* Follow the directions for stoma care given on page 160. In addition, rotate the button in a full circle during every cleaning. This helps reduce irritation around the stoma.

You can also lubricate the obturator, dome of the button and stoma site with a water soluble lubricant. This helps prevent dislodging of the button.

Summary

A gastrostomy is a surgical procedure used when certain health conditions prevent someone from feeding through the mouth.

In this procedure, an opening, or stoma, is made in the wall of the abdomen. Then a tube is inserted into the stoma. One end of this tube enters the stomach; the other end can be attached to another tube for feeding.

Follow the general guidelines in this chapter for feeding through a gastrostomy tube. However, also get specific directions for feeding from the student's parents or physician.

If you feed with the gastrostomy button, get specific training for this device. Use the procedure in this chapter as a guide.

References

California State Department of Education. guidelines and procedures for meeting the specialized health care needs of students. Sacramento, 1980.

Chapter 14

Communication and the Student with Physical Limitations

Marian Sheehan, Ph.D., C.C.C.

In This Chapter You'll Find:

Statistics about the extent of communication disorders in this country.

Information about the types of communication disorders.

An explanation of some communication devices used by people with these disorders.

Suggestions that can help you work more effectively with students with communication disorders.

Communication disorders are the most common disability in the United States. More individuals have speech, hearing or language disorders than have heart disease, epilepsy, blindness, cerebral palsy, muscular dystrophy and multiple sclerosis *combined*.

Between 5 and 10 percent of the American population has a speech or language disorder. About 25 percent of those with speech or language problems are school-aged children, between 5 and 21 years old.

Types of Communication Disorders

There are many different communication disorders. Problems of communication may occur in:

- Language content—the meaning of language, or what we say.

- Language form—the grammar and syntax, or how we say it.

- Language use—the pragmatics, or why and when we say it.

- Articulation—speech sound production.

- Fluency—the fluidity or flow of speech (such as stuttering or dysfluency).

- Voice—vocal pitch, loudness or vocal quality (hoarseness, breathiness, nasality).

- Hearing—transmissive or perceptive losses. (See Chapter 16 for an explanation of these terms.)

Communication problems may be present in any or all of these areas, and in any combination. They can range from mild to severe.

Speech and language pathologists are the professionals responsible for evaluating and treating communication disorders. These people frequently serve students with developmental delays, hearing impairments, mental disabilities, neurological disabilities and motor impairments.

Alternative Ways to Communicate

The goal of most treatment for communication disorders is to teach the student oral speech and language. Sometimes, however, a form of alternative communication—using a mode other than words—is needed.

For many years a total communication approach (manual sign language plus speaking) has been used successfully with hearing-impaired and deaf students. More recently, total communication has been used with severely language-impaired, nonverbal students to facilitate their learning oral language.

Some students may never be capable of producing intelligible speech. For students with cerebral palsy or other physical disabilities that limit oral communication, there is an increasing variety of nonverbal augmentative communication devices.

Augmentative communication systems vary widely: from simple, individually-designed picture boards for a student to indicate basic needs (eating, drinking, going to the bathroom) to much more elaborate, commercially-available electronic devices. (See Figure 14-1). Commercial communication devices differ in their language content, response or access mode, and portability. They also differ in output, using either synthetic voice output or visual display.

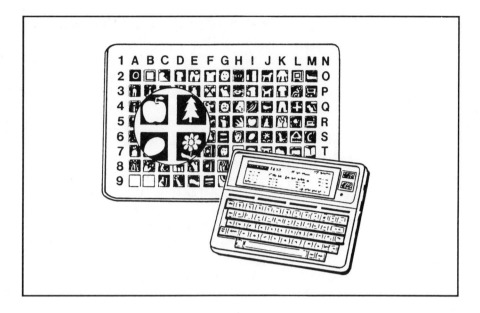

Figure 14-1: Picture communication board (top) and pocket size personal computer (bottom).

Almost any motor response a student makes can be used in accessing a communication system. Head pointers, foot pedals, even eyebrow and tongue switches—all can permit a student to use an augmentative communication system.

Augmentative communication systems are not appropriate for every student. Most importantly, a student must have the cognitive ability to communicate, be able to make choices and demonstrate communicative intent. A student must understand language before being able to use it.

Use a Team Approach

It's essential that people who routinely interact with a communicatively-impaired student be aware of the student's abilities and limits. This is especially important when a student is using augmentative communication. Families and school personnel should be team members in selecting and teaching the use of an appropriate device to meet the student's needs. Other professionals—such as an occupational therapist or rehabilitation specialist—may also provide valuable input.

The speech or language pathologist involved with a student is an excellent resource for assessing the student's communication capabilities and designing effective ways to interact with the student.

Summary

Communication disorders are the most common handicapping disability in the United States.

Many kinds of communication disorders exist, affecting anything from speech articulation and verbal fluency to hearing and syntax.

Speech and language pathologists specialize in treating communication disorders.

Many augmentative communication devices are available. They range from simple picture boards to electronic devices with keyboards.

To use an augmentative communication device, the student must have certain prior abilities.

All people who interact with a communicatively-impaired student should know about that student's abilities.

Chapter 15

Assessing and Managing Visual Impairment

Cyndy Schuster Silkworth, M.P.H., R.N., C.S.N.P.
Mary Billington, R.N.

In This Chapter You'll Find:

A brief guide to the types of visual impairment.

A list of the symptoms of visual impairment—symptoms you should carefully watch for.

Guidelines for referring a student with visual impairment to a health care professional.

Visual impairment is one of the most common disabilities students must cope with—a disability with obvious consequences for the quality of a student's education. Unfortunately, it may be difficult to tell that a student has a visual impairment unless the condition is severe. This is why regular vision assessments are essential.

Common Visual Problems

The term "visual impairment" really points to a diverse number of conditions. Those conditions in children include:

- Strabimus—eye deviation due to the lack of eye muscular coordination. The deviation may be constant (tropia), or it may occur only on occasion (phoria).

- Refractive errors including myopia (nearsightedness), hyperopia (farsightedness) or astigmatism (blurring).

- Nystagmus—recurring, involuntary eyeball movement. Such movement may be horizontal, vertical, rotating or mixed. It produces blurred vision and difficulty in focusing.

- Cataract—a gradually developing opacity (cloudiness) of the lens or lens capsule.

- Glaucoma—abnormally increased fluid pressure that may produce severe and permanent vision defects.

- Retinal degenerative diseases, including central or peripheral degeneration.

- Neuro-ophthalmological diseases, including optic nerve atrophy (degeneration), multiple sclerosis or optic neuritis (inflammation).

- Inflammatory diseases, including iritis (inflammation of the iris), uveitis (inflammation of the uveal tract), chorioretinitis (inflammation of the choriod and retina) and conjunctivitis.

- Tumors, including retinoblastoma (malignant tumor of the retina), rhabdomyosarcoma (skeletal muscle tumor) or neurofibromatosis (an inherited disease of the nervous system, muscles, bones and skin that causes multiple soft tumors).

Observing and Assessing for Visual Impairment

School personnel need to cooperate with designated health care providers in coordinating services for students with visual impairments. Both parents and teachers can make an important contribution to assessing the student with visual impairments: careful observation. Parents and teachers have the advantage of observing a student several hours a day, putting them in an excellent position to detect vision difficulties.

Any student manifesting one or more of the following behaviors consistently should go through vision screening. Refer if the problem persists after you discuss the problem with the parent or teacher—even though the student may pass the screening.

External abnormalities. Note any observed problem or change in the whites, lids, lashes, pupils or area around the eye.

Complaints of visual distress. Watch for these signs of difficulty expressed by the student:

- Sensitivity to light.

- Burning or itching of eyes or lids.

- Blurring or seeing double.

- Words or lines running together.

- Words jumping.

- Headaches.

- Nausea or dizziness.

Behaviors that indicate vision problems. These can include any of the following:

- Rubbing eyes frequently.

- Blinking frequently when reading or watching movies.

- Frowning or scowling when reading.

- Closing or covering any eye when reading or watching movies.

- Abnormal posture when doing close work.

- Squinting.

- Body tension while looking at near objects.

- Avoiding close work.

- Abnormally short attention span.

- Tilting the head to one side.

- Placing the head close to book or desk when reading or writing.

- Dislike for tasks requiring sustained visual concentration.

- Nervousness, irritability or restlessness after maintaining visual concentration.

- Losing place while reading.

- Using finger or other devices to keep place while reading.

- Moving head rather than eyes while reading.

- Poor eye-hand coordination.

Evaluating the student. The student with a possible visual impairment should be evaluated in several key areas. Among them is the student's own perception of his or her visual acuity. Another area is the health history, with special attention to visual problems. Here the relevant areas to consider are:

- Academic history—how well the student performs in classroom activities, and at what level.

- Visual screening—observation, acuity, corneal light reflex, cover test, alternate cover test, color vision. (All these tests should be done by trained personnel.)

- Ophthalmological assessment—visual fields, extraocular movements, red reflex and visual perception. This assessment should be done by trained personnel.

- Corrective lenses—perception, compliance, last exam and lens change.

- Treatments—medication or eye patching.

When to refer a student. Make a referral when the student fails visual screening and assessment. Other times to think about a referral are:

- When the student, parent or teacher becomes concerned about the student's ability to see.

- Blurred vision, double vision, eye injury and visual problems associated with head injury.

- Drainage, redness, itching, recurrent styes, pain and light sensitivity.

Summary

Visual assessments should be regularly performed on all students.

Visual impairments you may encounter in students vary greatly.

Members of the school staff should regularly work with a health care professional, taking a team approach for the student with visual impairment.

Observe the student with a visual impairment carefully. Parents and teachers are a key source information about a student's visual impairment.

Refer the student for further assessment when any signs of visual impairment occur.

For Further Reading

Vision and Hearing Conservation Unit, Maternal and Child Health Section, Minnesota Department of Health. *Pre-School and School Vision Screening Manual.* Minneapolis, MN, Minnesota Department of Health, 1980.

Bleck, Eugene E. and Donald A. Nagel. *Physically Handicapped Children: A Medical Atlas for Teachers*, 2nd ed., New York: Grune and Stratton, 1982.

Chapter 16

Hearing Impairment: Assessment and Management

Cyndy Schuster Silkworth, M.P.H., R.N., C.S.N.P.
Clara Gray, R.N.
Jennifer Phillips, B.S.

In This Chapter You'll Find:

A brief introduction to types of hearing impairment.

Guidelines for observing, assessing and referring the student with a hearing impairment.

Three checklists: one for classroom teachers who work with hearing impaired students, and troubleshooting guides for hearing aids, phonic ear receivers and microphones.

Hearing impairment is a sensory deficit that directly affects the student's ability to learn. Because this condition is so closely tied to learning ability, regular hearing assessments are essential.

Types of Hearing Deficits

Hearing impairments can be classified into types according to the site of interference:

Conductive—interference with sound transmission in the outer part of the middle ear. This is also known as transmission disturbance. The causes include wax accumulation, acute and chronic ear infections.

Sensorineural—dysfunction of the inner ear or the pathway from the inner ear to the brainstem. Another term for this condition is perception disturbance. The causes include abnormalities present at birth, injuries, toxic drug effects and prolonged exposure to noise.

Mixed—contains both conductive and sensorineural components.

Central—interference with transmission from the brainstem to the auditory cortex, or within the auditory cortex itself. The causes are many: brain tumors or abscess; stroke; or brain damage, acquired at birth or later in life through injury or infection.

Observing and Assessing the Student's Impairment

What factors should you consider when assessing the student with a hearing impairment? They include:

• The student's own perception of his or her condition.

• Perceptions of parents or guardians.

• Observations by the school staff.

• Behaviors that may indicate hearing problems:

  - Inattention or daydreaming, failure to respond to questions, requests that directions be repeated, saying "What?" frequently, and continual misunderstanding of directions.

  - Waiting to visually check with others before following directions and difficulty in completing tasks independently.

  - Aggressive physical behaviors and insensitivity to others' feelings.

  - Withdrawn, self-contained personality and blank expression.

  - Confusing words that sound alike, using immature speech or language, difficulty in formulating and expressing original ideas and difficulty in group discussions.

  - Seldom asking for help or clarification.

  - Tiring out easily, "tuning out," or playing alone.

  - Body language that indicates straining to hear or inattention to the public address system.

  - Behavior that expresses low self esteem and excessive self-criticism: "I can't do it; I'm too dumb."

- Refusing to wear a hearing aid or use assistive devices (auditory training units, note takers, interpreter services).

- Difficulty in understanding audio tapes and films.

- The student's health history—especially a history of frequent ear infections and slow speech development.

- Academic history.

- Use of hearing aids—prescription, compliance, monitoring.

- Audiometric screening and testing. This measures the student's capacity to hear sound.

- Tympanometry, which measures the eardrum's ability to vibrate.

- Otoscopic assessment. This refers to visual inspection of the ear canal and middle ear.

The last three assessments should be done by trained professionals.

When to refer a student. Make a referral when the following conditions occur:

- A failed threshold audiogram and failed tympanometry, with problems detected on otoscopic assessment. Again, these evaluations should be done by trained personnel.

- Parent or student concern regarding the student's ability to hear.

- Staff concern about any of the following: the student's inability to discriminate sounds; a voice pitch either too high or low; use of incomplete language; speech that is either abnormally soft or loud; difficulty in articulating certain speech sounds; and infantile or nonexistent speech.

- Reports of hearing difficulty that may be associated with a history of a head injury or exposure to loud noises.

- Health care provider's request for periodic follow-up, especially when it is past or nearly past the time frame for hearing reassessment. Encourage compliance by the student and parent or guardian.

- A history of familial deafness, with the student showing academic or social problems.

- Spells of dizziness or equilibrium problems.

Staff members who work with students with hearing impairments need appropriate training. Moreover, the school staff needs to cooperate with designated health care providers in coordinating the necessary services.

Summary

Hearing assessments should be regularly performed on all students.

Hearing impairments are classified according to the site of interference. That site may be in the inner ear, the pathway from the inner ear to the brainstem, or the middle ear. Interference can also occur as messages flow from the brainstem to the auditory cortex.

Members of the school staff should work closely with health care professionals to provide services for hearing impaired students.

Observe the student with a hearing impairment carefully. Refer the student for further assessment when any signs of hearing difficulty occur.

Following the "For Further Reading" section are three useful checklists:

- Is the Hearing Impaired Student in Your Class Learning?

- How to Troubleshoot a Hearing Aid Troubleshooting Guide for a Phonic Ear Receiver

- Troubleshooting Guide for a Phone Ear Receiver

For Further Reading

Bleck, Eugene E. and Donald A. Nagel. *Physically Handicapped Children: A Medical Atlas for Teachers.* 2nd ed., New York: Grune and Stratton, 1982.

E.A.R.S. (Educational/Audiological and Related Services) Program Publications. (Available from E.A.R.S., 916 Area Vocational Technical District, 1130 West Country Road B, Roseville, MN 55113.)

Levine, Melvin D., Robert Brooks and Jack Shonkoff. *A Pediatric Approach to Learning Disorders.* New York: John Wiley and Sons, 1980.

A Checklist for the Classroom Teacher

Is the Hearing Impaired Student in Your Class Learning?

Hearing Aids

1. Does the student wear a hearing aid? He or she should be wearing the aid consistently to get maximum benefit from it.

2. Do you check to make sure the aid is in working order? Is the aid on? Is the battery charged? Check this every day.

3. Do you keep a supply of batteries at school? It's a good idea.

4. Do you understand the purpose of a hearing aid and how it works? Contact your nearest hearing aid dealer or speech and hearing center for information.

5. Do you know who to contact when having problems with the aid? The parent, a school nurse, a speech and hearing therapist, an audiologist, or a hearing aid dealer will be able to help you.

6. Is the hearing aid worn both at home and at school? It should be.

7. Are batteries taken out of the aid each night? This is recommended, as well as storing the batteries in a cool dry place.

Class Situation

8. Does the student watch your face all the time while you are talking? Consistent watching is essential for a hearing impaired student.

9. Do you keep eye contact with your class or do you lose it by using a blackboard and looking down? Lack of constant eye contact by the teacher can be a great handicap to the hearing impaired student.

10. Is the student seated about 5 to 10 feet from where you talk to the class (first or second row) so that he does not have to strain to watch your face?

11. Do you avoid standing with your back to the window? Facing light makes lip reading difficult, if not impossible, for the hearing impaired student.

12. Do you check to make sure the hearing impaired student understands before beginning a new lesson? Please do if you can.

13. Do you use an overhead projector throughout the day to write "key" ideas (words, phrases, sentences) as you talk to the class? This technique of visual teaching can help all students in your class!

14. Do you avoid talking to the class with your back turned? The hearing impaired student must see your face.

15. Do you enunciate clearly when you talk?

16. Do you speak in simple, clear language?

17. Do you always make sure hearing impaired students are watching you before you begin talking? Developing a good habit of watching will help the student learn.

18. Do you label objects in your classroom? Constant visual exposure can help a student learn new words he or she does not hear.

19. Do you ask questions other than "Do you understand?" to make sure the student is learning? Coming from the student, the answer "Yes" may mean nothing. Ask meaningful questions beginning with how, when, where, what or why.

20. Do you avoid having students read aloud in front of the class? This is meaningless to the hearing impaired student: He or she cannot read along in a book and read the lips of the reader at the same time. Even this assumes that students doing the reading have "readable" lips and their faces are not expressionless and buried in the book!

21. When the lights in your classroom are dimmed for a film or filmstrip, do you write what you say to the class on an overhead projector so that the hearing impaired student also received the information? This additional visual exposure to the written language should help some of the slow learners in the class as well as the hearing impaired student.

22. Do you understand the hearing impaired student's deficit of language, the cause, the problem, and how you can help? Write to the Volta Bureau, 1537 35th Street N.W., Washington, D.C. 20007 for information on hearing loss and education for persons who are deaf.

23. Do you know what language sounds like to the hearing impaired student? The record *How They Hear*, Gordon N. Stowe and Associates, Northbrook, Illinois, explains this clearly.

Parent Involvement

24. Have you communicated regularly with the parents about a) specific ways they can help the student at home and b) what the student is learning at school?

25. Are the parents consistent in the student's management?

26. Do the student's parents have a realistic outlook on the student's future?

27. Does the student have equal responsibilities at home with siblings?

28. Does the family interact and communicate effectively with the student as a functioning member of the family?

(Courtesy the E.A.R.S. Program, 916 Area Vocational Technical District, White Bear Lake, Minnesota.)

How to Trouble-Shoot a Hearing Aid

Problem	See Paragraphs
Hearing aid dead	1, 2, 3, 4, 5, 7, 10, 14, 15
Working, but weak	1, 2, 3, 4, 5, 6, 7, 8, 9, 10, 13
Works intermittently or fades	1, 3, 4, 5, 10, 15, 16
Whistles	6, 9, 11, 12, 13, 15, 17, 18
Sounds noisy, raspy, shrill	1, 3, 4, 5, 8, 9, 10, 11, 12, 17
Sounds hollow, mushy muffled	1, 2, 7, 15, 16
Other kinds of bad sound quality	1, 7, 10, 15, 17
Makes noise when the student moves	19, 20, 21

Causes, Tests and Remedies

1. **Cause:** Dead, run-down or wrong type of battery.
   Test: Substitute new battery.
   Remedy: Replace old battery.

2. **Cause:** Battery reversed in holder, so that (+) terminal is where (-) terminal should be.
   Test: Examine battery replacement.
   Remedy: Insert battery correctly.

3. **Cause:** Poor contacts on receiver-cord plugs, due to dirty pins or springs.
   Test: Turn on the hearing aid; wiggle the plugs in the receptacles and withdraw and reinsert each plug.
   Remedy: Rub accessible contacts briskly with lead pencil eraser; then wipe them with a clean cloth slightly moistened with Energine or a similar cleaning fluid. Inaccessible contacts can usually be cleaned with a broom straw moistened with cleaning fluid.

4. **Cause:** Break or near break inside receiver cord.

    Test: While listening to the hearing aid, flex all parts of the cord by running your fingers along their entire length; while doing this, wiggle the cord at the terminals. Intermittent or raspy sounds indicate broken wires.

    Remedy: Replace the cord with a new one. Worn cords cannot be repaired satisfactorily.

5. **Cause:** Plugs not fully or firmly inserted in receptacles.

    Test: While listening to the hearing aid, withdraw and firmly insert each plug in turn.

    Remedy: Testing should solve the problem.

6. **Cause:** Ear tip too small or not properly seated in ear.

    Test: With your fingers, press the receiver firmly into the student's ear. Twist the receiver back and forth slightly to make sure that the ear tip is properly aligned.

    Remedy: Testing should solve the problem.

7. **Cause:** Ear tip plugged with wax or with a drop of water from cleaning.

    Test: Remove the ear tip. Examine it visually and blow through it to determine if the passage is open.

    Remedy: If the ear tip is obstructed with wax, wash it in lukewarm water and soap. Use a pipe cleaner or long-bristled brush to reach down into the canal. Rinse with clear water. Use a dry pipe cleaner to dry out the canal, or blow through the canal.

8. **Cause:** Loose receiver cap.

    Test: Examine the cap. Shake it.

    Remedy: If it's a screw-type cap, turn it finger-tight. If the cap was cemented on or crimped and has become loose, it can repaired only by the manufacturer.

9. Cause: Insufficient pressure of bone vibrator on mastoid.

   Test: While listening to the hearing aid, press the bone receiver more tightly against the head with your fingers.

   Remedy: Bend the bone-vibrator headband to provide greater pressure. This should ideally be done by the dealer.

10. Cause: Battery leakage (resulting in poor battery connections) or corroded battery contacts.

    Test: Examine the battery and battery holder for evidence of leakage: a powder or corrosion.

    Remedy: Discard the battery and wipe the terminals carefully.

11. Cause: Receiver close to a wall or other sound-reflecting surfaces.

    Test: Examine your position.

    Remedy: Avoid sitting with the fitted side of the hearing aid near a wall or other similar surface. These surfaces tend to reflect sound from the receiver; the sound is more picked up by the microphone. The result is whistling.

12. Cause: Microphone worn too close to the receiver.

    Test: Try moving the microphone to provide wider separation between microphone and receiver.

    Remedy: Avoid wearing microphone and receiver close together or on the same side of the body.

13. Cause: Microphone facing the body.

    Test: Reposition the microphone.

    Remedy: Testing should solve the problem.

14. Cause: Telephone-microphone switch is in the wrong place.

    Test: Place switch in the desired position.

    Remedy: Testing should solve the problem.

15. Cause: Faulty receiver.

    Test: Examine the receiver for possible breaks, cracks, etc.

    Remedy: Replace with a new receiver.

16. Cause: Collapse of tubing.
    Test: Check to see if the tube bends, either when the head is in a satisfactory position or is moved.
    Remedy: Shorten or replace the tube.

17. Cause: Volume control turned too high.
    Test: Reduce volume until speech sounds clearer.
    Remedy: Testing should solve the problem.

18. Cause: Air leak between ear mold and receiver.
    Test: Reduce volume until speech sounds clearer.
    Remedy: Testing should solve the problem.

19. Cause: Clothing noise from loose clothing clip.
    Test: Check clothing clip.
    Remedy: Testing should solve the problem.

20. Cause: Clothing noise from improper placement of hearing aid.
    Test: Experiment by placing the aid in different positions on the body.
    Remedy: Testing should solve the problem.

21. Cause: Clothing noise present because garment bag is not used.
    Test: Use garment bag.

If the above tests do not disclose the source of the trouble, the difficulty is probably in the receiver, microphone or amplifier. The instrument should be serviced by your dealer.

(Courtesy the E.A.R.S. Program, 916 Area Vocational Technical District, White Bear Lake, Minnesota.)

Troubleshooting Guide For A
Phonic Ear Receiver

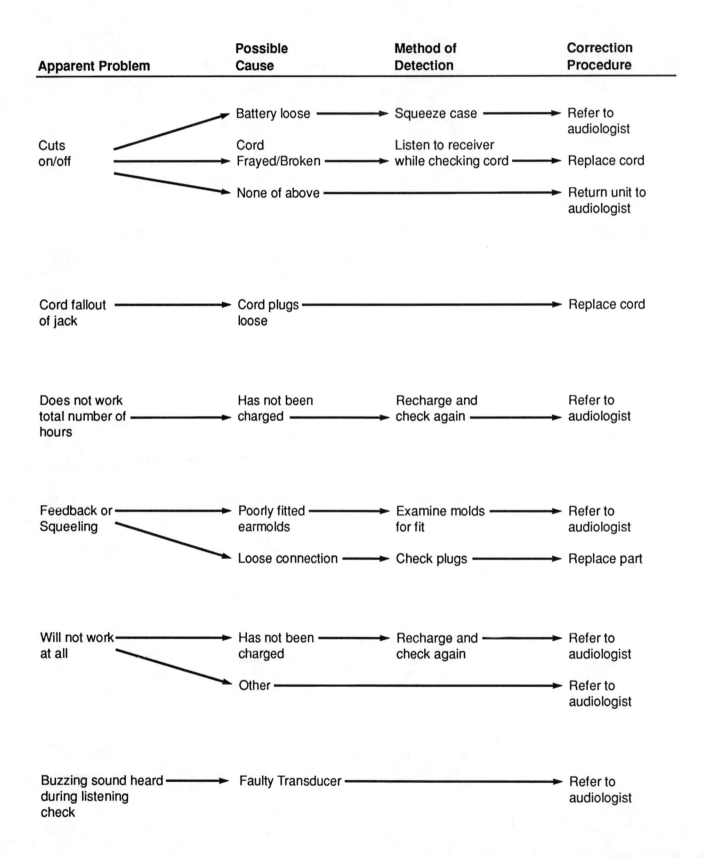

Apparent Problem	Possible Cause	Method of Detection	Correction Procedure
Cuts on/off	Battery loose	Squeeze case	Refer to audiologist
	Cord Frayed/Broken	Listen to receiver while checking cord	Replace cord
	None of above		Return unit to audiologist
Cord fallout of jack	Cord plugs loose		Replace cord
Does not work total number of hours	Has not been charged	Recharge and check again	Refer to audiologist
Feedback or Squeeling	Poorly fitted earmolds	Examine molds for fit	Refer to audiologist
	Loose connection	Check plugs	Replace part
Will not work at all	Has not been charged	Recharge and check again	Refer to audiologist
	Other		Refer to audiologist
Buzzing sound heard during listening check	Faulty Transducer		Refer to audiologist

Troubleshooting Guide For
Microphone For The Phonic Ear Receiver

Apparent Problem	Possible Cause	Method of Detection	Correction Procedure

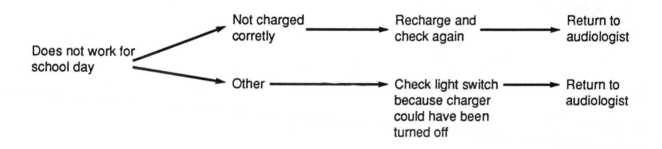

Signal cuts off/on through receiver

- Antenna broken → Check antenna → Return to audiologist
- Battery loose → Squeeze case → Return to audiologist
- Receiver malfunction → Recharge and check again → Return to audiologist if still malfunctioning

Does not work for school day

- Not charged corretly → Recharge and check again → Return to audiologist
- Other → Check light switch because charger could have been turned off → Return to audiologist

Chapter 17

Assessing and Managing Tactile Deficit

Barbara White, O.T.R.
Mary Coleman, O.T.R.
Cyndy Schuster Silkworth, M.P.H., R.N., C.S.N.P.
Clara Gray, R.N.
Mary Billington, R.N.

In This Chapter You'll Find:

A definition of tactile deficits and the possible consequences of this condition.

Guidelines for assessing and working with the student who has a tactile deficit.

Children with altered sensations of touch—tactile deficits—are at risk: They cannot use their sense of touch to accurately evaluate their environment. They are not aware of pain, pressure areas or extreme temperatures, all of which may be harmful.

Types of Tactile Deficit

Alterations in touch sensation are manifested in several ways:

- Paresthesia—the sensation of burning, crawling, tingling or prickling.

- Hyperesthesia—exaggerated sensitivity of the skin to touch.

- Hypoesthesia—diminished sensation to touch.

- Anesthesia—absence of sensation to touch.

The Danger of Pressure Sores

Pressure sores are one of the biggest health hazards for persons with disabilities, particularly if they lack sensation. These sores, also known as decubitus ulcers, result from a lack of blood supply and consequent lack of nourishment to the skin and underlying tissue. They can be serious.

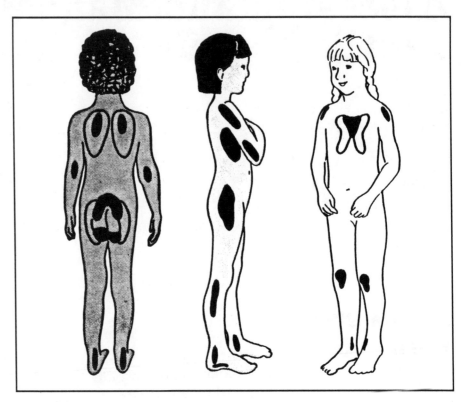

Figure 17-1: Areas susceptible to pressure sores.

Pressure sores most commonly occur over bony prominences such as heels, knees, lower back and buttocks. Often the cause is unrelieved pressure, such as occurs when one sits or lies in one position for an extended time. A student with limited mobility often endures the discomfort of being in one position for too long because he or she is unable to move.

Pressure sores can also be caused by friction under braces, moisture from perspiration, and, in an incontinent student, by the moisture and chemical content of urine and stool.

In the early stages, a pressure sore appears as a warm, tender red spot that turns white when you push it with your finger but becomes red when the pressure is released. Any area that stays red over 15 minutes is a potential problem area. In later stages, the skin becomes blue or purplish-red and is often mottled. It is no longer warm and does not pale (whiten) when pressure is applied with a finger.

Ensuring good circulation is the best prevention of pressure sores, particularly through frequent change of position and nonrestrictive clothing.

Assessing the Student with a Tactile Deficit

Tactile deficits may place a student at risk for injury, because altered sensations to touch create immobility in the affected area. Management aims to prevent muscle atrophy (wasting), contractures of joints (stiffening) and pressure areas.

Carefully observe the student with a tactile deficit. This is an essential aid to assessing the student's condition. Assessments should be done by the school nurse or other qualified health professional and include several elements:

- The student's own perception of his or her condition.

- The parent or guardian's perception of the condition.

- The perceptions and observations of the school staff, covering both behavioral and educational concerns.

- Health history—including causes of the deficit, life style modifications and associated physical impairments.

- The student's academic history.

- Treatments given—therapy or medications.

Whenever you work with a student who has a tactile deficit, apply the guidelines shown in Table 17-1.

Table 17-1

Safety Considerations for Students with Tactile Deficits

School personnel should exercise special care when working with a student with a tactile deficit. The most important points are these:

1. Observe the student's skin. Keep it clean and guard it from bruising, rashes, lesions and pressure sores.

2. Make sure the student wears clothing that fits properly and is appropriate for the weather.

3. Take special safety precautions when the student is in the kitchen or chemistry lab or around exercise and playground equipment. Have the student use protective devices such as hot mitts, goggles, gloves and aprons.

4. Practice environmental safety: Clearly mark hot water pipes, hot water faucets, and cold or frozen equipment or articles.

5. Monitor the student's use of equipment—saws, sewing machines, paper cutters, scissors, stoves and carving knives. Offer instruction in their proper use, storage, maintenance and safety precautions.

When to Refer the Student to Health Care Professionals

Make a referral when you observe these conditions:

- Loss of tactile sensation, whether it occurs as a new development or merely increased loss.

- Injury to a body part or area accompanied by sensation loss.

- Concern about sensory deficit as expressed by the student, parents or teachers.

Summary

Tactile deficits are altered sensations to touch in certain areas of the body.

Students with tactile deficits cannot accurately evaluate their environment. Muscle atrophy, stiffening of joints and pressure sores are possible consequences of tactile deficit—all of them serious.

Carefully observe the student with a tactile deficit. When working with such a student, follow the safety precautions listed in this chapter.

Make sure the student with a tactile deficit receives a thorough assessment. Refer the student to a health professional if you have a concern about any sensory deficit.

For Further Reading

Bleck, Eugene E. and Donald A. Nagel. *Physically Handicapped Children: A Medical Atlas for Teachers*, 2nd ed., New York: Grune and Stratton, 1982.

Levine, Melvin D., Robert Brooks and Jack P. Shonkoff. *A Pediatric Approach to Learning Disorders.* New York: John Wiley and Sons, 1980.

Malasanos, Lois, et al. *Health Assessment.* St. Louis: C.V. Mosby, 1981.

Jones, Monica Loose. *Home Care for the Chronically Ill or Disabled Child.* Philadelphia: Harper and Row, 1985.

Chapter 18

The Bowel Training Program

Kathleen Lytle, R.N., B.A.

In This Chapter You'll Find:

An explanation of encopresis, the condition that underlies chronic fecal soiling.

Guidelines for setting up a bowel training program.

An outline of a sample bowel training program, including suggestions for diet.

A bowel training program may become necessary for the student with a chronic health condition or disability. As a member of the school staff, you might be involved in such a program. This chapter, consisting mainly of guidelines for setting up a bowel program, should help you.

The Condition: Encopresis

Some children have problems with chronic fecal soiling. This is known as encopresis, and it occurs when a child is unwilling or unable to have a bowel movement in the toilet. Such voluntary or involuntary withholding of stool can lead to chronic constipation and loss of muscle tone in the lower bowel and rectum. Liquid stool from higher up in the bowel then leaks down around the constipated stool and results in soiling.

There can be several causes of encopresis, including physical abnormality in the bowel or rectum. A constipating diet may result in painful bowel movements which then lead to holding back stool. Over time this causes a loss of muscle tone, which then reinforces the cycle. Encopresis may also be a symptom of underlying emotional or psychosocial problems. Frequently encopresis is caused by a combination of the above factors.

Setting Up a Bowel Program

Before setting up a bowel program for a child with encopresis, ask that a pediatrician evaluate the student and recommend a bowel training procedure. This step is important in ruling out a medical cause and prescribing a bowel cleansing routine. Also ask for a psychological assessment to look at emotional factors and set up a behavior program that positively rewards the child for successful use of the toilet.

Good communication between the psychologist, pediatrician, school personnel and parents is essential for continuity and consistency of the program. The role of the school nurse or other qualified health professional could be to assume several tasks: serving as a liaison between all the people involved, monitoring the effectiveness of the program and teaching the parents and child the steps of the bowel program.

Achieving a satisfactory bowel program requires "trial and error," time and patience. Keep in mind that each bowel program is different and highly individualized.

Goals of the program. Some goals of bowel management include:

- Emptying the lower bowel at regular intervals.

- Preventing accidents between regular emptying.

- Preventing constipation.

- Promoting independence when carrying out the bowel program.

Remember, the bowel program must be individualized for each student's needs, patterns and neurological deficits.

Stimulating the bowel. These are some methods to try for stimulating the bowel and achieving successful bowel evacuation:

- Ask the student to drink a large amount of fluid. This stimulates peristalsis, which occurs when the intestine contracts and helps move stool down to the large intestine and out.

- Use natural laxatives, food substances that trigger evacuation. These include prunes and raw apples.

- Use stool softeners. These prevent hardening of stools, and students can take them on a regular basis.

- Use suppositories. These stimulate the bowel and cause it to contract. There should be no stool in the rectum; this allows the suppository to come in contact with the rectal wall.

- Use digital stimulation. This relaxes the sphincter and allows for movement of the stool. To do this, insert a gloved finger about 1/2 to 1 inch into the rectum. Use gentle circular motion for 1 minute to stimulate evacuation.

- Use laxatives. This is a medication that comes in pill, liquid and suppository form. Laxatives also stimulate the bowel to cause evacuation.

- Start manual evacuation, the removal of stool within the rectum with a gloved finger. This could be necessary if the student is unable to pass stool and other techniques are not successful.

- Use an enema. This is one of the last choices in bowel evacuation because it tends to make the bowel more sluggish. An enema should be used only if other choices prove unsuccessful. Enemas distend the bowel, which in turn irritates the bowel and causes it to contract.

General suggestions for the program. Some helpful tips to remember when carrying out the bowel program are these:

- Sitting is better than lying down for a bowel movement. If the student's feet don't touch the floor when sitting on the toilet, put a box under the feet so the knees are higher than the hips. This "squat" position promotes evacuation.

- It's best for the student to start a new routine with a clean bowel. For this purpose, give a very mild laxative or a small enema.

- Diet is important. Fiber foods such as bran cereals, breads, fruits and raw vegetables all help stimulate the bowel by adding bulk to the diet. Avoid foods that cause constipation: chocolate, cheese and bananas.

- Drinking plenty of fluids, especially water and fruit juices, keeps the stool from becoming hard.

- The student should go no more than three days without a bowel evacuation.

- Good skin care is essential after each bowel movement or accident. This prevents skin breakdown.

- Activity is crucial for normal bowel function. Inactivity tends to slow it down.

Remember above all that good bowel management and preventing constipation depend on time, patience and hard work. Try various programs until you find the successful one, always working under the guidance of a physician.

Summary

Encopresis is chronic fecal soiling that occurs when a child is unwilling or unable to have bowel movements in the toilet.

Bowel training programs may be needed to overcome encopresis.

Good communication between all personnel involved in the bowel program is essential.

Achieving a successful bowel program requires time and patience. The program must be designed specifically for the individual student.

You can use various methods to stimulate the bowel, including laxatives, suppositories, asking the student to drink large amounts of fluid, digital stimulation and manual evacuation. Enemas can be used too, though they are a last choice.

Bowel training programs should always be administered under the guidance of a physician. The general suggestions offered in this chapter will help you toward a successful bowel program.

Chapter 19

Guidelines for Diapering

Cyndy Schuster Silkworth, R.N., M.P.H., C.S.N.P.

In This Chapter You'll Find: Guidelines for avoiding cross-contamination when changing diapers.

Some students with a chronic health condition or disability may use diapers. These students are unable to control urination or bowel movements, the result of conditions such as quadraplegia, spina bifida or profound mental retardation.

At first glance this may seem a simple, everyday task. Actually, it's possible to spread infection when changing diapers, so the task must be performed with care. This chapter offers step-by-step instructions for changing diapers safely.

Equipment You'll Need We'll begin with the supplies you'll need. Have the following items on hand before starting the procedure:

- Changing table.

- Disposable cover for changing table.

- Supplies (soap, water, cotton balls or soft tissue) for cleaning the student's skin.

- Plastic bags for student's soiled clothing.

- Covered receptacle lined with disposable plastic bags for soiled cloth diapers.

- Plastic bag ties or masking tape for sealing disposable plastic bags at time of discard.

- Disposable plastic gloves (medium or large size, nonsterile).

- Disinfectant for cleaning the changing table.

Changing the Diaper

Next follows the main steps involved in careful diaper changing.

Procedure:

1. *Place the student on a clean changing table* or other appropriate surface. Do not leave the student unattended.

2. *Remove the soiled diaper* and place it in double-bagged plastic in a covered pail.

   If the diaper is cloth and soiled with feces, leave it on the changing table until the student returns to the classroom.

3. *If other clothing is soiled, remove it* and place it directly into an identifiable plastic bag which can be secured and sent home at end of day.

4. *Cleanse the perineum (area between the buttocks and rectum) and buttocks* thoroughly with soap and water.

   Use ointments and powders only when authorized and provided by parent.

5. *Rinse and dry the skin* before applying the clean diaper.

6. *Return the student to the classroom.*

7. *While wearing disposable plastic gloves, rinse and wring out in the toilet any cloth diaper soiled with feces.*

   Use only disposable diapers unless the physician orders cloth diapers for a specific reason.

8. *After rinsing, place the cloth diaper in appropriate receptacle.*

9. *Remove the gloves* and discard them in an appropriate receptacle.

   Wash your hands after wearing gloves.

10. *Report abnormal conditions* to appropriate person.

    Abnormal conditions may be:

    • Blood or streaks of blood on diaper.

    • Watery, liquid stool.

    • Mucus or pus in stool.

    • Clay-colored stool.

    • Skin rashes, bruises or breaks in skin.

11. *Use a disinfectant* to clean the changing table.

    Household bleach and strong chemical cleaners work well.

Summary

It's possible to spread infection when changing diapers, so perform the procedure carefully.

Before you change a diaper, have the necessary equipment on hand.

When changing the diaper, follow the step-by-step procedure listed in this chapter.

References

California State Department of Education. *Techniques for Preventing the Spread of Infectious Disease.* Sacramento, CA: California State Department of Education, 1983.

Chapter 20

Stoma Care for Students with Ostomies

Eileen Stever, R.N., B.S.N., P.H.N.

In This Chapter You'll Find:

A definition of ostomies and information on the different types of ostomies.

Guidelines for promoting good stoma care.

Step-by-step instructions for changing a stoma bag.

Ostomies are surgical procedures used to treat some intestinal diseases in children and adults. Other conditions can make also an ostomy necessary, such as cancer or accidents.

The ostomy creates an opening in the gastrointestinal or urinary systems to allow for the elimination of body wastes--stool or urine. The actual opening is called a stoma. Although there are several kinds of ostomies, the three main types of abdominal ostomies are colostomy, ileostomy and urostomy.

Types of Ostomies

Colostomy. In a colostomy (the most common type), part of the colon is removed or disconnected. All or part of the rectum may be removed as well. The end of the remaining colon is brought to the surface through the abdomen, folded back like a turtleneck and stitched in place.

Discharge from a colostomy will vary in consistency, depending on the location of the colostomy. The colon absorbs water as stool passes through it; the more usable the colon remains after surgery, the more likely the discharge is to be solid with predictable frequency.

Ileostomy. In an ileostomy, the entire colon is removed. An ileostomy is created by bringing a portion of the ileum, or smaller intestine, through an opening in the abdomen. The discharge is fairly constant and watery, containing large amounts of water and salts. Active digestive enzymes are present in the discharge as well, and they are highly irritating to skin around the stoma.

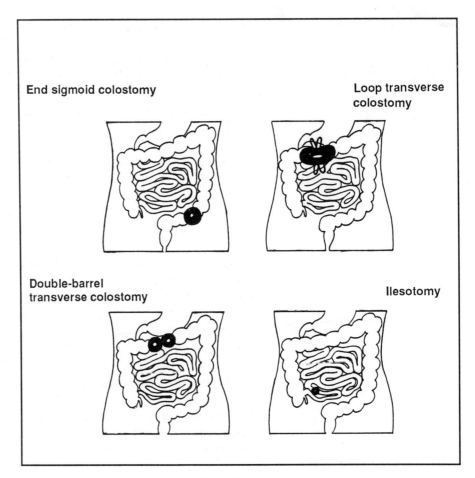

Figure 20-1: Anatomic placements of stomas.

Urostomy. A urostomy, or urinary diversion, is performed when the bladder is removed or bypassed. Urine is then redirected to an external pouch, or bag. A urostomy is the most common ostomy among teenagers, often performed to correct conditions at birth.

Urostomies may be of two kinds: an ileal conduit or ureterostomy. With ileal conduit, the ureters, which carry urine from the kidneys, are attached to a short piece of intestine. This piece in turn is attached to the abdomen to form a stoma. With the ureterostomy, one or both ureters are brought directly to the surface of the abdomen.

Promoting Good Stoma Care

For students with ostomies, the basic goal is to promote personal habits and techniques that keep the skin and stoma healthy. There are related goals as well: for students to assume self-care of the stoma and bag according to their ability, and to ensure that students are socially acceptable. Reaching these goals means working with both the student and family.

Our basic goals translate into more specific objectives:

- To promote personal awareness and educate the student about personal hygiene and proper skin care.

- To provide education in diet and promote proper food and fluid intake.

Skin care. Skin care is a major concern for all people with ostomies, because discharge from the stoma can be destructive to skin tissue. For this reason, a properly measured skin barrier must be applied around the stoma to protect the skin and provide a leakproof seal with the bag.

Ongoing education. Because an ostomy may be a permanent condition for the student, it is important for the student and parents to learn as much as they can about appliances. Urge them to keep abreast of the continuing new developments.

You can try several devices when teaching ostomy care to younger children. One is to make an educational toy by drilling holes in a "Chatty Cathy" doll where the stoma is located. You can then add a realistic-looking abdominal stoma. Practicing with catheters, tubes, appliances, and bandages can also prepare toddlers for their own treatments and help initiate self-care.

Use two bags. The student should have at least two reusable bags: While one is being worn, the other one can be cleaned and dried. This approach requires less time in changing bags and can assure a completely clean bag with each change. The care that you give to reusable equipment will determine how long it lasts.

Who should change the stoma bag? Whenever possible, the student should perform this procedure. However, it may also be done by designated school personnel, under supervision of the school nurse or other qualified health professional.

How to Change a Stoma Bag

Equipment needed. Before changing a stoma bag, have the following equipment on hand:

- Mild soap and water.

- Skin preparations such as stomahesive wafers, karaya washers, powders, cement, or sealants which are recommended by the doctor or student's interostomal therapist.

- Short-bladed, curved scissors.

- The bag or pouch recommended.

- A guide for measuring stoma size.

- A container for cleaning a reusable bag.

- Recommended disinfectant solution for cleaning and soaking the bag, either commercial or a home remedy: one part vinegar to three parts water for soaking the reusable bag.

Changing the stoma bag.

Procedure:

1. *Assemble all needed equipment.*

   Doing this promotes efficiency, teaching the student organizational skills related to self-care. It also promotes personal hygiene.

2. *Make sure you use clean supplies for cleaning the stoma equipment.*

   These supplies don't have to be sterile. The stoma and surrounding skin are not sterile and require only the same cleanliness as the rest of the body exterior.

3. *Wash your hands.*

4. *Empty the contents of the bag the student is wearing.*

5. *Measure the stoma size* accurately, and regularly, with a measuring guide to assure a good fit for the skin barrier.

   Consider also the outer dimensions of the pattern on the measuring guide. Take care to avoid hip bones, ribs, pubic area, and folds near the waist and navel.

   Stomas tend to shrink during the first few months after surgery. A proper appliance fit does not leak, prevents skin irritation and breakdown, is odorless, is comfortable in all activities and is not noticeable under clothing.

6. *Carefully remove the old bag and skin barrier* from the abdomen. Push the skin from the bag rather than pulling the bag from the skin.

   Prevent irritation and tearing of skin around stoma.

7. *Wash the stoma area* using a soft, nonabrasive cloth and gentle strokes. *Do not scrub.*

   Stomas are shiny, wet and dark pink in color—similar to the lining of your mouth. They have no nerve endings and do not transmit sensation or pain. Stomas are, however, rich in blood vessels and may bleed easily if nicked with a fingernail or brushed with a coarse cloth or gauze pad.

8. *Observe for the skin around the stoma* for redness, blistering or weepy skin—reddened skin with a pinpoint rash.

   These may indicate leakage of the discharge on the skin around stoma. Signs of pinpoint rash may indicate a monilial or yeast infection similar to "diaper rash."

9. *Also observe the skin for allergies* to cement, adhesive, karaya, tape or other pouch materials.

10. *Pat the skin dry* and place a skin barrier on the skin around the stoma.

    Follow the directions for the specific appliance being used. Directions will vary.

11. *Remove the backing* of the stomahesive faceplate and peel the paper backing from the adhesive on the new bag.

    Save the backing and use it as a pattern for the next change.

12. *Center the new bag* directly over the stoma. Press the bag to the barrier so there are no wrinkles.

13. *Open the bag* and allow a little air to enter. Follow the specific directions for sealing off the bottom of the bag.

    Allowing a small amount of air in the bag provides for better drainage.

14. *Tape the top, sides and bottom adhesive areas* of the bag with paper tape.

Figure 20-2: Basic steps in stoma care.

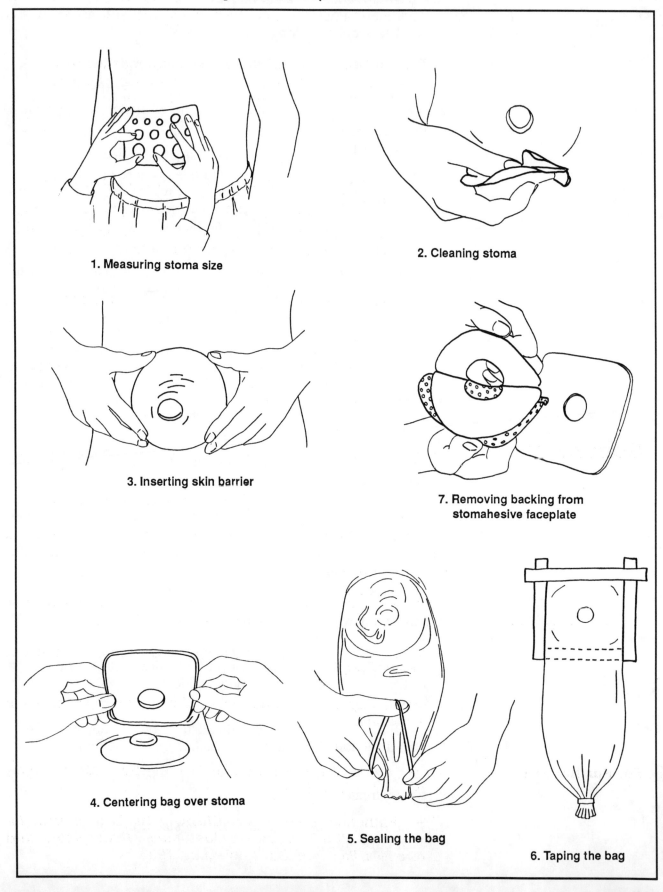

1. Measuring stoma size

2. Cleaning stoma

3. Inserting skin barrier

7. Removing backing from stomahesive faceplate

4. Centering bag over stoma

5. Sealing the bag

6. Taping the bag

Follow-up steps. The preceeding steps complete the basic procedure. However, some follow up is needed to make sure it goes well the next time.

15. *Remind the student about proper food and fluid intake.* Students with a colostomy or ileostomy should choose foods to reduce flatulence (gas) from the stoma site. Students with a urostomy need to remember that skin irritation and breakdown can be caused by acidic or concentrated urine.

    Encourage the student to drink cranberry juice frequently, which retards odor. In addition, these students can take oral ascorbic acid (vitamin C) in a dosage recommended by the physician. To avoid concentrated urine, encourage the student to drink the proper amount of fluid each day.

16. *Always rotate two or more bags.* Keep reusable bags.

    Clean bags prevent infection and skin ulcerations. Clean the bags by soaking them in the prescribed disinfectant. Or use a 1:3 solution—one part white vinegar to three parts water; soak the bag for 10 to 15 minutes. Rinse thoroughly before applying.

Summary

A stoma is an opening in the abdomen that allows for eliminating body wastes.

The stoma is created by a procedure known as an ostomy.

The goal of stoma care is to keep the skin and stoma clean and healthy. This requires working with both the student and family. Encourage self-care for the student with an ostomy.

Skin care is a major concern for everyone with an ostomy. Use a properly applied skin barrier around the stoma.

Help the student and parents keep abreast of new techniques in stoma care.

When changing a stoma bag, follow the procedure explained in this chapter.

For Further Reading

Gross, Linda, *Ileostomy: A Guide.* Los Angeles: United Ostomy Association, Inc., 1979.

Jeter, Katherine. *These Special Children: The Ostomy Book for Parents of Children with Colostomies, Ileostomies and Urostomies*, Palo Alto: Bull Publishing, 1982.

Mullen, Barbara and Kerry McGinn, *The Ostomy Book*, Palo Alto: Bull Publishing, 1980.

Ostomy and Your Child - A Parent's Guide. Princeton: E.R. Squibb and Sons (Convactec), 1984.

Wood, Lucille and Beverly Rambo ed. *Nursing Skills for Allied Health Services.* Philadelphia: W.B. Saunders, 1978.

Chapter 21

Intermittent Catheterization for Urine

Eileen Stever, R.N., B.S.N., P.H.N.

In This Chapter You'll Find: Step-by-step instructions for safe use of a catheter.

The term "catheter" merely means a tube for injecting or emptying fluids. The main purpose of using a catheter is to help empty urine from the bladder. The catheter also helps prevent infection and regulate urine flow.

Students with some chronic health conditions or physical disabilities will find it difficult or physically impossible to empty their bladders. These students may need catheterization during the school day.

Most often these students will use the catheter to empty the bladder intermittently—rather than continuously with an indwelling catheter. Studies indicate that there is less chance of kidney or bladder infection with periodic use of a catheter.

Whenever possible, the student should perform this procedure. As with any specialized health care procedure, however, catheterization needs to be administered by or done under direct supervision of a qualified health professional.

Intermittent catheterization may be done with either clean or sterile technique. The choice depends on recommendation from the student's physician. Both techniques are described in this chapter.

How to Do the Catheterization

What follows are step-by-step instructions for performing a catheterization. The main section of these instructions are divided into three categories: procedures for a female, for a male and for self-catheterization. In any case, the first step is careful preparation.

Equipment Needed

Have the following supplies on hand before you begin the catheterization:

- A container to collect the urine.

- A properly-sized straight catheter. Ask the student's parent or physician for the correct size.

- Cleaning equipment: washcloth, soap, and water.

- Water soluble lubricant for the catheter tip.

- Gloves—clean or sterile, depending on recommendations from the child's physician.

Preparatory Steps

The following steps apply to either the sterile or clean technique.

Procedure:

1. *Set up needed the materials.* (See the equipment checklist above.)

2. *Reassure the student and explain the procedure* at the student's level of understanding.

   A doll adapted with urethral, vaginal and anal openings may be helpful initially in teaching the proper procedure. Adequate explanation reduces apprehension and promotes a trusting relationship.

3. *Provide privacy* for this procedure.

4. *Wash your hands and the student's hands.*

   Teach good hand washing techniques before and after catheterization. Promote its importance as the student begins a self-catheterization program.

5. *Put on clean or sterile gloves,* depending on the preferred technique. If sterile technique is recommended, contact the student's physician for specific procedural guidelines; these will vary.

Instructions for the Female Student

1. *Ask the student to lie down* on her back with knees flexed and legs spread apart.

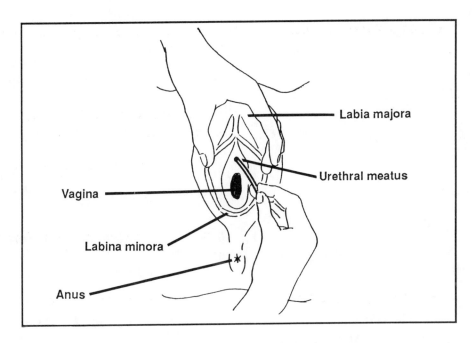

Figure 21-1: Inserting catheter—female.

2. *Cleanse the area around the urethra meatus.* Assess the area for redness, skin eruptions, swelling or discharge or drainage of any kind.

3. *With your thumb and middle finger, separate the labia minora.* Maintain uninterrupted separation with a slight backward and upward tension. You must clearly see the meatus in order to introduce the catheter without injuring the student.

4. *Position the open end of the catheter tube over the collection container.*

5. *Ask the student to breathe deeply. Then slowly insert the catheter* into the meatus until urine begins to flow.

Inserting too much catheter may cause looping and incomplete emptying. Deep breathing promotes relaxation and facilitates insertion of catheter.

6. *Measure and record the amount of urine obtained.*

7. *Observe the urine,* noting color, density and any foreign particles. Document these observations and tell the student, parents or physician about anything that merits medical attention.

8. *Withdraw the catheter slowly* to avoid injury to urethra.

9. *Teach the importance of proper cleansing* of the catheter, following instructions from the physician or parent.

   This applies especially with the clean technique when the catheter is used for repeated catheterizations.

10. *Properly dispose of the urine.* Wash your hands and the student's hands.

11. *Remind the student of the importance of drinking enough liquids.* The amount of liquid a student should drink is based on body weight and health status.

Instructions for a Male Student

1. *Ask the student to lie down on his back* with legs extended.

2. *Cleanse the area around urethral meatus. Assess the perineum* for redness, skin eruptions, swelling or discharge or drainage of any kind.

   The perineum is the area between the anus and genitals.

   You must clearly see the meatus to introduce the catheter without injury to the student.

3. *Lift the penis perpendicular to the body* to straighten the urethra. Retract the foreskin as necessary.

4. *Position the open end of the catheter over the collection container.*

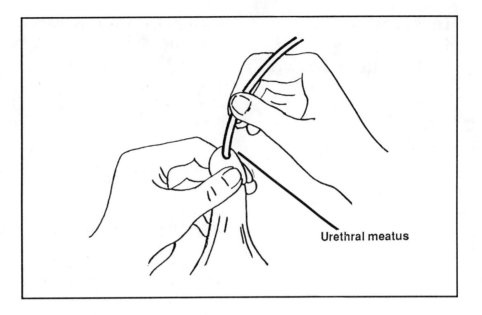

Urethral meatus

Figure 21-2: Insertion of catheter—male.

5. *Ask the to student breathe deeply; then insert the catheter into the meatus slowly until urine begins to flow.*

   Deep breathing promotes relaxation and eases insertion of catheter.

6. *Measure and record the amount of urine obtained.*

7. *Observe the urine,* noting color, density and any foreign tissue. Document your observations and tell the student, parent or physician of anything that merits medical attention.

8. *Withdraw the catheter slowly* to avoid injury to urethra.

9. *Teach the importance of proper cleansing* of the catheter used in intermittent catheterization. Use the clean technique when the catheter is to be reused.

10. *Properly dispose of the urine. Wash your hands and the student's hands.*

**Instructions
for Teaching
Self-catheterization.**

1. *Use a mirror to indicate the location of urethral opening. Teach the student to observe for abnormal appearance of the perineum.*

   Besides providing an orientation to body function, this step promotes self-care skills and early detection of abnormal conditions.

2. *Help the student get in proper position* on the toilet for self-catheterization.

   Optional use of a clean pan over the toilet enables the student to see the flow of urine.

3. *Help the student proceed through the steps for catheterization.* (See the two preceding sections.)

Summary

Intermittent catheterization promotes regular urine flow and prevents infection.

Whenever possible, have the student perform his or her own catheterization. Anyone doing this procedure, however, should be directly supervised by a health care professional.

Follow the instructions in this chapter when performing the catheterization.

Chapter 22

Guidelines for Handling Body Fluids in Schools

Elaine Brainerd, M.A., R.N.

In This Chapter You'll Find:

Answers to common questions about the spread of infectious disease through contact with body fluids.

Specific guidelines to help you guard against the transmission of disease.

Recent concern about how children with Acquired Immune Deficiency Syndrome (AIDS) should be educated has raised several questions about the exposure of teachers and children to potentially infectious body fluids—especially from children with communicable diseases in the school setting.

- Does contact with body fluids present a risk of infection?

- What should be done to avoid contact with potentially infected body fluids?

- What should be done if direct contact with body fluids is made?

- How should such fluids when spilled be removed from the environment?

The following guidelines provide simple and effective precautions against transmitting disease. They apply to all persons, including pregnant women, potentially exposed to the blood or body fluids of any student. No distinction is made between body fluids from students with a known disease and those from students without symptoms or with an undiagnosed disease.

Before explaining the guidelines in detail, we offer answers to common questions about contact with body fluids.

Does Contact with Body Fluids Present A Risk?

We should consider the body fluids of all persons as containing potentially infectious agents (germs). The term "body fluids" includes: blood, semen, drainage from scrapes and cuts, feces, urine, vomitus, respiratory secretions (for example, nasal discharge) and saliva.

Contact with body fluids presents a risk of infection with a variety of germs. In general, however, the risk is very low and depends on a variety of factors—including the type of fluid and the type of contact made with it.

One thing must be emphasized: With the exception of blood, which is normally sterile, the body fluids you may come in contact with usually contain many organisms. Some of those organisms may cause disease. Furthermore, many germs may be carried by individuals who have no symptoms of illness. These individuals may be at various stages: at the beginning stages of infection, mildly infected without symptoms, or chronic carriers of certain infectious agents, including the AIDS and hepatitis viruses.

In fact, transmission of communicable diseases is more likely to occur from contact with infected body fluids of unrecognized carriers than from contact with fluids from recognized carriers. Why? Because simple precautions are not always carried out.

What Should Be Done To Avoid Contact With Body

When possible, avoid direct skin contact with body fluids. If you make contact with body fluids, you should wash your hands afterwards.

At the least, disposable gloves should be available in the office of the custodian, nurse, or principal. Gloves are recommended when direct hand contact with body fluids is anticipated—for example, when treating bloody noses, handling clothes soiled by urine or feces, or when cleaning any spills by hand. Gloves used for this purpose should be put in a plastic bag or lined trash can, secured and disposed of daily.

What Should Be Done if Direct Skin Contact Occurs?

In many instances, unanticipated skin contact with body fluids may occur in situations where gloves are not immediately available. Examples are the teacher wiping a runny nose, applying pressure to a bleeding injury outside the classroom or helping a child in the bathroom.

In these cases, wash the hands and other affected skin areas of all exposed persons with soap and water after direct contact has ceased. Clothing and other nondisposable items that are soaked through with body fluids (such as towels used to wipe them up) should be rinsed and placed in plastic bags. Presoaking in cold water may be required to remove blood, feces or other stains. Use gloves when rinsing or soaking the items in cold water prior to bagging.

Send clothing home for washing with appropriate directions to parents and teachers. Contaminated disposable items— tissues, paper towels, diapers—should be handled with disposable gloves.

How Should Spilled Body Fluids Be Removed From the Environment?

Most schools have standard procedures already in place for removing body fluids such as vomitus. Review these procedures to determine whether appropriate cleaning and disinfection steps have been included.

Many schools stock sanitary absorbent agents specifically intended for cleaning body fluid spills. (An example is ZGOOP from Parsens Manufacturing Co., Philadelphia, PA.) The dry material is applied to the area, left for a few minutes to absorb the fluid, and then vacuumed or swept up.

Wear disposable gloves when using these agents, and dispose of the vacuum bag or sweepings in a plastic bag. Rinse the broom and dustpan in a disinfectant. No special handling is required for vacuuming equipment.

Hand Washing Procedures

Proper handwashing requires the use of soap and water and vigorous washing under a stream of running water for about 10 seconds. For detailed instructions on hand washing, see Chapter 11.

Soap suspends easily removable soil and micro-organisms, allowing them to be washed off. Running water is necessary to carry away dirt and debris. Remember to use paper towels to thoroughly dry your hands.

Disinfectants

Use an intermediate-level disinfectant to clean surfaces contaminated with body fluids. Such disinfectants will kill vegetative bacteria, fungi, tubercle bacillus and viruses. The disinfectant should be registered by the U.S. Environmental Protection Agency (EPA) for use as a disinfectant in medical facilities and hospitals.

Various classes of disinfectants are listed below. Hypochlorite solution (bleach) is preferred for cleaning objects that may be put in the mouth. Brand names are listed only for examples of each type of germicidal solution and should not be considered an endorsement of a specific product.

- Ethyl or isopropyl alcohol (70 percent).

- Phenolic germicidal detergent in a 1 percent aqueous solution (such as Lysol®).

- Sodium hypochlorite with at least 100 ppm (parts per million) available chlorine (1/2 cup household bleach in one gallon water). This needs to be freshly prepared each time it is used.

- Quaternary ammonium germicidal detergent in 2 percent aqueous solution (for example, Tri-quat®, Mytar® or Sage®).

- Iodophor germicidal detergent with 500 ppm available iodine (such as Wescodyne®).

Disinfecting Hard Surfaces and Caring for Equipment

After removing the soil, apply a disinfectant. Soak mops in the disinfectant after use; rinse them thoroughly or wash them in a hot water cycle before rinsing.

Disposable cleaning equipment and water should be placed in a toilet or plastic bag as appropriate. Remove disposable gloves and discard them in appropriate receptacles. Nondisposable cleaning equipment (dust pans, buckets) should be thoroughly rinsed in the disinfectant. Promptly dispose of the disinfectant solution down a drain pipe.

Disinfecting Rugs

To disinfect a rug, apply a sanitary absorbent agent; let it dry and then vacuum. If necessary, mechanically remove the agent with dust pan and broom; then apply rug shampoo (a germicidal detergent) with a brush and revacuum. Rinse the dust pan and broom in a disinfectant. If necessary, wash the brush with soap and water. Dispose of nonreusable cleaning equipment as noted above.

Laundry Instructions for Clothing Soiled with Body Fluids

When laundering clothing contaminated in the school setting, the most important factor is eliminating potentially infectious agents by soap and water. Adding bleach will further reduce the number of potentially infectious agents. Clothing soaked with body fluids should be washed separately from other items. Presoaking may be required for heavily soiled clothing. Otherwise, wash and dry as usual.

If the material is bleachable, add 1/2 cup household bleach to the wash cycle. If the material is not colorfast, add 1/2 cup nonclorox bleach (for example, Clorox II or Borateem) to the wash cycle.

Summary

Body fluids from all persons contain potentially infectious germs. However, that risk is generally low and depends on a variety of factors. Those factors include the type of fluid involved, the kind of contact made with it, and the stage of infection of the carrier.

Avoid direct contact with body fluids. Use disposable gloves when you anticipate extensive contact.

If you make direct skin contact with body fluids, wash affected skin areas with soap and water. Rinse clothing and other nondisposable items and place them in plastic bags before washing. Handle soiled items with disposable gloves.

Follow your school's procedures for cleaning up body fluids. Make sure those procedures include thorough instructions for disinfecting.

(This chapter was prepared by Elaine Brainerd, M.A., R.N., Connecticut Department of Education, in consultation with James Hadler, M.D., M.P.H., Chief, Epidemiology Section, and Patricia Checko, M.P.H., Epidemiology Program, Connecticut Department of Health Services. Used by permission of the authors.)

Chapter 23

Respiratory Therapy

Susan Lapakko, C.R.T.T.
Georgianna Larson, R.N., P.N.P., M.P.H.

In This Chapter You'll Find:

What respiratory therapy is and why it's done.

Techniques that moisten and condition the airway.

General guidelines and safety precautions for respiratory therapy.

Respiratory therapy is useful for students who are unable to swallow or cough effectively, and for students who have thick or sticky secretions from the airway, or windpipe. Chronic health conditions that can lead to these airway problems include cystic fibrosis, emphysema, muscular dystrophy and bronchial pulmonary dysplasia.

A respiratory therapy program is always prescribed by the student's physician and should never be performed without specific training from a respiratory therapist or other trained health professional.

The student's respiratory therapy program may include many or all of the following:

- Conditioning and moistening the airway and secretions with fluid intake, moist air and prescribed medication.

- Postural drainage with percussion and vibration to help loosen secretions and move them from the lungs.

- Suctioning to remove secretions when the student is unable to cough effectively.

Each of these factors is discussed in the next section.

Figure 23-1: Basic postural drainage positions showing areas of the lungs drained in each position.

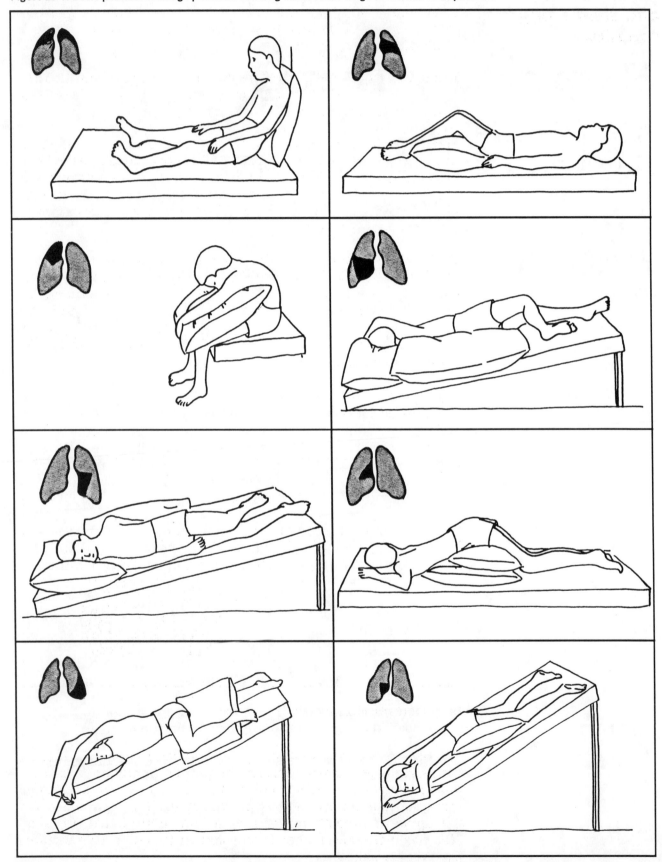

Conditioning and Moistening the Airway

Adequate fluid intake. Fluid intake is important for keeping secretions thin. Ask the student's parents or physician for the recommended daily amount of fluids, taking into account the student's size and condition.

Breathing moist air. Moistening of the airway can also be done by using a room humidifier or mist tent. This therapy is usually done at night while the student sleeps.

Medications. Administered directly into the airway through a nebulizer, these medications are like an aerosol. They are extremely potent. Such medications should be given only by qualified personnel who have had instruction from the student's physician. In addition, they should be administered before postural drainage therapy.

Postural drainage. This therapy encourages lung secretions to move by gravity into the large airway, where they can be coughed or suctioned out. To accomplish this, the student is put in a sequence of positions that encourage the secretions to drain. The student's physician will indicate which positions to use, and in what sequence. Figure 23-1 illustrates basic postural drainage positions.

Percussion and vibration. Both percussion and vibration are often prescribed in conjunction with postural drainage to loosen secretions.

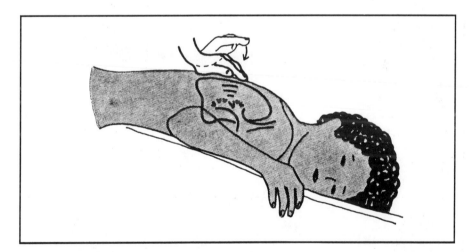

Figure 23-2: Performing percussion.

Percussion is done by clapping with cupped hands on the student's rib cage. Instruction on the proper technique is essential for safety and effectiveness; this can from a respiratory therapist or other appropriate professional. Never percuss over the spine or breastbone, or over a female student's breasts. Also avoid the lower ribs: Percussion in this area can irritate the liver and kidneys.

Vibration, which is done after secretions have been loosened by percussion, moves secretions through the airways. From that point, the aim is for the student to cough the secretions out—or to have them suctioned out. Again, you must have proper training before doing this procedure.

Suctioning is done to remove secretions if the student is unable to cough adequately. For more information, see Chapter 24.

Summary

Respiratory therapy promotes efficient use of respiratory muscles. Besides helping students to swallow and cough more effectively, it clears the airway of thick or sticky secretions.

Specific techniques used are postural drainage, chest percussion and vibration, coughing and suctioning.

Conditions that indicate a need for respiratory therapy include cystic fibrosis, emphysema and muscular dystrophy.

Any respiratory therapy should be performed—or directed—by a qualified health professional. The therapy must be prescribed by a physician.

Chapter 24

Care of the Student with a Tracheostomy

Susan Lapakko, C.R.T.T.

In This Chapter You'll Find: Information on what a tracheostomy is, why the procedure is done and the types of tracheostomy tubes.

Special considerations for the student with a tracheostomy.

Guidelines for controlling infections.

Instructions for daily care of the tracheostomy.

Emergency and safety measures to use.

A tracheostomy keeps a person breathing when physical changes make it difficult for air to pass through the nose, mouth and trachea into the lungs. In this simple surgical procedure, an incision is made through the neck into the windpipe (trachea). The actual hole made is called a stoma. A tube, called the tracheostomy tube, is then inserted into the stoma.

Tracheostomy care keeps the tracheostomy tube free of mucus build-up, ensuring a clear airway. There are other benefits as well: maintaining good mucus membranes, good skin condition and preventing infection.

This chapter presents instructions for these daily care procedures:

- Suctioning the tracheostomy tubes.

- Cleaning the inner cannula (for metal tubes).

Before providing step-by-step instructions for each procedure, we'll cover some important preparatory material. This includes types of tracheostomy tubes, special care considerations for the student with a tracheostomy and how to control infections.

Tracheostomy care involves specialized procedures. Improperly done, they can result in a life-threatening emergency. For this reason, tracheostomy care needs to be administered or directed by the school nurse or another qualified health professional.

Types of Tracheostomy Tubes

Both plastic and metal tracheostomy tubes are used in pediatrics. Metal tubes consist of two hollow tubes called cannulas: a larger tube called the external cannula, and a smaller tube, called the inner cannula. The inner cannula fits inside the external cannula. The inner cannula serves as a lining that can be removed for cleaning while the external cannula holds the airway open. To lock the inner cannula in place, you turn a button at the top of the cannula.

Plastic tracheostomy tubes are usually one piece and do not have an inner cannula.

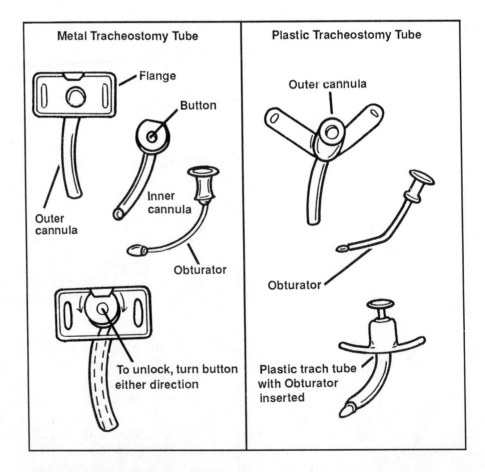

Figure 24-1: Types of tracheostomy tubes.

Special Considerations for the Student with a Tracheostomy

Safety precautions. Tracheostomy care can be done with either a sterile or clean technique. To determine which method to use, consult the student's primary physician.

All persons who work with a student with a tracheostomy should be certified in cardiopulmonary resuscitation (CPR).

Retractions. Retractions take place when the skin between the ribs or above and below the breast bone is being pulled in. They signal difficulty in breathing and indicate a need for suctioning.

Suctioning. The body produces mucus as a means of cleansing the lungs. During the first weeks after a tracheostomy, more mucus is usually produced. This is a natural response to the irritation of the trachea caused by the tracheostomy tube. Afterwards, mucus production usually decreases to a more normal amount.

Accumulated secretions, however, may make breathing more difficult. Suctioning is necessary to remove secretions that accumulate in the tracheostomy tube. Suctioning consists of inserting a small catheter into the tracheostomy tube. The catheter is in turn connected to a suction pump to remove secretions.

It is essential that suctioning be done only when necessary. If done too often or incorrectly, suctioning can be traumatic. As an alternative, encourage the student to expel secretions by coughing into a tissue.

Normal mucus color is clear to white. If you observe green or yellow mucus, notify the student's doctor.

Humidity. Students with tracheostomies may not need additional humidity at all times; however, most will benefit from extra humidity during naps and at bedtime. An ultrasonic nebulizer (USN) or another type of humidifying device will deliver adequate humidity.

Tracheostomy humidifying filters act as an "artificial nose," connecting directly to a plastic tracheostomy tube. (They will not fit most metal tubes.) The filters prevent the loss of moisture and heat from the lungs during exhalation, using the same moisture and heat for the next breath.

Lavage. If the student's mucus is very thick and sticky, it may be hard to remove by suctioning. Tracheal lavage consists of instilling normal saline into the tracheostomy tube and then suctioning it out—a procedure that loosens the mucus. Use only a small amount of saline—about 1/2 to 1 teaspoons. Never use water instead of normal saline: This may cause spasms.

Assess the student regularly. Regular assessment of a student with a tracheostomy is important. Check these key factors:

- Color of the lips and fingernails—A bluish color suggests problems with breathing.

- Breathing—Look for a comfortable exchange of air. In a student having problems, you'll see breathing retractions.

- Need for suctioning—Look and listen for excess mucus that needs to be cleared from the tracheostomy tubes.

- Tracheostomy ties—Check to see if they're secure. Ties are too loose if the tracheostomy tube moves up and down with each breath—or if the tube comes far enough out of the stoma so that you can see the stoma and tube behind the flange. (See Figure 24-1 for the location of the flange.)

Controlling Infections

The tracheostomy tube is a direct "pipeline" to the lungs. What's more, all the equipment you'll be using has the potential to grow harmful bacteria. These facts mean you must know how to control infection. The three things that you'll have the most control over are clean hands, clean equipment and aseptic technique.

Aseptic technique means that you handle things so as not to introduce any extra possibility of contamination: "Clean" never touches "dirty." More specifically, aseptic technique is:

- Using a fresh suction kit every time you suction.

- Realizing that anytime something "clean" touches something "dirty" it is no longer "clean." The item must now be thrown away or re-cleaned.

- Discarding disposable suction catheters after each use.

- Emptying the suction collection bottle at the end of every school day.

Note that special training is required to use aseptic technique.

Suctioning Using Sterile Technique

When to suction. Certain signs indicate a need for suctioning:

- The "gurgly" sound of secretions.

- Difficulty in breathing, including retracting or sweating.

- Breathing accompanied by a whistle noise.

- A blue or gray color around the eyes, mouth, fingers and toenails.

- Sleepiness for no reason.

Be sure to check with the student's physician to get approval for the procedure. The person who does the suctioning must be trained in the proper technique.

Choosing between clean or sterile technique. Clean technique can also be used for all tracheostomy care, if that is what the student's physician recommends. Check with the child's parents if you are in doubt as to whether to use clean or sterile technique.

Equipment needed. Have three items on hand before you begin suctioning: the suction catheter kit, normal saline vials for lavage and a suction pump.

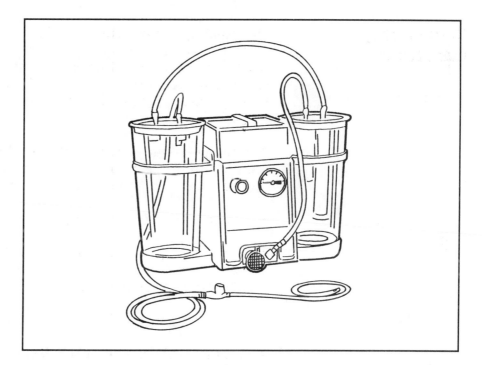

Figure 24-2: Suction machine.

Instructions. What follows are instructions for suctioning the tracheostomy tube.

Suctioning the Tracheostomy Tube

Procedure:

1. *Wash your hands.*

   For instructions on hand washing, see Chapter 11.

2. *Turn on the suction machine.*

3. *Open the suction catheter kit.*

   Everything inside the suction kit is sterile when you first open it.

4. *Put on the sterile glove.* Don't touch anything that is not sterile: This will contaminate the glove.

   For clean technique, you do not need to use a sterile glove.

5. *Pick up the sterile suction catheter* with your gloved hand. Attach the catheter to the connecting tube of the suction machine.

6. *Insert the suction catheter* about 2 inches into the tracheostomy tube with the catheter vent (thumb port) open.

   To avoid oxygen loss and tissue trauma, do not cover the catheter vent or apply suction during insertion of the catheter.

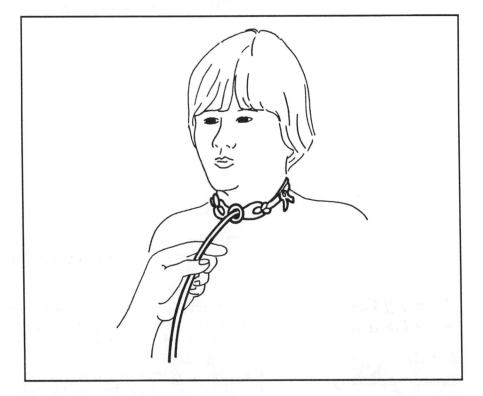

Figure 24-3: Inserting the suction catheter.

7. *Cover the air vent* with the thumb of your ungloved hand to apply suction. Withdraw the catheter slowly and gently rotate the catheter between your thumb and forefinger. Do not apply suction longer than 5 seconds.

   This rotating motion prevents the catheter from grabbing tissue as it is withdrawn, avoiding tissue trauma.

8. *Observe suctioned secretions* for color, amount and consistency.

   Normal mucus color is clear to white. A yellow or green color indicates infection, meaning that you should notify the student's physician. The presence of blood-tinged mucus should also be reported to the physician.

9. *Let the student rest* for a few minutes before another suctioning. Observe the student carefully.

   This enables the student to catch his or her breath. The timing of each suctioning and the length of rest period is determined by the student's tolerance for the procedure.

10. *Repeat the suctioning* if necessary.

11. *Discard the catheter and the glove.*

12. *Turn off the suction pump.*

13. *Wash your hands.*

14. *Offer oral hygiene as needed.*

    The student's mouth can become dry and malodorous or develop sores due to encrusted secretions.

Cleaning the Inner Cannula

As explained under "Types of Tubes" on page 224, metal tracheostomy tubes include an inner cannula that you can remove for cleaning. The outer cannula holds the airway open.

Care for the inner cannula is often done by the parents at home. If you are called on to clean the inner cannula during the school day, however, these are the basic steps to follow.

Equipment needed. Have the following equipment and supplies on hand:

- Suction catheter kit.

- Suction pump.

- Two small paper cups.

- Hydrogen peroxide.

- Distilled water.

- Pipe cleaners.

- Tweezers.

Instructions. What follows are step-by-step instructions for cleaning the inner cannula.

Cleaning the Inner Cannula

Procedure:

1. *Wash your hands* thoroughly with soap and water.

   Sterile technique is described in this procedure. If clean technique is used for the student, contact the parents or primary physician for guidelines.

2. *Fill one paper cup with hydrogen peroxide and distilled water in a 1:1 solution*—1/2 hydrogen peroxide and 1/2 distilled water.

3. *Fill the other paper cup with distilled water only.*

4. *Have the student assume a comfortable position,* either sitting or lying down.

5. *Open the suction kit.*

6. *Using a clean tweezers, remove two pipe cleaners* from their container.

7. *Place the pipe cleaners in the sterile field* provided by the suction kit.

8. *Suction the student, then put the catheter on the sterile field.*

   Observe suctioned secretions (through the suction catheter) for amount, color and consistency. Normal mucus color is clear to white. Yellow or green mucus indicates an infection; notify the student's physician.

9. *Using your ungloved hand, unlock the inner cannula* by turning the button clockwise.

10. *Remove the inner cannula* with your ungloved hand and place it in the hydrogen peroxide and distilled water solution.

    Soaking the cannula in hydrogen peroxide will loosen encrusted materials.

11. *Suction the student again if needed.*

12. *Remove the inner cannula from the hydrogen peroxide solution* with your ungloved hand. Pick it up by the button.

13. *Pick up a pipe cleaner with your gloved hand and run it through the inner cannula.* Do this twice.

14. *Place the inner cannula in the distilled water cup.*

    This rinses the cannula and provides a thin film of solution to lubricate it for replacement.

15. *Remove the inner cannula from the distilled water with your ungloved hand.* Pick it up by the button.

16. *Replace the inner cannula* in the external cannula, and lock in the inner cannula in place.

17. *Suction the student again if necessary.*

18. *Wash your hands.*

19. *Discard all equipment, supplies, solutions and trash.*

20. *Repeat the procedure* at least once every eight hours, or as needed.

Emergency Procedures

All people who work with a student with a tracheostomy should be certified in cardiopulmonary resuscitation (CPR). As you perform the procedures described in this chapter, observe the student carefully. Notify the student's physician if you see any of these conditions:

- The student coughs up, or you suction fresh blood.

- The student seems to be having difficulty breathing.

- The amount of mucus produced by the student increases.

- The student's mucus changes color.

- Student's mucus becomes thicker and does not thin with lavage.

- The student has a fever.

- The student's lips or nail color becomes darker.

What to do if the Tube Plugs

First of all, work fast and don't panic. You have a number of options:

Procedure:

1. *Suction the tubes*, as explained in the above section.

2. *If you can't pass the catheter, lavage to soften the plug and try to suction again.*

3. *If the catheter still won't go down, place your mouth on the student's tracheostomy tube and give a soft blow from your cheeks.* This should dislodge the plug from the tube.

4. *If these attempts fail,* pull the tube out and replace it with a clean tube. Note: only trained health professionals should attempt this procedure. Notify student's parent's and physician if if you have difficulty with procedure.

What to do if the Tube Comes Out

Procedure:

1. *Insert a clean tube* in the stoma using the obturator.

   If a clean tube and obturator are not available, use the dirty tube. At this point, keeping the airway open is more important than aseptic or clean technique.

2. *Hold the tube in place with your fingers.*

3. *If you used an obturator, pull it out now.*

4. *Replace the ties.*

5. *Replace the inner cannula* (for metal tubes).

If a clean tube and obturator are not available, replace the old tube. Hold the new tube in place until you can secure it with ties. *Do not waste time looking for a clean tube or ties.* You can use a shoelace, ribbon or yarn to temporarily secure the tracheostomy tube if ties are not available.

If the tube comes out—or even if it cannot be found—the stoma may stay open and the student may be able to breathe for a short period of time.

If the stoma does not stay open, insert a straw into the stoma—or anything hollow that the student can breathe through. The most available hollow item may be a suction catheter inserted about 1 inch into the stoma. Replace this with a tracheostomy tube as soon as possible.

Note: Only trained health professionals should attempt this procedure.

An emergency phone list should be easily visible on the wall next to each telephone. This list should include the 911 number if you live in an area where 911 is the emergency number. If not, list numbers for the fire department, rescue squad, ambulance, hospital emergency room and student's physician.

Special Safety Measures for a Student with a Tracheostomy

A student with a tracheostomy should have an emergency kit available at all times. This kit should include:

• A spare tracheostomy tube with obturator.

• Extra tracheostomy ties.

• A round-tipped bandage scissors. These are used to cut the ties if the tube is dislodged while tied to the neck.

• An extra suction catheter.

Keep the emergency kit at school in a location known by everyone who works with the student. The kit should also go with the student during transportation to and from school, and during field trips.

Don't use powders or talc on the student. These could easily be inhaled into the lungs.

Cover the tracheostomy tubes with a cloth diaper or a cloth bib when the student is outside in wind or dust.

Don't use plastic bibs when feeding the patient. When feeding, do cover the tracheostomy tubes with a cloth bib to prevent inhaling food into the tubes.

Avoid blankets or toys with fuzz.

Don't use aerosol sprays around the student.

Don't use any ointments around the student's tracheostomy unless ordered by the physician.

No foreign objects should ever enter the student's tracheostomy tube. These include lint, food, water, baby powder, aerosols, small toys, sand, dust and so on.

Never allow the student's playmates to touch or pull on the tracheostomy tube.

Remember that a student with a tracheostomy may be unable to speak—and thus unable to summon help. For such students, a "call system"—a bell, buzzer or toy clicker—may help.

Students with tracheostomy tubes cannot play in sandboxes or go swimming.

Develop a plan of care with the parents and student's physician.

Summary

A tracheostomy is a surgical procedure where an incision (stoma) is made through the neck into the windpipe (trachea). A tube is then inserted through the stoma. This procedure is done when it becomes difficult for air to pass through the person's nose, mouth and trachea into the lungs.

Both plastic and metal tubes are used in tracheostomies, and each is cleaned differently.

Suctioning is needed to remove secretions from the tube. This should be done only when necessary, however. Some mucus can't be removed by suctioning. In that case, saline is instilled in the tube to loosen the mucus up; then the tube is suctioned. This latter procedure is called a tracheal lavage.

When assessing the student with a tracheosotmy, check the key indicators. These include color of the lips and fingernails, excess mucus and ease of breathing. Also make sure the tracheostomy ties are secure.

Control infections by washing your hands carefully, using clean equipment and using aseptic technique.

Ensure that appropriate daily care for the tracheostomy is done. This includes: suctioning the tube, cleaning the inner cannula (metal tubes) and changing the tracheostomy ties. Instructions for each are listed in this chapter.

Know what to do in emergencies—for example, if a tube plugs or comes out. Also follow the safety measures listed in this chapter.

Part Four

Mobility and the Student with Physical Limitation

Part Four

Mobility and the Student with Physical Limitation

Walkers, wheelchairs, crutches, canes—all of these devices have one purpose: to aid mobility. This is a major concern for many students with a chronic health condition or disability that impairs mobility. A student's ability to move from one location to another is obviously crucial, not only for learning but for feeling "a part of the group." You may be called on to help.

This raises a whole series of questions: What is the best way to transfer a student from a wheelchair to another surface, such as a chair or toilet? What students are good candidates for power wheelchairs? A student with no mobility may need lifting to be placed on a toilet seat; how do we do that without injuring the student—or caregiver? How can we put the student in a sitting or standing position so he or she can take part in classroom activity?

Such questions are the concern of the chapters that follow.

Chapter 25 gives an overview of this topic. Focusing on students at five different levels of mobility, it offers a guide to planning transfers and increasing student independence.

Chapter 26 reminds us of an essential point: All students can benefit from taking part in sports and related activities. The question is, How do we make this experience possible for students with a chronic illness or disability? Here you'll find answers for students at all levels of mobility.

Chapter 27 introduces you to equipment that helps with the activities of daily living. For many students, these will include special toilet and shower seats, as well as lapboards.

Chapter 28 will help you work with students who cannot sit or stand without support. Many adaptive devices are available for these purposes. This material offers guidelines for using the devices safely.

Chapter 25

Levels of Mobility: Using Equipment and Making Transfers

Karen Ostenso, R.P.T.

In This Chapter You'll Find:

Instructions for aiding mobility of the student with a physical limitation. These instructions are presented for students at five different levels of mobility.

Students with physical limitations vary widely in mobility. Some are totally dependent. These students, for example, may use a wheelchair; you would have to lift them when transferring them from a wheelchair to a toilet. In contrast, other students will never use a wheelchair. They will walk and transfer themselves independently, perhaps with the aid of an orthosis, a supportive device or both. (Orthoses are appliances that provide support to a limb or joint).

You may become directly involved with a student's transfers and any equipment needed for that purpose. Before you do, gather information about:

- Medical diagnosis, including special problems such as susceptibility to fractures.

- Equipment currently being used, such as wheelchairs, orthoses or walkers.

- General level of mobility.

- Any recent surgery that may affect handling techniques.

The rest of this chapter is divided into five sections. Each section gives guidelines for students at differing levels of independence. The levels of independence we've identified are:

- Level I—the student who is totally dependent.

- Level II—the student in a wheelchair who assists with some mobility.

- Level III—the student who is independent in wheelchair mobility.

- Level IV—the household ambulator. ("Ambulatory" refers to the ability to walk.)

- Level V—the community ambulator.

Level I: Totally Dependent

Students at Level I may have voluntary head control, but require support to sit. They need to be totally lifted for transfers and are dependent for all care. Examples are students severely involved with cerebral palsy, students with a high level myelomeningocele (spina bifida) or spinal cord injury, or those in the advanced stages of Duchene's muscular dystrophy.

Your goal at this level is to safely transfer the student and to promote self-care.

Many students who need total lifting are severely spastic. For example, students with cerebral palsy tend to hold their bodies in a totally extended position. In order to place them in the sitting position, it is best to bend them sharply at the hips. Hold them in this flexed position as you place their buttocks down and back. Then secure any lap belt.

Safety precautions. Because these students require extensive lifting, the greatest safety concern is that the caregivers not harm their backs by lifting too much weight. If you have any doubt, get help before starting to lift. Always have two people present if you are transferring a student for the first time.

How to Transfer

These are the steps you should take to safely transfer a student at Level I.

Procedure:

1. *Plan the transfer carefully.* Place the student as close as possible to the surface to be occupied.

   Make sure there are no obstacles and that the surface is stable.

2. *Lock any wheels* on the chair or buggy in which the student is sitting.

   Do the same to any chair or buggy in which you're placing the student.

3. *Unfasten any straps or buckles.*

4. *Bend your knees and keep your back as straight* as possible.

   Do the majority of the lifting with your legs, not your back.

5. *Reach behind the student at the shoulders and under the buttocks.* Support the head and legs with your arms.

6. *Keep the student as close to your body as possible. Lift* and come to a full standing position.

7. *Move to the new surface and lower the student by bending your knees.* Keep attending to the student until the straps have been secured.

8. *Coordinate the moves* of the two people lifting by using verbal cues.

A *two-person transfer* may be needed for lifting a larger student, and the procedure is similar. There is a difference, however: One person lifts under the shoulders and low back. The second person lifts under the buttocks and knees.

Level II: The Student in a Wheelchair

A student in this category would be seated in a wheelchair most of the time. This student, though probably unable to propel a manual wheelchair, could manage a powered chair. He or she could assist with self-feeding and dressing. Examples would be a student with mild cerebral palsy or muscular dystrophy less advanced than Level I.

Your goal at this level is to safely transfer and assist the dependent student, allowing him or her to help as much as possible.

Safety precautions. This student provides minimal help in transferring. Still, proper lifting techniques are essential to help caregivers avoid back strain. If you have any question about this, get more help before starting to lift.

How to Transfer

These are the steps you should take to safely transfer a student at Level II.

Procedure:

1. *Plan carefully to minimize the distance the student must be moved.* It's best to move from one surface to another without taking any steps.

2. *If possible, ask the student to do a standing pivot transfer.*
   Start by locking the wheelchair in such a position that a quarter-turn will get the student from one surface to the other.

   This works best when the student is able to bear a little weight on his or her legs, and is not obese or excessively tall.

3. *Unfasten any straps or buckles:* Face the student. Put a transfer belt on him or her if necessary. Help the student to slide forward as much as possible.

4. *Ask the student to put his or her arms around your neck, if possible. Grip the transfer belt* behind the student, or get your hands well under the student's buttocks.

   Bend at your knees, not your waist.

5. *Agree on a prearranged signal. At the signal, the student should try to stand as you lift by* straightening your knees. When the student is in full stance, he or she can be supported by leaning against your body. Come to a full stand before beginning to turn.

6. *Pivot together.* Help move the student's feet with your own if necessary.

7. *Slowly lower student onto the surface* by bending your knees.

8. *Adjust the student's position in new location,* making sure that buttocks are well back. Attach any buckles or straps.

Level III: The Student Who is Independent

Students at this level are mobile in the community in a wheelchair. They can accomplish transfers essentially without assistance and are independent in feeding and dressing. Examples are the student who has cerebral palsy that only minimally affects the arms and hands, or the student who is paraplegic from a spinal cord injury.

Your goal at this level is to monitor the progress of the student in mobility and transfers. To help plan for any further steps in independence, be alert to changes in the student's skill level.

Safety precautions. Be aware of the student's limitations to eliminate any possibility of injury.

These are the steps you should take to safely transfer a student at Level III.

How to Transfer

Procedure:

1. *Accompany the student to all places he or she would regularly go.* Make sure that these facilities are accessible.

2. *Observe the student* doing transfers and assess their safety.

3. *Be aware of student's speed and endurance* so that you can provide help for difficult terrain or long distances, if needed.

4. *If possible, ask the student to do sliding transfers*, side-to-side with the new surface to be occupied. These transfers can be done at an angle or by having the student turn completely around. A sliding board may help.

   As an alternative, ask the student to independently do a standing pivot transfer with grab bars.

   If you think complete independence is a possibility for the student, even though it hasn't been achieved yet, ask for consultation from therapists.

5. *Make sure grab bars are accessible.* This is essential when the student is able to take a few steps—for example, from wheelchair to bathroom.

6. *Check the condition of the wheelchair frequently.* The student's position in the wheelchair and mechanical maintenance of the wheelchair are significant for the student at Level III. When needed, recommend changes or repairs.

Level IV: The Household Ambulator

Students at Level IV can move about home and school on their own power, using some combination of prescribed assistive devices. These students might require extra time to get from place to place, but they need no help or supervision with toileting. When going long distances or on rough terrain, these students can use a wheelchair and self-propel it.

Such students would most likely have mild or moderate cerebral palsy. However, they might also have lumbar myelomeningocele (spina bifida) or one of the low incidence disabilities, such as dwarfism.

Your goal at this level is to monitor the safety and accessibility needs of a student who primarily walks around school.

Points to Remember

Safety precautions. Be aware of the student's limitations to eliminate any possibility of injury.

Keep the following in mind when you evaluate mobility at Level IV:

• Accompany the student to all places he or she would regularly go. Make sure that all facilities are accessible.

• Observe the student in all areas to assess safety—especially on stairways and terrain that must be covered in bad weather.

• Be aware of circumstances requiring the student's speed or endurance. Determine whether or not the wheelchair is appropriate in such circumstances.

• If the student uses any orthoses, see Chapter 29.

• If the student uses a walker, make sure it provides the most support available. When using the walker, the student should put it forward less than arm's length, then take a step with each foot. After stepping, the student's body should still not be in contact with the front cross bar.

  - Test for ideal walker height. Ask the student to stand erect, in line with the rear legs of the walker. The student's elbows should be flexed about 30 degrees with hands on grips.

• If the student uses axillary crutches, make sure he or she uses proper technique. The student can advance crutches simultaneously and then take a step with each foot or hop forward.

  - An alternate way is to advance one crutch, step with the opposite foot, advance the other crutch and then advance the other leg.

  - Test for ideal crutch height. A crutch is at an ideal height when the student, standing erect, has two fingerbreadths between armpit and top of crutch pad.

- The legs of the crutches should be several inches forward and to the side of the toes. The child's elbows should be flexed about 30 degrees with hands on grips.

• If the student uses four-point canes, forearm crutches or any other assistive devices, make sure he or she uses proper technique. The walking patterns can be similar to those in the previous step (crutch walking).

- For some students, consider a less supportive device. This issue comes up when a student is using an assistive device and appears to be totally safe and efficient, or uses it only partially.

- Students are never ready for a less supportive device until they are skilled with the one that offers more support for balance.

- The most support is provided by parallel bars. Next comes the walker, followed by axillary crutches, forearm crutches, four-point canes and single point canes. Axillary crutches are most commonly used by persons with a cast or broken leg; they are not usually meant for long-term use.

- Make the change to a new assistive device in consultation with the student's medical facility or the school's physical therapist. Direct treatment in therapy may be needed to make the transition.

Level V: The Community Ambulator

Students at Level V never use a wheelchair. They participate fully in all age-appropriate social activities. These students may use lower extremity orthoses or assistive devices. They need no help for self-care activities. However, they may need to make some adaptations to participate in sports. Examples of students at this level are those with mild cerebral palsy, or those with one or more limbs missing.

Your goal at Level V is to monitor the student's progress in mobility. Keep track of changes in equipment or adaptations needed for mobility, sports or recreation.

Safety precautions. Be aware of the environmental hazards such as uneven floors, dark corridors, loose stair treads, etc. These may interfere with safe mobility. Prevent disrepair or breakdown in assistive devices or orthoses.

Points to Remember

Keep the following in mind when you evaluate mobility at Level V:

- Accompany the student to all places he or she would ordinarily go. Make sure that all facilities are accessible.

- Observe the student in all areas to assess safety, particularly on stairs, rough terrain and in crowded places.

  Be aware of circumstances requiring speed or endurance from the student. This helps determine if the student needs to start early or be allowed to arrive late.

- If the student uses any orthoses, see Chapter 29.

  Be aware of changes in the student's status, such as use of a walker, cane or other device that may call for different accommodations.

Summary

Students with physical limitations vary widely in mobility. This chapter identifies five different levels of independence.

Before you become involved in transferring a student, gather the relevant information: medical diagnosis, equipment currently being used, general level of mobility and any recent surgery that may affect transfer techniques.

Follow the safety precautions and transfer instructions provided in this chapter for each level of mobility.

Chapter 26

Sports and Leisure Activities

Rebecca G. Lucas, M.S., R.P.T.

In This Chapter You'll Find:

A list of the information you'll need to plan activities for students with a chronic illness or disability.

Safety precautions and activity guidelines for students at each level of mobility.

All students—regardless of their physical abilities—can benefit emotionally, intellectually and physically from sports and leisure activities. The type of activity, level of involvement and need for adapting the activity will vary greatly, depending on the student's ability level.

Before a student is programmed for sports and leisure activities, obtain the following information:

- Medical diagnosis, including restrictions on certain activities—for example, contact sports or trampoline jumping. Also find out directions for use of equipment such as helmets.

- Equipment needed for mobility and positioning, with directions for its use.

- Any recent medical procedures that may affect functioning level, temporarily or permanently.

- The student's general mobility level.

- The student's overall skills: gross motor, intellectual, fine motor and visual perception.

This chapter uses a scheme for classifying students according to their general level of mobility. Based on this criterion, students are grouped into five levels. For a full explanation of each level, see Chapter 25.

Level I: Totally Dependent

Students at Level I may have voluntary head control but require support to sit. They need to be totally lifted for transfers and are dependent for all self-care. Examples are students who are severely involved with cerebral palsy, those with a high level of myelomeningocele (spina bifida) or spinal cord injury, or students in the advanced stages of Duchene's muscular dystrophy.

These students, who have minimal motor control, cannot be expected to participate normally in standard sports or leisure activities. However, in adapted environments, they can often power electric toys or operate computers with simple switches.

Level I students are also excellent candidates for pool programs: water supports them and counteracts the effects of gravity, making it easier to move freely. Swings, merry-go-rounds, tandem bike seats and other movement equipment can also be adapted for their enjoyment.

Level II: The Student in a Wheelchair with Some Mobility

Students at Level II are primarily sitters: in a wheelchair nearly all the time but able to assist with some mobility. These students could probably not propel a manual wheelchair but could manage a powered chair. They could also help with self-feeding and dressing. Examples would be students with moderate cerebral palsy or those with muscular dystrophy less advanced than in Level I.

Activity planning at this level aims to maximize the student's fitness and motor skills through enjoyment of appropriate sports and leisure activities. Possibilities include water activity (standing and swimming), power equipment, floor exercises, hand-driven tricycles with seat adaptations and adapted bowling.

Level III: The Student Who is Independent in Wheelchair Mobility

Students at Level III are mobile in the community using a wheelchair. They transfer to and from the wheelchair essentially without assistance and are independent in feeding and dressing. Students in this group might have cerebral palsy that only minimally affects the arms and hands, or be paraplegic from a spinal cord injury or spina bifida.

The goal in working with students at Level III is to maximize overall fitness, wheelchair skills and independence through sports and leisure. Activities include most sports adaptable to sitting posture: wheelchair basketball, tennis, golf, pool, floor games using hand propelled equipment and standing games using standing support equipment.

Level IV: The Household Ambulator

Students at Level IV move about home and school on their own power, using some combination of assistive devices such as walkers or canes. They might require extra time to get from place to place, but would need no help or supervision. When going long distances or on rough terrain, students at Level IV may use a wheelchair. Examples of students at Level IV are those with mild or moderate cerebral palsy or spina bifida.

The goal at Level IV is to maximize the student's fitness and independence through sports and leisure activities. This group may include a wide variety of students who are better suited for wheelchair sports, even though they have some walking abilities. Use of a wheelchair to encourage fitness and enjoyment is appropriate at this level; these students' ambulation skills can be practiced in other settings.

Level V: The Community Ambulator

Students at Level V take part fully in all age-appropriate social activities. They may use lower extremity orthoses, assistive devices or both. These students need no help for self-care activities, though they may require some adaptations to participate in sports. Examples of students at Level V are those with mild cerebral palsy or those with one or more limbs missing.

Your goal at this level is to maximize the student's fitness and independence through sports and leisure activity. Through careful planning, almost any activity can be adapted for these students. They may even be candidates for competitive sports involvement, but this need not be a specific goal.

Safety Precautions

Level I. The inability to direct their activities because of limited motor abilities will cause these students to be at risk for difficulties in the pool. Consequently, they will need standby assistance at all times. All pool activities should be supervised by trained personnel current with cardiopulmonary resuscitation (CPR) and life saving skills.

There are few strict indications that a student cannot use a pool program, but open wounds and acute ear infections are two. Some tracheostomies and gastrostomies can be covered for pool involvement; consult the student's physician. Students with seizure disorders can use the pool. However, a physician should approve this, and you should monitor the student carefully.

Level II. Because of their limited motor abilities, these students require close supervision during sports activities, use of power equipment (chairs, tricycles) and use of other adapted equipment.

Programs for students at Level II can allow for increased motor abilities over Level I. You can plan for movement that involves the respiratory and cardiac systems. Monitor this activity to increase fitness and not overstress the student's endurance. This is especially crucial for students with muscular dystrophy.

Levels III, IV and V. Monitor the student carefully to ensure safety and be aware of limitations. Be aware of limited sensation.

Planning Activities

Here are the steps to follow when planning activities for students at any level.

Procedure:

1. *Evaluate the student's mobility skills.* This should be done with consultation from the student, parents, physical and occupational therapist and physical educator.

2. *Develop a program.* Incorporate as many sports and leisure activities as possible that allow the student to participate actively.

3. *Make sure the program allows movement and motor stimulation at least three times a week.*

4. *Monitor the student's progress toward goals.* Work to increase the student's independence, skill and enjoyment.

5. *Monitor the student's endurance and fitness* during gross motor activities.

Summary

All students-regardless of their physical ability—can benefit from sports and leisure activities.

To effectively plan these activities, you need certain information beforehand, such as: the student's motor abilities, necessary equipment and activity restrictions.

When planning activities, take into account the student's general level of mobility.

Make sure the activity program allows motor stimulation at least three times a week. Monitor the student's progress, fitness and endurance.

Chapter 27

Devices to Assist with Daily Living

Rebecca Lucas, M.S., R.P.T.

In This Chapter You'll Find: Guidelines for using shower chairs, special toilet seats and lapboards—tools that aid daily living for the student with a physical disability.

Many students with a physical disability are familiar with equipment that enhances their activity in daily life: wheelchairs, crutches, orthoses, etc. Beyond this kind of equipment, most of which increases mobility, there is an array of devices for used for other purposes. Some of these devices can directly enhance the student's experience in the classroom.

This latter group could include a large variety of equipment. We will focus on two fundamental tools: equipment needed for toileting, and lapboards for the classroom.

Toileting Equipment The purpose of toileting equipment is to make the standard bathroom accessible to all students. With this equipment, the student with a physical disability gains independence in performing routine skills—and does it safely and efficiently.

For students with a chronic illness or physical disability, toileting equipment offers added advantages. Proper support for their bodies can free their arms and hands for other activity. Support also allows body muscles to relax, helping with use of the toilet. And along with increased independence in the toilet comes increased privacy for body care.

Two common pieces of toileting equipment are special toilet seats and shower chairs. Their use is discussed in the sections that follow.

Figure 27-1: Equipment that assists with tasks of daily living.

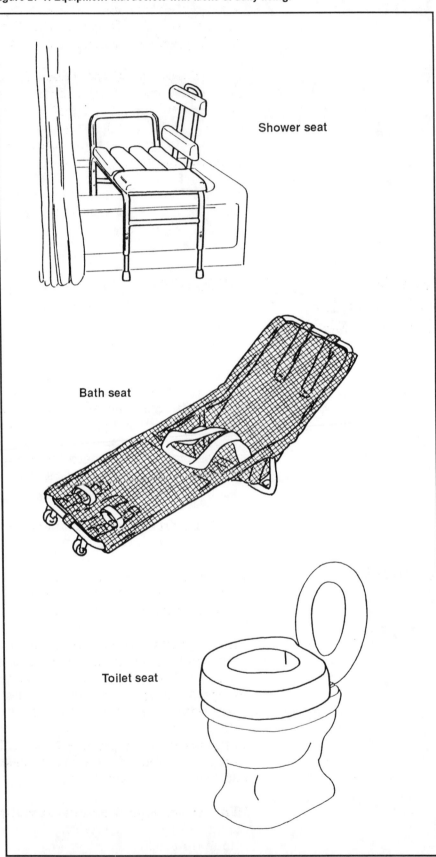

Shower seat

Bath seat

Toilet seat

Safety precautions. When using a toilet seat or shower chair, the student should be stable. You want to eliminate any risk of falling if the student is left alone for bathroom activities.

Procedures for a transfer. Transferring the student to and from the shower chair or toilet seat calls for special care. Make sure the wheelchair, toilet seat or shower chair is locked in place. (For more information on transfers, see Chapter 25.) Because bathroom floors could be wet, special safety precautions are needed.

Many toilet seats and shower chairs are available, so specific instructions for using them will vary slightly. These are some general guidelines.

Transfer to/from Toilet or Shower Seat

Procedure:

1. *Stabilize the toilet or shower seat.*

2. *Transfer the student appropriately.* Make sure you know the standard transfer used by the student.

3. *Fasten all belts snugly.* If appropriate, check any fasteners before leaving the student alone.

4. *Know the student's abilities.* Stand by or assist as needed.

Lapboards

Lapboards provide a work surface at an appropriate level for the student. They can also incorporate communication systems or feeding equipment. The surface can be level or elevated.

Safety precautions. Apply the lapboard carefully so the student's fingers or arms are not pinched. Remember that a lapboard isolates the student socially; it should not be in place except for a specific activity or for housing a communication system the student actively uses.

Procedures for using the lapboard. The number of uses and variety of lapboards is endless. Learn the rationale for the student's use of any lapboard.

Here are some guides to using the lapboard effectively.

Using a Lapboard

Procedure:

1. *Place the lapboard on the student's seating system and fasten it securely.*

2. *Follow the specific instructions* for the lapboard's use.

3. *Share any suggestions* for using or adapting the lapboard with the student's family—as well as the people who designed or prescribed the lapboard.

Summary

Equipment such as specially-designed toilet seats, shower chairs and lapboards offer many advantages to students with a disability—including more independence and privacy.

Know the student's abilities to use this kind of equipment. Stand by or help as needed.

When using this equipment, follow the safety precautions and guidelines listed in this chapter. In addition, follow any specific directions for the equipment's use.

Chapter 28

Supportive Standing and Sitting Devices

Karen Ostenso, R.P.T.
Rebecca Lucas, M.S., R.P.T.

In This Chapter You'll Find:

General suggestions for using a supportive sitting device.

General guidelines for proper use of a supportive standing device.

Children are fitted with supportive devices for a variety of purposes. These devices make it easier to transport the student, and they provide the normal experience of sitting or standing for a student who cannot do it alone. Such equipment allows for more normal social experiences, promotes interaction with other students and allows the student to take part more fully in academic and social activities.

Sitting devices aid crucial tasks such as feeding. They can maintain the student's body alignment and distribute weight in a way that avoids pressure sores. With these devices, many students gain greater use of their arms.

Supported standing devices include a variety of equipment: standers, prone standers, supine standers, crutchless standing orthoses, parapodiums and more. All of them allow students to be in an upright position when interacting with the environment.

Using Supportive Sitting Devices

Safety precautions. For the student who uses a support or sitting device, the main concern is that no pressure areas develop. See Chapter 18 for information on preventing pressure sores.

Procedures for applying the device. Many types of special seats are available, so follow the provider's specific directions when using them. Common principles are these:

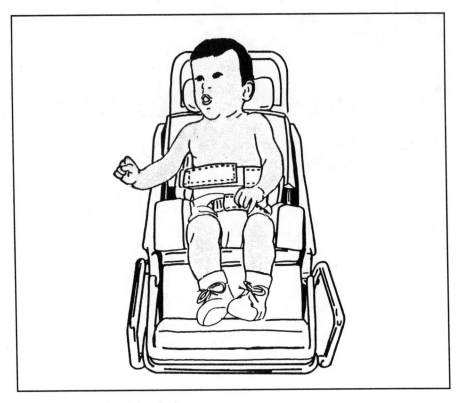

Figure 28-2: Adaptive sitting device.

Using Supportive Sitting Devices

Procedure:

1   *Do not lift a student alone if it's unsafe for you.*

2.   *Begin by bending the student at the hips* and placing his or her buttocks back as far as possible.

3.   *If there is a hip or lap belt, fasten it first*, and snugly.

4.   *Attach any upper straps* while holding student's shoulders as erect as possible.

5.   *Next, move down and fasten any lower straps.*

6.   *Make sure that the seat is securely fastened* in the wheelchair, classroom chair or whatever base is used.

7   *Observe the student's position* for alignment of trunk and support of the arms. Make sure the student's head is upright, midline in the body.

8. *Place the lap tray,* if one is used.

9. *Report to parents any concerns about pressure areas.* Make suggestions for improving the student's position—or for any other modifications that might improve the device's utility.

Using Supportive Standing Devices

Get preliminary information. You need to know certain things to help the student use a supported standing device correctly:

• The specific reasons the student uses the device. These should be documented.

• The protocol for wearing the device. Generally, supported standing devices are used for a limited time during the day. There may be a specific time limit, and you should know what it is.

• Names, phone numbers and addresses for medical personnel who recommend this equipment. Keep this information in the student's records in case any concerns arise.

• The student's responsibility for putting on and taking off the device, and the student's particular needs for care. Any staff member who assists with the student must know this information. If appropriate, consider a program to increase the student's independence in using the device.

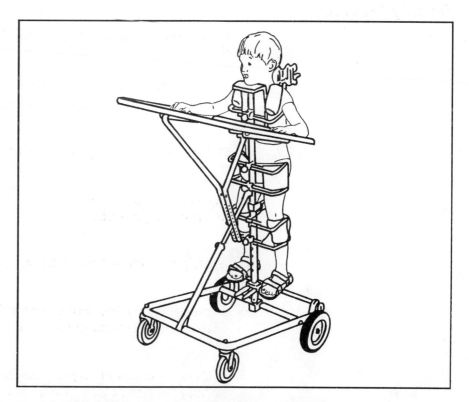

Figure 28-2: Adaptive standing device: prone stander with desk.

Safety precautions. Proper fit for the student and skin care are the primary safety concerns. A small sore or blister may temporarily prevent the use of a standing device. Share any concerns about fit with the student's family or medical care-givers as soon as possible. See page 188 for information on pressure sores.

The student's leg length must also be watched carefully during growth. Again, share any of your concerns so the standing device can be properly lengthened. Students should be regularly followed by their physicians during the school years until the student's growth has stopped.

Putting on the device. Instructions for using any supported standing device will vary, so follow specific directions for any particular device. These are some general guidelines:

Putting on the Supportive Standing Device

Procedure:

1. *Make sure the stander is well stabilized* — locked in place if it's on wheels, with straps undone. A crutchless standing orthosis is laid down.

2. *Align the student in the stander* to allow appropriate posture of the trunk and legs. If possible, the arms and hands should be free for manipulating toys or classroom materials. Trunk and leg alignment should resemble the anatomically correct posture as closely as possible—unless for medical reasons it needs to vary. Any rationale for variance should be documented.

3. *Make sure the student's feet are well positioned* before pelvic or thoracic supports are applied. The supports used should maintain appropriate posture without restricting movement more than necessary.

Taking off the device and checking for pressure sores. Again, follow any specific directions for the device the student is using.

Taking off the Supportive Standing Device

Procedure:

1. *Loosen straps slowly* while supporting the student.

2. *Carefully lift the student out* of the stander. Some students may be able to get out of a crutchless standing orthosis independently.

3. *Check the student for redness or pressure* in areas where straps are fastened. This is possible while the student is still in the stander or immediately after removing it.

Summary

Supportive standing and sitting devices offer many advantages to the student. Beyond the immediate physical benefits are increased opportunities to interact with other students and take part in activities.

The guidelines offered in this chapter will help you use a supportive standing device. In addition, follow specific directions for the device the student uses.

Help the student use the device correctly, so that pressure areas don't develop. If you think of a way to improve the student's position or adapt the device, suggest it to the student, physician and parents.

To help the student use one of these devices, you must have certain information: the student's reason for using the device; protocol for its use; how to contact the student's medical caregivers; and the student's responsibility for using the device.

Proper fit and skin safety are primary concerns.

Part Five

Guidelines for Orthopedic Care

Part Five

Guidelines for Orthopedic Care

Some students with a chronic health condition or disability may be without a hand, foot, arm or leg. Others may need help with proper positioning and posture. Fortunately, many alternatives exist for these students. Such options fall under the category of orthopedic care.

Part Five outlines some of the commonly used devices in orthopedic care. These include prostheses (appliances that replace a missing body part) and orthoses (devices that straighten or correct a body part).

Chapter 29 is an introduction to orthoses, providing basic definitions and care guidelines.

Chapter 30 focuses on proper use of prostheses, including those for the upper limb, lower limb, hip and spine.

Chapter 31 offers guidelines for cast care.

Chapter 29

The Student with an Orthosis

Mary Kay Albanese, B.S., Mechanical Engineer

In This Chapter You'll Find:

General information about orthoses, including:

- What these devices are.

- What they accomplish.

- Proper fitting, skin care and hygiene for their use.

Guidelines for proper application of an upper-limb orthosis.

Guidelines for safe use of a lower limb orthosis.

Guidelines for using common orthoses in hip treatment. These include the Pavlik harness, plaster casts and the Scottish Rite orthosis.

Guidelines for helping a student use a spinal orthosis.

An orthosis is a common orthopedic device. Its basic purpose is to support or stability to a limb, joint or body segment. Orthoses prevent movement to promote healing. These devices also counteract deforming forces, such as those from spasticity, abnormal bone growth or paralysis. An orthotist is the professional who designs, fits and repairs these devices.

Another use for orthoses is to maintain normal alignment for a body segment during growth or healing. Orthoses can also provide a starting position for voluntary activity, such as walking.

Besides offering general information about orthoses, this chapter offers basic guidelines for using four types of orthoses: those for treating an upper limb, lower limb, hip or the spine.

It's essential to remember one thing, however: You should discuss the specific about any orthopedic device—prescription, schedule of use and objectives—with the student's parents and physician. The product manufacturer can also be a source of information.

Why Orthopedic Devices are Used

Both orthoses and prostheses (see Chapter 30) may be used by students to compensate for lack of complete independence in several areas:

Sitting. External trunk and head support is provided by these devices. They increase the student's interaction with the environment and participation in social and academic experiences. Achieving a normal eating position and better mobility are other advantages.

Standing and walking. Paralysis can prevent a student from standing or walking. Orthoses, sometimes in combination with assistive devices (walkers, crutches), allow the student to regain these abilities. When lack of muscle control prevents standing or walking, a positioning device can provide the ability to hold the body properly for these activities.

Reaching and grasping. Upper extremity orthoses are used to stabilize joints or assist in arm, wrist or hand movement.

Self care. Adaptive toileting, bathing, dressing and feeding equipment helps caregivers. This equipment also gives the student the maximum independence in activities of daily living.

Development. Various orthoses and adaptive devices have a primary or secondary goal of enhancing development. When the prerequisites for a specific developmental skill have been reached, devices can be used to stimulate progress in:

- Gross motor activities—Support for sitting and standing has a developmental purpose as well as a functional purpose. The student's lack of independent floor mobility can be compensated for with a caster cart or wheelchair. Both upper and lower limb prostheses are fit when needed to approximate normal developmental milestones.

- Fine motor activities—A student's weak or uncoordinated grasp may be overcome with upper limb orthoses that control hand position or provide passive grip. Scissors, pencils and similar tools may be placed in easy-to-hold devices.

- Psychosocial development—Mobility and independence are essential to social interaction. Alternative and augmentative communication devices can decrease a student's isolation. Special controls for driving a car can help a teenager keep pace with his peers.

**Two Major
Concerns with
any Orthosis:
Pressure Points
and Hygiene**

Before you get to the specifics of using a particular orthosis, learn about two basic areas: proper fit and skin hygiene. Making sure the orthosis fits properly—both initially and as the student grows—is essential. This precaution, along with good hygiene, prevents skin breakdown and rejection of the device by the user.

Check for pressure sores. One sure indicator of improper fit is a pressure sore. Any orthopedic device that's in intimate contact with the skin or that bears weight should be checked at least once a day. If it's a new device, check it several times a day until you're sure there are no pressure sores, as explained in the instructions below.

**Check for
Pressure Sores**

Procedure:

1. *Remove the orthosis and any other covering.*

2. *Look at all skin surfaces covered by the orthosis.*

   Note any redness, particularly over bony prominences.

   A large area of redness on well-padded skin is of relatively little concern, unless it is extremely red. A small point of redness over a bony prominence is more likely to cause a problem later.

3. *If there is no red area,* put the orthosis back on.

4. *If there is some redness,* leave the device off for 20 to 30 minutes.

5. *If redness persists beyond 30 minutes,* notify the student's parents. There may be a potential problem.

6. *If there is a blister or skin breakdown,* do not use the device.

   Notify parents immediately to make necessary alterations.

Practice good hygiene. Make sure the body part to be covered is dry and clean before an orthosis is put on. That body part should be covered with a stocking, stockinette, t-shirt or similar item.

Clean the device according to the manufacturer's instructions. Most of the plastic orthoses can be cleaned with soap and water.

Self care. The student you're working with may start managing hygiene independently. It's important to observe the student's progress in this area. Lack of sensation over a body part can cause a delay in the development of a student's body image; it may even lead to total neglect of the body part. You may need to intervene and provide training in personal hygiene.

Upper Limb Orthoses

As stated above, orthoses are commonly used by children with conditions such as abnormal bone growth, paralysis or spasticity. The upper limb orthosis stabilizes or corrects position in a specific area of the body: the hand or hand and wrist joints.

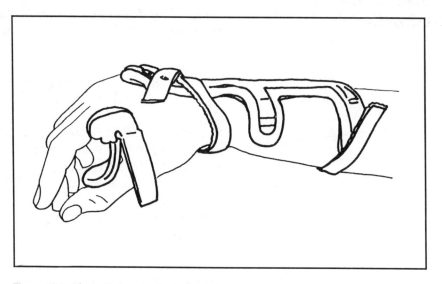

Figure 29-1: Upper limb orthosis (wrist splint).

Safety precautions. The primary concern with these close-fit orthoses is that no pressure sores develop. Frequent checks, especially after initial fit, are required to do this. Someone should check the orthosis every time it's removed.

Be sure the orthosis is properly applied to the student's upper limb. The correct fit of the device is not always obvious to a person who is unfamiliar with its use. Improper fitting can lead to incorrect anatomical positioning, excessive pressure areas and related problems. If you're unsure of correct position, contact the student's parents for instructions.

Typically, upper limb orthoses are made of a temperature-sensitive material. So keep the orthosis away from heat or flame; otherwise the orthosis may melt and lose its shape. For example, avoid exposing the device to hot water or the heat of a closed car on a hot day. Should the orthosis lose its shape, ask the parents to contact the orthotist for repair.

Parents should also contact the orthotist if the orthosis causes any other problems: swelling, pain, changes in skin color lasting longer than 30 minutes or excessive stiffness.

How to put on (don) the upper limb orthosis. Instructions for applying an upper-limb orthosis will vary. Follow specific instructions for the device the student uses. These are some general guidelines to keep in mind:

Putting on the Upper Limb Orthosis

Procedure:

1. *Make sure the skin is clean and dry* before putting on the orthosis.

2. *Use a stockinette* or sock between skin and the orthosis. This keeps the skin free of prolonged moisture from perspiration.

   Use of a stockinette is particularly important for night-time wearers of an upper limb orthosis. Many daytime wearers use the stockinette also.

3. *Be sure orthosis is put on correctly.* It should fit snugly at the web of the thumb space.

4. *Securely fasten the straps.* This avoids slippage or displacement of the orthosis from its proper alignment with the student's hand.

5. *Check for pressure points* each time the orthosis is removed. (See Chapter 17.)

Lower Limb Orthoses

The purpose of a lower limb orthosis is to correctly position and support a lower extremity joint, such as an ankle or foot joint. These orthoses may be constructed of rigid plastic or of leather and metal.

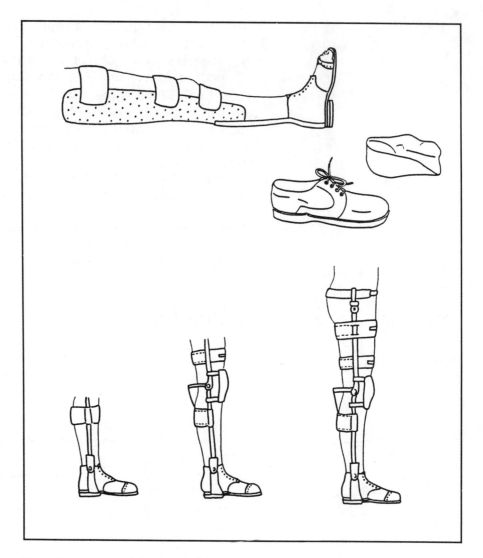

Figure 29-2: Lower limb orthoses: night leg splint (top left), foot orthosis (top right), ankle-foot (bottom left), knee-ankle-foot (bottom center), hip-knee-ankle-foot (bottom right).

Types of lower limb orthoses. Lower limb orthoses are named to define the joints that they cross. These are the basic types:

- Foot orthosis (F.O.)—This orthosis stabilizes joints of the foot in proper anatomical position.

- Ankle-foot orthosis (A.F.O.).—This device supports the ankle and foot. It also limits undesirable motion and encourages desirable motion. Design typically aims for a rigid ankle, but may allow a flexible ankle.

- Knee-ankle-foot orthosis (K.A.F.O.).—This orthosis supports the knee, ankle and foot, and it may have locked or unlocked knee joint. The hip is left free.

- Hip-knee-ankle-foot orthosis (H.K.A.F.O.).—With this orthosis, motion is controlled at the hip, knee, ankle and foot. Hip and knee-joint designs may unlock, allowing the student to both sit and stand. Or, they may allow for standing only.

Safety precautions. As with other orthoses, the primary safety concern is that no pressure problems develop. These problems can occur with inappropriate fit or improper application, especially in body areas without sensation. As the student grows, both fit and application will obviously change. For these reasons, take extra care in putting on the orthosis.

How to put on (don) the lower limb orthosis. Specific application procedures for each device is different, but they do have common considerations:

Putting on the Lower Limb Orthosis

Procedure:

1. *Before putting on the orthosis, check the body part it will cover.* The skin should be dry and clean.

2. *Apply a stockinette or sock over the limb.* Carefully cover all areas the orthosis will contact.

   These coverings are worn beneath the orthosis to allow some air circulation and keep skin as dry as possible. Prolonged moisture causes skin to break down.

3. *Make sure the orthosis is put on the correct limb.*

   Most are marked "R" for right or "L" for left. If you're unsure, have orthoses labeled by parents or the supplier.

4. *Position the orthosis beneath the lower limb.* Have the student sit or lie comfortably.

5. *When applying all lower limb orthoses, properly position the foot first.* Bend the leg at the knee and slip the lower leg into the calf cuff. Bend down the ankle and place the heel of the foot snugly into the heel of the orthosis; use firm frontal pressure.

   If there is an instep strap, secure it while holding the heel down and back into place. If no instep strap exists, put the student's shoe on at this time.

6. *Gently place the limb into the remaining orthosis shell.* Secure the calf cuff straps and remaining straps from further to closer part of the body.

Removing (doffing) the lower limb orthosis. Again, these procedures will vary for different orthoses. Here are some general guidelines:

Removing the Lower Limb Orthosis

Procedure:

1. *Loosen all the straps and attachments* of the orthosis.

2. *Carefully lift the limb out of orthosis.* Avoid scraping the skin on the orthosis edge. If the student can remove the device independently, allow him or her to do so. Be sure to supervise the procedure, however, and ensure cautious care of the skin—especially in areas when no sensation is present.

3. *Check for pressure sores* each time you remove the orthosis. Look at the limb carefully for signs that the limb may be receiving an excessive amount of pressure from the orthosis.

Hip Treatment Orthoses: the Pavlik Harness and Plaster Cast

Orthoses for hip positioning have two distinct applications. The first is for treating congenital dislocation of the hip (CDH), or general infantile hip dysplasia. This condition is usually diagnosed in infancy or when the child starts to walk. A second application is for treatment of Legg Perthes Disease, a bone disease that commonly occurs in children between ages 3 and 10. (This condition and its treatment are explained in the next section.)

The goal of treatment for CDH is to return the femoral (thigh bone) head to its normal relationship within the hip socket and to maintain this position until pathological changes reverse. Orthotic treatment usually begins during infancy.

Many orthotic restraints have been designed to treat CDH and Infantile Hip Dysplasia. The Pavlik Harness is one device often used for this purpose. The harness fits over the trunk and has straps that embrace the legs down to the heels. The hips are held in a slightly bent position.

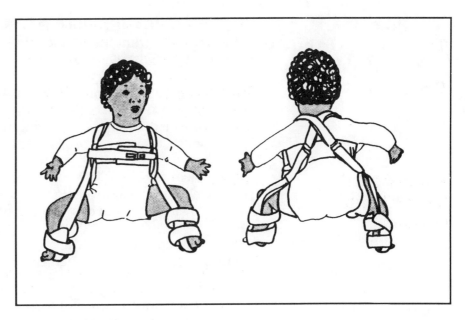

Figure 29-3: Pavlik Harness.

Safety precautions. Be sure the harness is applied correctly. Improper application or adjustments can cause problems such as dislocation or necrosis (death in areas of bone).

Watch for hip irritation or loss of motion. If either develops, ask the parents to have the student see a physician or orthotist.

Sometimes a plaster cast is used to treat CDH. Again, some safety precautions are essential:

- Keep the student's perineum as clean and as dry as possible. An adequate perineal opening should be provided to aid diapering and cleaning.

- Pay particular attention to the possibility of food or debris falling under the cast. This can lead to serious skin irritation.

- Never place sharp objects or powders beneath the cast.

- Take care to keep the cast from becoming soiled. A soiled cast will soften and accumulate odors, and both conditions could lead to skin irritation.

- Tell the student's parents to return to the hospital quickly if the cast becomes cracked, wet or softened.

Putting on and taking off the Pavlik harness. Instructions on how to apply this device are lengthy. If you will be working with a Pavlik harness, ask for a demonstration from the student's parents.

Another Hip Treatment Orthosis: The Scottish Rite Orthosis

Treatment of Legg Perthes Disease also aims to contain the thigh bone within the hip socket. This allows remodeling in the correct anatomical position.

Several devices are commonly applied to treating Legg Perthes Disease. One device used with school age children is the Scottish Rite orthosis. It places minimal restriction on a student's activities, allowing for roller skating, bicycling, running, etc.

The typical Scottish Rite orthosis is worn snugly over the student's clothes. However, it may also be worn under clothing. The following sections describe the specifics of using this device.

Safety precautions. These are the most important safety points to keep in mind when using a Scottish Rite orthosis.

* Be sure the orthosis is applied correctly.

  • Watch for irritation or decreased movement. Report any problems you observe to the student's parents.

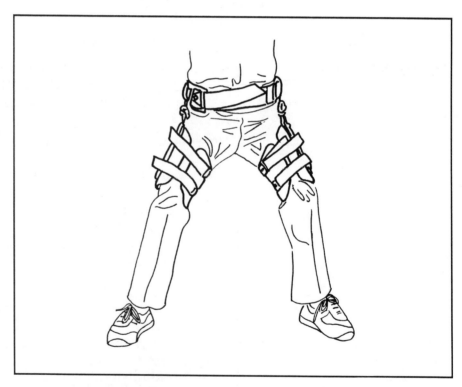

Figure 29-4: Scottish Rite Orthosis.

Putting on the Scottish Rite orthosis. Help the student put on the orthosis correctly by following these steps:

Putting on the Scottish Rite Orthosis

Procedure:

1. *Secure the thigh cuffs* snugly over each knee.

2. *Secure the pelvic belt,* which is rigid, firmly below the anterior superior iliac spine but above the trochanters.

3. *Make sure the metal hip joint of the orthosis falls directly over the trochanter.*

Other guidelines. The length of this orthosis must be properly adjusted as the student grows. These adjustments are made regularly by the supplier of the orthosis.

Check typical problem areas—the ankle bones—for signs of too much pressure.

Remember that the student will wear this orthosis continuously, day and night. The exceptions are periods of bathing or swimming, where a life preserver is worn to prevent weight bearing.

Spinal Orthoses

An increasing curve of the spinal column (scoliosis) can occur at anytime in a student's development. Notably, however, this condition is common in teenage girls who have no other orthopedic problem.

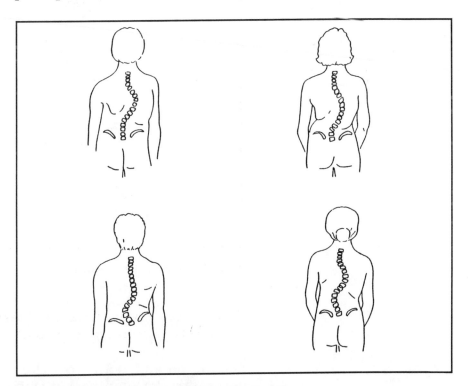

Figure 29-5: Types of abnormal spinal curve (scoliosis).

A spinal orthosis is a nonsurgical way to either correct an increasing spinal curve or provide spinal stability. The orthosis, in this case, applies forces that counteract and halt a growing curve. An orthosis is also used with students following a surgical procedure to the spine; here the orthosis provides spinal stability during the healing process.

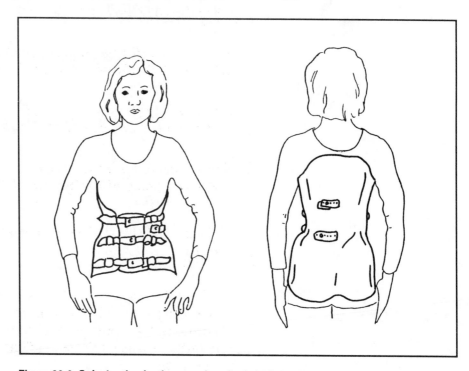

Figure 29-6: Spinal orthosis: the one-piece body jacket.

Safety precautions. Each time the spinal orthosis is removed, check the torso carefully to discover areas that may be receiving too much pressure from the orthosis. It's particularly important to monitor how well the orthosis fits as the student grows.

Preparing to put on (don) the spinal orthosis. Before helping the student put on the orthosis, go through these steps:

Putting on the Spinal Orthosis

Procedure:

1. *Be sure the skin is clean and dry.*

2. *Help the student put on a wrinkle-free stockinette or t-shirt beneath the orthosis.* These absorb perspiration and allow the skin to "breathe." Change the t-shirt daily—more frequently if perspiration is a problem. Prolonged moisture causes skin breakdown.

Putting on and taking off the orthosis. Application procedures differ for each type of spinal orthosis. General instructions are briefly discussed below. Consult the parent or orthotist if specific questions arise. To remove the orthosis, simply reverse these steps.

Procedure for the one-piece body jacket:

1. *Spread the orthosis* enough for student to enter. This orthosis typically opens at the back.

2. *Position the orthosis down on the pelvis.* Align the waist groove on the orthosis with the student's waist line.

3. *Secure the straps* at the posterior opening snugly. The correct strap position is often marked. Do not over tighten.

Instructions for the two-piece body jacket:

1. *First put the posterior part of the orthosis in correct position.* To do this, roll the student on his or her side. The waist groove of the orthosis should be aligned with the student's waist line. When this is done, roll the student onto his or her back.

2. *Position the matching front portion of the orthosis.* Be careful not to pinch skin between the front and back pieces. Check again to be sure the orthosis is positioned snugly over pelvis and is not "riding up."

   Align the pelvis to be level and not rotated, using the anterior superior iliac spine as a reference. Check this again during the day to provide an accurate fit.

3. *Secure the straps as snugly as possible.* Do this in steps, making sure that skin is not caught in the overlap. The correct position is often marked on the straps.

Summary

Orthoses are common orthopedic devices. Their purpose is to provide support or stability to a limb or joint.

Orthoses help compensate for a student's lack of independence in sitting, walking, standing or grasping. They also aid self care and development.

Make sure the orthosis fits properly; check it at least once a day. Follow the instructions in this chapter on examining for pressure sores and maintaining proper hygiene.

An upper-limb orthosis stabilizes the hand or wrist joints for proper position. The primary safety concern in using an upper-limb orthosis is avoiding excess pressure. Because many orthoses are temperature-sensitive, keep them away from heat or flame.

A lower limb orthosis supports and correctly positions a lower body joint. When the orthosis is removed, check for signs of improper pressure.

Hip orthoses are commonly used to treat two conditions: congenital hip dislocation (CDH) and Legg Perthes Disease. An orthosis often used to treat CDH is the Pavlik harness. If one of your students uses this device, get detailed instructions for its application from the student's parents or physician. Watch for any hip irritation or loss of motion. Plaster casts are also applied in treating CDH. To use these correctly, follow the safety precautions listed in this chapter.

The Scottish Rite Orthosis is a common orthosis for treating Legg Perthes Disease. Again, get detailed instructions for it use.

A spinal orthosis is a nonsurgical way to either correct an increasing spinal curve or provide spinal stability. Check the student's torso carefully to discover areas that may be receiving too much pressure from the orthosis.

Ask the student's parents to contact the orthotist if you suspect any orthosis doesn't fit properly. Watch for changes of skin color, redness, pain, stiffness or swelling caused by an orthosis.

Follow the guidelines in this chapter for putting on and taking off orthoses. In addition, get specific directions from the parent or orthotist for the specific orthosis the student is wearing.

If the student can put on and take off the orthosis properly, let him or her do that. Encourage correct technique and hygiene.

For Further Reading

Atlas of Orthotics, Biomedical Principles and Application. St. Louis: C. V. Mosby, 1975.

Durr-Fillauer Orthosis Comparison Guide. Chattanooga, TN: Durr-Fillauer. (Available from Durr-Fillauer Medical, Inc., Orthopedic Division, P. O. Box 1678, Chattanooga, TN 37401.)

"Home Care for a Child with an Ankle/Foot Orthosis," from Gillette Children's Hospital, St. Paul, MN.

"Instructions for Use and Care of Your Upper Extremity Orthosis," from Gillette Children's Hospital, St. Paul, MN.

Chapter 30

The Student with a Prosthesis

Rebecca Lucas, M.S., R.P.T.

In This Chapter You'll Find:

General information about prostheses, including:

- What these devices are.

- What they accomplish.

- Proper fitting, skin care and hygiene for their use.

Guidelines for helping a student use an upper limb prosthesis.

Guidelines for helping a student use a lower limb prosthesis.

Along with orthoses, prostheses are orthopedic devices. As pointed out in Chapter 29, orthoses provide stability to a limb or joint; they prevent movement to promote healing. In contrast, a prosthesis actually replaces a body part—such as arm or leg—to help restore normal body function. The professional who designs, fits and repairs these devices is called a prosthetist.

Besides offering general information about prostheses, this chapter offers basic guidelines for using them. It's essential to remember one thing, however: You should discuss the specifics about any orthopedic device—prescription, schedule of use and objectives—with the student's physician and parents. The product manufacturer can also be a source of information.

Two Major Concerns with any Prosthesis: Pressure Points and Hygiene

Before you get to the specifics of using a particular prosthesis, learn about two basic areas: proper fit and skin hygiene. Making sure the prosthesis fits properly—both initially and as the student grows—is essential. This precaution, along with good hygiene, prevents skin breakdown and rejection of the device by the user.

Check for pressure sores. One sure indicator of improper fit is a pressure sore. Any orthopedic device that's in intimate contact with the skin or that bears weight should be checked at least once a day. If it's a new device, check it several times a day until you're sure there are no pressure sores, as explained in the instructions below.

Check for Pressure Sores

Procedure:

1. *Remove the prosthesis and any other covering.*

2. *Look at all skin surfaces* covered by the prosthesis.

3. *Note any redness,* particularly over bony prominences.

   A large area of redness on well-padded skin is of relatively little concern, unless it is extremely red. A small point of redness over a bony prominence is more likely to cause a problem later.

4. *If there is no red area,* put the prosthesis back on.

5. *If there is some redness,* leave the device off for 20 to 30 minutes.

6. *If redness persists beyond 30 minutes,* notify the student's parents. There may be a potential problem.

7. *If there is a blister or skin breakdown,* do not use the device. Notify parents immediately to make necessary alterations.

Practice good hygiene. Make sure the body part to be covered is dry and clean before a prosthesis is put on. That body part should be covered with a stocking, stockinette, t-shirt or similar item.

Clean the device according to the manufacturer's instructions. Most of the plastic prostheses can be cleaned with soap and water.

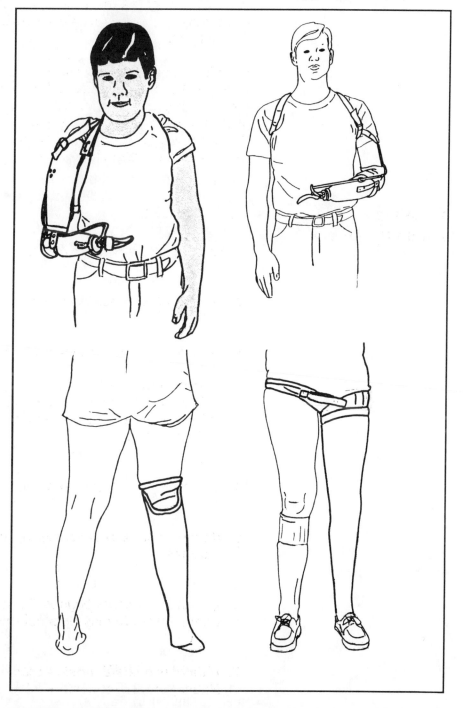

Figure 30-1: Types of prostheses: above elbow (top left), below elbow (top right), below knee (bottom left) and above the knee (bottom right).

Self care. The student you're working with may start managing hygiene independently. It's important to observe the student's progress in this area. Lack of sensation over a body part can cause a delay in the development of a student's body image; it may even lead to total neglect of the body part. You may need to intervene and provide training in personal hygiene.

General Guidelines

Understand the specifics. Loss of a limb results from a wide range of causes: trauma, absence at birth, cancer and others. Each of them will have different effects on the student, the use of prosthesis and other health issues. Be aware of the specific reason a student uses a prosthesis; document this fact and and try to make sure its implications are understood.

Know the procedures. Proper procedures for wearing the prosthesis are especially important for the new user. Most long-term users have built up their tolerance for full-time application of a prosthesis. Still, periods of non-use may be necessary due to repair, replacement or skin problems. Everyone involved should anticipate and plan for this.

Arrange for therapy. Students with a prosthesis should also receive physical or occupational therapy throughout their development years. These services become important as questions arise or new skills are required, particularly in the preschool and grade school years. Make sure that contacts with a therapist are documented in records to help the school staff.

Make information available. School staff members also need to know the student's responsibility for using and caring for the prosthesis and limb. This information, along with goals for occupational and physical therapy, should be available to everyone who works with the student. Progress toward these goals can be encouraged, if applicable, through therapist consultation with the school staff.

Most students who use a prosthesis can become completely independent in its use, and this should be encouraged.

Upper Limb Prostheses

An upper limb prosthesis replaces a part of the arm, wrist and hand. The aim is to help the person wearing the prosthesis take part in activities that require two hands.

An upper limb prosthesis cannot completely replace the skill and dexterity of a normal hand. But with practice and training, many people with this type of prosthesis learn to write or play a musical instrument. Persons who cannot use either hand often develop dexterity in another body part—such as the feet—to assist in daily skills.

Upper limb prostheses are grouped according to how much of the body they replace, falling in three major categories: below elbow, above elbow or shoulder. When only part of the hand is missing, a prosthesis is rarely used. That way, the person can benefit from the sensation still present in the body area.

At this point, it's useful to repeat a general guideline: Get the specifics. There are many upper limb prostheses—for example, myoelectric and manual devices, passive hooks or cosmetic hands. One student may have many different components for a prosthesis, or even two prostheses. Some students may need daily therapy programs or help in using the prosthesis. Parents can help you define these needs.

Safety precautions. Proper fit and skin care are the primary concerns. Development of a small blister or sore may mean the prosthesis can not be used. Share any concern about fit with the family, therapist or prosthetist as soon as possible. Both physician and prosthetist must follow the student regularly throughout his or her growing years to monitor fit. The prosthesis should come off when the student showers or swims.

Putting on (donning) the upper limb prosthesis. Specific considerations for putting on the prosthesis should be clearly established by the medical care givers. In turn, the student, parents and any school staff members who help with the procedure should know what these considerations are. Two important points to keep in mind are these:

Putting on the Upper Limb Prosthesis

Procedure:

1. *Check the skin of the limb.* It should be clean and dry. Some users prefer powder on the skin, but this is not necessary. Do not use abrasive soaps.

2. *Apply a stockinette* and then the prosthesis, as prescribed. Make sure it is aligned correctly.

Taking off (doffing) the upper limb prosthesis. This procedure may not be required during the average school day. However, school staff members should know about it if the student must remove the prosthesis for swimming or other activities. Perform a skin check each time after removing the prosthesis.

Lower Limb Prostheses

Lower limb prostheses may replace the leg or parts of the hip, knee or foot, making activities such as walking possible.

Again, these prostheses are grouped according to how much of the body limb they replace. There are four major types: those applied to the foot, below the knee, above the knee and for hip disarticulation. (The latter term refers to total absence of the femur, or thigh bone.)

The more the natural limb is missing, the more difficulties a person can have in imitating a normal gait and taking part in gross motor activities. A condition that involves both legs is also more restrictive.

Remember that there may be times when the student cannot use the lower limb prosthesis. Crutches or some alternative aid will be needed if the student has limited tolerance—or if the prosthesis needs repair, lengthening or replacement.

The student should receive physical therapy for gait and mobility guidance when first fitted with a lower limb prosthesis. Make sure the therapist's name is in the school records if questions arise.

Safety precautions: Fit and skin care are the primary precautions: A small sore or blister may mean the prosthesis can't be used until the limb heals. Share any concern about the fit should with family and prosthetist as soon as possible.

Leg length also needs careful monitoring as the student grows. Again, refer any concerns about length to the prosthetist. Both physician and prosthetist should regularly follow the student during the school years.

The prosthesis should come off for showers and swimming, unless it is especially fabricated for water use.

Putting on (donning) the lower limb prosthesis. Specific considerations for putting on the prosthesis should be clearly established by medical caregivers. In turn, the student, parents and school staff members who help with the procedure should know what these considerations are.

Two important points to keep in mind are these:

Putting on the Lower Limb Prosthesis

Procedure:

1. *Check the skin of the limb.* It should be clean and dry. Some users prefer some powder on their skin, but this is not necessary. Do not use abrasive soaps.

2. *Apply a stockinette* on the limb as prescribed. Make sure it is aligned appropriately.

Taking off (doffing) the lower limb prosthesis. This procedure may not be required during the average school day. However, you should know about it if the student needs help in removing the prosthesis for swimming or other activity.

Summary

Prostheses are common orthopedic devices. Their purpose is to replace a missing body part.

Prostheses compensate for a student's lack of independence in sitting, standing, walking and grasping. They also aid self care and development.

Make sure the prosthesis fits properly; check it at least once a day. Follow the instructions in this chapter for examining for pressure sores and maintaining proper hygiene.

An upper limb prosthesis replaces a part of the arm, wrist and hand. The aim is to help the person wearing the prosthesis to take part in activities that require two hands.

Lower limb prostheses replace a leg or parts of the hip, knee or foot.

Learn the specifics: the student's reason for wearing a prosthesis and the procedures for using it. Make sure that anyone who works with the student has this information.

Help the student arrange for physical therapy or occupational therapy.

The main safety concerns are proper fit and skin care. Check skin condition each time the prosthesis is put on or removed. To assure proper fit, both physician and prosthetist should monitor the student's growth. The prosthesis should come off for showering or swimming.

The following document, "Taking Care of Your Affected Limb and Prosthesis," **can be used as a handout to give to students and parents.**

Taking Care of Your Affected Limb and Prosthesis

Bathing

Your affected limb should be washed daily with mild soap. It's important that the soap be rinsed off completely and the skin dried thoroughly before applying your prosthesis.

It's also important to wear a clean prosthetic sock every day. The socks may be washed in Dreft, Ivory or any mild soap—as long as they are rinsed well. You might find it necessary to do this by hand; some rinsing machines will not rinse them well enough.

Dry skin

If your skin has a tendency to be dry, you may use greaseless lotions such as Noxema. This should be done at night rather than just before putting on your prosthesis.

Perspiration

Some people perspire more than others. You may find it necessary to wash your affected limb two or three times each day. Use powders or cornstarch sparingly; it's best to avoid them completely.

Pressure sores

Many sores can be prevented by using good hygiene and common sense. Before applying your prosthesis, make sure the prosthetic sock is wrinkle-free over your affected limb. You can toughen your skin by using witch hazel, available in most drug stores. You can use it following each bath—more frequently if you desire. Witch hazel should be applied like shaving lotion: pat it on the affected limb vigorously.

Pressure sores that occur repeatedly should be examined by the prosthetist and your doctor. That way your prosthesis can be adjusted to make you more comfortable and to prevent the pressure area from becoming an open sore.

If you do develop an open sore, try to keep it exposed to air as much as possible. Using bulky bandages on sores while wearing your prosthesis will only cause pressure on on the affected parts of your limb. A piece of Tefla is relatively thin and will have less tendency to stick to the sore. Adhesive bandages can be used for small open sores; apply them vertically so they have less tendency to rub off when you put your prosthesis on.

Odors

Odors usually result from repeated perspiration. The socket of your prosthesis can be washed out with any kind of soap, as long as it is rinsed thoroughly afterwards. If you prosthesis is made of material that does not readily dry, you may use a hair dryer to help. It's best to do this at night before you go to bed—you'll have additional aeration before putting the prosthesis back on. If odors persist, try rubbing the socket with baking soda or vanilla extract.

With time you'll find some home remedies that work best for you. We would appreciate it if you would share your ideas with us, as well as your questions.

(Courtesy of Gillette Children's Hospital, St. Paul, Minnesota.)

Chapter 31

Guidelines for Cast Care

Georgianna Larson, R.N., P.N.P., M.P.H.

In This Chapter You'll Find: A checklist for proper cast care.

Plaster casts are molded to a body part—for example, an arm or leg—and used to cover and immobilize a large area. Immobilizing the area promotes healing of the condition involved, such as a fracture or improper joint placement occurring with Congenital Hip Dysplasia (CDH).

To do their job efficiently, plaster casts need daily care. You may become involved in that care for a a particular student. This chapter lists the essentials you'll need to check.

Safety precautions. It's important to keep the cast clean and dry at all times. A wet cast becomes soft and does not give support. The student should not put small objects inside the cast, including coins, pencils, clips or small toys. These objects can cause pressure sores.

What to Watch for Daily

Carefully observe the student's fingers or toes.

Daily Observations for Students with Casts

Procedure:

1. *Check to see if the fingers or toes are pink.* If the fingernail or toenail is pressed, the nail should turn pink again immediately as soon as the pressure is released. Compare the plastered and free body parts; they should be similar in color.

2. *Touch the fingers or toes. They should be warm.* Ask the student if there is any numbness, tingling or pain in the fingers and toes. These sensations should be prevented.

   In general, look out for any changes in color, temperature, or feeling in toes or fingers.

3. *Check to make sure there is no swelling.*

4. *Find out if the fingers or toes can move.* They should be able to do so. Compare their motion before and after cast application. Check for toes that have slipped back into the cast.

5. *Check the cast for unusual odors.* If you detect any odor such as a foul or musty smell, report this to the parent immediately. Clean between toes with a Q-tip applicator moistened with witch hazel once a day.

In addition to the condition of the fingers and toes, check for these signs:

• Excessive student irritability without apparent reason.

• Swelling around the cast.

• Skin irritations or rashes.

• Elevated temperature.

• Softening or cracking of the cast.

• Pain.

If any of the above occurs, immediately notify the student's parent or guardian and responsible physician.

Summary

Plaster casts need daily care. Keep the cast clean and dry, and make sure no small objects are inserted in it.

Noting the points listed in this chapter, monitor the condition of the skin and toes—as well more general signs of pain and irritation.

Part Six

Guidelines for Emergency Conditions

Part Six

Guidelines for Emergency Conditions

Would you know how to respond to a health emergency in the classroom—for example, a severe allergic reaction, cardiac arrest or seizure? As students with chronic health conditions or disabilities enter your classroom, it becomes essential to give a positive answer to this question.

Obviously it's important to have a standard procedure for handling an emergency. Many school systems, recognizing this fact, provide training in cardiopulmonary resuscitation (CPR) and related procedures. This is commendable.

Still, we need to go beyond the immediate emergency and ask other questions: Did you let the parents know exactly what happened when their child had a medical emergency? Did you tell them how you intervened? Did the student's physician get this information? What will you do to prevent another such emergency? And do the other students in the classroom understand what happened? How do they feel about it?

The chapters in Part Six offer both general emergency procedures and guidelines for follow up. Each focuses on a different condition: severe allergic reactions (**Chapter 32**), autonomic hyperreflexia (**Chapter 33**), cardiac arrest (**Chapter 34**), obstructed airway (**Chapter 35**), asthma attacks (**Chapter 36**), hypoglycemia and hyperglycemia (**Chapter 37**) And seizures (**Chapter 38**).

Chapter 32

Dealing with Allergic Reactions

Cyndy Schuster Silkworth, M.P.H., R.N., C.S.N.P.

In This Chapter You'll Find:

A definition of allergic reactions and a list of symptoms.

Suggestions for preventing emergencies caused by allergic reactions.

Instructions for handling an emergency.

Allergies are a common health problem in school-aged children and adolescents. The students affected—and their parents—may be unaware of all the things that can trigger an allergic reaction.

Allergic reactions can happen at any time and can range from very mild to life threatening. Schools must therefore have an established procedure for dealing with a severe reaction.

Symptoms of a Severe Allergic Reaction

Severe allergic reactions are responses to a foreign protein from a variety of sources: food, medication, pollen or insect stings. These reactions (also known as anaphylactic reactions) can cause death if not properly handled. Thus, an allergic reaction is a medical emergency that requires immediate action. Symptoms include one or more of the following:

- Swelling, flushing, and itching skin.

- Irritability.

- Tightness of throat and chest.

- Rash—hives, diffuse or wheal-like pattern.

- Breathing difficulty, wheezing or both.

- Bluish color to the skin (cyanosis).

- Hard to find or weak pulse (circulatory collapse).

- Seizures.

- Loss of consciousness.

Prevention is Essential

Take several steps to avoid life-threatening allergic reactions. Members of the school staff need education about these reactions and the procedures for handling them. Beyond this, the school nurse should:

- Identify students with known allergies to medications, foods, pollens, insect stings, etc.

- Tell appropriate staff members about students with known severe allergies and past anaphylactic reactions.

- Encourage students with known allergies to wear identification (medical alert bracelets or necklaces).

- Encourage parents of students with known severe allergies or past severe allergic reactions to send a supply of the student's prescribed medication to school. Get a written authorization from the student's parent or guardian and physician.

Managing Severe Allergic Reactions

Work with the health care professional. Members of the school staff need to cooperate with designated health personnel when handling an emergency. Medications need to be administered or directly supervised by the school nurse or other qualified health professional.

What to do in an emergency. This section explains the essential steps in managing a severe allergic reaction.

Managing a Severe Allergic Reaction

Procedure:

1. *Determine if the student is having a severe allergic reaction.* Ask these questions:

- Has there been exposure to allergens?

- Are the symptoms present?

- Have the symptoms appeared suddenly (within minutes)?

If in doubt, treat it as a severe allergic reaction.

2. *Give the prescribed amount of the student's prescribed medication.*

The student should respond within 15 minutes. Repeat the dosage as indicated in the instructions from the parent and physician.

Note: Only designated and trained personnel should administer medication.

3. *Establish and maintain vital body functions:*

- Airway and breathing—administer artificial respiration if indicated. Activate your school's procedure for handling a medical emergency.

- Circulation—administer cardiopulmonary resuscitation (CPR) if indicated.

4. *If you do send the student to an emergency medical facility, also send along the student's health and allergy information:*

- Suspected or known allergens.

- Medication that has been administered.

5. *Notify the student's parent or guardian and physician.*

6. *Document the reaction* through a:

- Daily log.

- Incident report.

- Pupil Health Record.

7. *Follow-up by documenting the:*

- Medical intervention—any medication, resuscitation or hospitalization.

- Allergen that triggered the reaction.

- Medications prescribed.

8. *Encourage the student's parents to send a supply of the prescribed medication to school to be given if another reaction occurs.* Obtain a written authorization for medication from the student's parents or guardian and physician.

9. *Help the staff and other students deal with the incident:*

- Talk about what a severe allergic reaction is and why it happens.

- Describe what to do if a reaction occurs.

- Talk about attitudes and feelings caused by the incident.

Methods for accomplishing these include health education, health counseling and small group discussion.

Summary

Severe allergic reactions are responses to a foreign protein. They can be life-threatening emergencies.

Take steps to prevent these reactions. Identify students with known allergies. Tell appropriate staff members about these students and encourage students with known allergies to wear identification. Encourage parents to send allergy medication to school.

Work with a health professional to administer medication. With that person, set up a standard procedure for handling allergic reactions. Use the instructions in this chapter as a guide.

For Further Reading

Merck Manual, 14th ed. Rathway, NJ: Merck, Sharp and Dohme Laboratories, 1982.

California Department of Education. *Guidelines and Procedures for Meeting the Specialized Physical Health Care Needs of Students.* Sacramento, CA, 1980.

American Red Cross. *Advanced First Aid and Emergency Care*, 2nd ed. Garden City, NY: Doubleday, 1979.

Chapter 33

Dealing with Autonomic Hyperreflexia

Cyndy Schuster Silkworth, M.P.H., R.N., C.S.N.P.

In This Chapter You'll Find:

Information on what autonomic hyperreflexia is and why it constitutes a medical emergency.

Suggestions for preventing the condition.

What is Autonomic Hyperreflexia?

Students who have certain kinds of spinal cord injury are at potential risk for sudden increase in blood pressure that can lead to stroke and death. This condition is called autonomic hyperreflexia, and it is a medical emergency that requires immediate action.

A stimulus, internal or external, causes a generalized spread of activity in the nervous system. For a person with a spinal cord injury above the sixth thoracic level (see Figure 33-1), certain stimuli lead to increased blood pressure. Because of the injury, however, the body can't take steps to decrease the blood pressure.

What kind of stimuli are we talking about? They include:

- Distended bladder—that is, filled with urine.

- Spastic bladder, meaning an inability to urinate.

- Urinary tract infection.

- Distended bowel or fecal impaction.

- Pressure sores.

- Irritating clothing.

- Skin temperature changes.

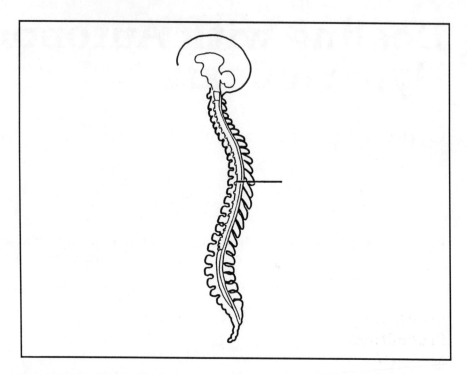

Figure 33-1: Location of the sixth thoracic level.

These factors can easily be beyond your control. For this reason, it's essential that the school to have an established procedure for dealing with autonomic hyperreflexia.

Safety precautions. Since this condition is a medical emergency, it should be managed only by a trained health professional. This person should get specific instructions from the student's parents or physician if autonomic hyperreflexia is a recurring emergency for the student. General guidelines are provided in the following section.

Staff members who work with spinal cord-injured students should be trained in the correct procedures to help autonomic hyperreflexia.

Preventing Autonomic Hyperreflexia

Other measures to take include:

- Identify students with spinal cord injuries who are at potential risk for autonomic hyperreflexia. Get a baseline blood pressure for students with spinal cord injuries.

- Encourage students with spinal cord injuries to perform weight shifts every 20 minutes to prevent pressure sores from forming.

- Check these students to make sure their clothes, especially pants, are not too tight or causing undue pressure on a specific area.

- Monitor urinary catheters used by these students. Look for kinks in tubing. Check the collection bag for adequate drainage. Each time the drainage bag is emptied, check the urine for signs of urinary tract problems, including cloudy or bloody urine.

- Monitor the student's bowel program for indications of constipation or bowel obstruction.

Members of the school staff need to cooperate with the school nurse or designated health professional in handling autonomic hyperreflexia.

The major steps in handling autonomic hyperreflexia are listed below.

Emergency Procedures

Procedure:

1. *Determine if the student is having autonomic hyperreflexia.*

   Symptoms include:

   - *Flushing of the face.*

   - *Sweating,* especially above the level of the spinal cord injury.

   - *Elevated blood pressure*—20 mmHg above the student's normal blood pressure. The normal blood pressure for a quadraplegic person in a sitting position is 90/60. Get a baseline measurement for all students with spinal cord injuries at or above the sixth thoracic level.

   - *Pounding headache.*

   - *Abnormal slowness of heartbeat.*

   - *Distended neck veins.*

2. *If symptoms of autonomic hyperreflexia are present,* activate your school's procedure for handling a medical emergency.

3. *Follow up:*

- Note the procedures and medications needed to decrease the hypertension and resolve the reflexia.

- Make any indicated changes in the student's daily care to decrease the risk of autonomic hyperreflexia.

4. *Help other students and staff members deal with the incident:*

- Talk about what autonomic hyperreflexia is and why it happens.

- Explain what to do if it happens again.

- Talk about attitudes and feelings caused by the incident. Also discuss attitudes toward people with physical disabilities, including those with quadraplegia. Methods for doing this include health education, health counseling and small group discussion.

Summary

Autonomic hyperreflexia is a medical emergency that results from certain kinds of spinal cord injury. In this condition, certain stimuli cause a dramatic rise in blood pressure. Because of the spinal cord injury, the body cannot control the increase.

A student with autonomic hyperreflexia should be taken to the nearest emergency room.

Identify students with spinal cord injuries who are at potential risk for autonomic hyperreflexia. Take steps to prevent autonomic hyperreflexia. Make sure the school staff gets appropriate training.

Encourage students with spinal cord injuries to perform weight shifts every 20 minutes. Check these students to make sure their clothes are not causing undue pressure on a specific body area. Monitor urinary catheters and bowel programs used by these students.

References

California Department of Education. *Guidelines and Procedures for Meeting the Specialized Physical Health Care Needs of Students.* Sacramento, CA, 1980.

For Further Reading

Bedbrook, George M. *The Care and Management of Spinal Cord Injuries.* New York, NY: Springer Verlag.

Downey, John A. and Niels L. Low, Ed. *The Child with Disabling Illness: Principles of Rehabilitation.* New York: Raven Press.

Chapter 34

Handling Cardiac Arrest

Patti L. Jacobson, M.S., R.N., C.P.N.P.

In This Chapter You'll Find:

A definition of cardiac arrest and a list of its symptoms.

Guidelines for preventing cardiac arrest.

Instructions on what to do when cardiac arrest occurs.

Cardiac arrest is the absence of heart contractions or the presence of inadequate contractions. The clinical signs of cardiac arrest are absence of heart sounds, pulse or blood pressure. In any case, cardiac arrest is a medical emergency that requires immediate action.

What might cause cardiac arrest? The answer is cardiovascular collapse, which may stem from severe hemorrhage, shock or various drugs. Another cause is rapid and uncoordinated heart contraction, also known as ventricular fibrillation. This can occur after a heart attack or low-voltage electrical shock. Severe lack of oxygen to the heart muscle can also trigger cardiac arrest.

Cardiac arrests in students start primarily with the latter problem: a lack of oxygen in the respiratory system. This in turn leads to cardiac arrest.

Safety precautions. Because the cause can sometimes be identified before the event occurs, some cardiac arrests can be prevented. Schools must, however, have an established procedure for administering basic life support when the situation does occur.

Preventing Cardiac Arrest

One of the most potent means of preventing cardiac arrest is training for the school staff. That training should focus on the causes and symptoms of cardiac arrest and respiratory failure.

Emergency procedures for dealing with these conditions should also be covered. In any case, certain staff members should become certified in Basic Life Support, including cardiopulmonary resuscitation (CPR).

Beyond training, you can take other steps to prevent cardiac arrest:

- Identify students known to be higher at risk for cardiac or respiratory complications. These include students with respiratory disorders, cardiac disorders, and those who are on routine medication for chronic problems.

- Inform the appropriate staff members who these students are.

- Encourage students with known cardiac and other medical problems to wear identification (medical alert bracelets or necklaces).

- Encourage early interventions when medical problems arise.

Managing Cardiac Arrest

Work with a health professional. As mentioned above, selected school personnel need to obtain and maintain Basic Life Support certification. (CPR should only be performed by people with such training.)

Develop a CPR plan. Make sure your school has in place a clear procedure for dealing with cardiac arrest.

Following are the essential steps to include in the plan.

Develop a CPR plan

Procedure:

1. *Determine if the student is having a cardiopulmonary arrest.* Symptoms include absence of respiration and pulse.

   You must establish that there is no respiration or pulse before beginning CPR. Artificial respirations can be given if only respiratory failure has occurred.

2. *If the student is still conscious, give the prescribed amount of the student's prescribed medication.* The student should respond within five minutes.

   Repeat the dosage, as indicated by directions from the parent and physician. Monitor the student's condition constantly.

Note: Medication should be administered or directly supervised by the school nurse or other qualified health professional.

3. *If a cardiopulmonary arrest has occurred, establish and maintain vital body functions:*

• Airway and breathing—administer artificial respiration, if needed. Activate your school's system for dealing with a medical emergency.

• Circulation—administer CPR if needed. Again, activate the emergency medical system.

4. *Continue CPR* until you receive instructions to stop from a physician.

5. *When the student is sent to an emergency facility, also send along the student's health information:* identification of known problems and medication that has been administered.

6. *Notify the student's parent or guardian and physician.*

7. *Document the situation.* Note it in a daily log, incident report and Pupil Health Record.

8. *Follow up.* Note the medical intervention received by the student: medication; resuscitation and/or hospitalization.

   If identified or suspected, record the cause of the student's health problem and the precipitating cause of the arrest.

9. *Help the staff and other students deal with the incident.*

   Methods for doing this include health education, health counseling and small group discussion. Topics to cover include: what a cardiopulmonary arrest is and why it happened; what to do in the future if an arrest occurs; attitudes and feelings about the incident.

Summary

Cardiac arrest is the absence of heart contractions or the presence of inadequate contractions. As a medical emergency, it needs immediate attention.

Take steps to prevent cardiac arrests. Arrange for the school staff to receive appropriate training, and make sure some staff members are certified in Basic Life Support.

Also, identify students known to be higher at risk for cardiac or respiratory complications. Inform the appropriate staff members who these students are. Encourage these students to wear identification.

Working with a health professional in your school, develop and learn a plan for managing cardiac arrest. Use the steps listed in this chapter as a guide.

For Further Reading

American Red Cross. *Advanced First Aid and Emergency Care*, 2nd ed., Garden City, NY: Doubleday, 1979.

Barkin, Roger M. and Rosen, Peter. *Emergency Pediatrics*. St. Louis: C.V. Mosby, 1984.

Behrman, R.E. and Vaughn, V.C. *Nelson's Textbook of Pediatrics*, 12th ed., Philadelphia: W.B. Saunders, 1983.

Chapter 35

Dealing with an Obstructed Airway

Cyndy Schuster Silkworth, M.P.H., R.N., C.S.N.P.

In This Chapter You'll Find:

Information on the causes and symptoms of an obstructed airway.

Guidelines for preventing incidents of obstructed airway.

Emergency procedures for dealing with an obstructed airway.

An obstruction of the airway can happen to anyone, and for a variety of reasons. Students with disabilities may have a greater potential for obstruction of the airway—especially if their ability to swallow is changed or they have conditions that compromise their respiratory system.

In any case, schools need to have an established procedure for handling airway and breathing problems. An obstructed airway is a medical emergency that requires immediate action.

What Causes an Obstructed Airway?

An obstructed airway is partial or complete blockage of the air passages. The blockage may be caused by a number of conditions.

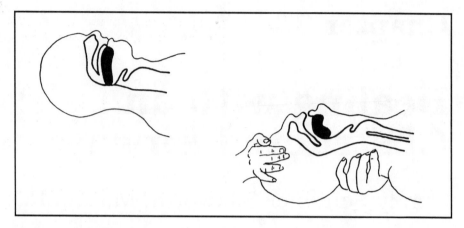

Figure 35-1: Anatomical obstruction of the airway (top) and opened airway (bottom).

Anatomical obstruction. Narrowing of the air passages can occur when the tongue drops back in the throat or tissues swell. Either of these conditions can be due to illness, such as asthma or croup; spasm of the larynx; swelling after facial burns; swallowing corrosive poisons; or a direct blow to the throat.

Mechanical obstruction. Objects can also obstruct the airways. These include food, solid foreign objects (bones, toys, coins, etc.) and the accumulation of fluids (mucus, blood or saliva).

Preventing Obstructed Airway

You can work directly with students to prevent obstructed airway:

• Restrict students and staff from walking, running or playing with food or foreign objects in their mouths.

• Encourage students and staff to avoid laughing and talking while chewing or swallowing.

• Identify students with alterations in their ability to swallow or conditions that compromise their respiratory system. Determine their needs for maintaining an open airway.

• Help with special procedures: bronchial drainage, inhalation therapy or suctioning. Also, assist the student who takes medication during the school day.

• Observe students who have alterations in their ability to swallow. These students may need help with eating.

• Tell appropriate staff members about students with an increased risk for airway obstruction.

- The student may use medication to help maintain an open airway. If so, encourage the student, parent or guardian to authorize and provide a supply of the medication at school.

What To Do When Obstructed Airway

Establish a procedure for dealing with an obstructed airway. Make sure that at least some staff members know this procedure, cardiopulmonary resuscitation (CPR), artificial resuscitation.

Staff members need to cooperate with school health personnel in performing emergency procedures. Special procedures and medications need to be administered or directly supervised by the school nurse, public health nurse or physician.

The actual emergency procedures for obstructed airway follow on the next three pages.

Step 1

Does the student have the symptoms of obstructed airway?
Look for coughing, wheezing, gasping or choking.

• Bluish or gray color to the skin and fingernails.

• Grasping at the throat with one or both hands.

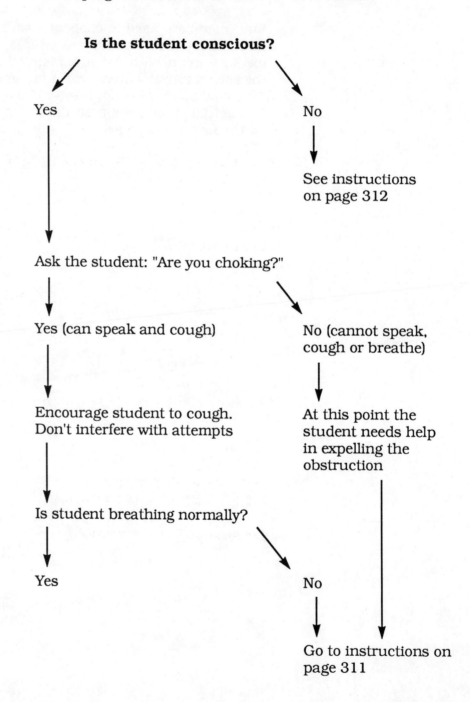

Is the student conscious?

Yes

No

See instructions
on page 312

Ask the student: "Are you choking?"

Yes (can speak and cough)

No (cannot speak,
cough or breathe)

Encourage student to cough.
Don't interfere with attempts

At this point the
student needs help
in expelling the
obstruction

Is student breathing normally?

Yes

No

Go to instructions on
page 311

(Step 1, continued)

Student is not breathing, speaking or coughing.

↓

Start your standard procedures for a medical emergency.

↓

Administer abdominal thrusts
(Repeat as many times as necessary.)

↓

Continue until object is expelled or student becomes
unconscious.

↓

Is student breathing?

Yes	No
↓	↓
Monitor the student. Have the student sit down and relax.	Student is unconscious. Go to instructions on page 312
↓	
Notify the student's parents or guardian. Recommend that the student be evaluated by a physician as soon as possible.	

(Step 1, continued)

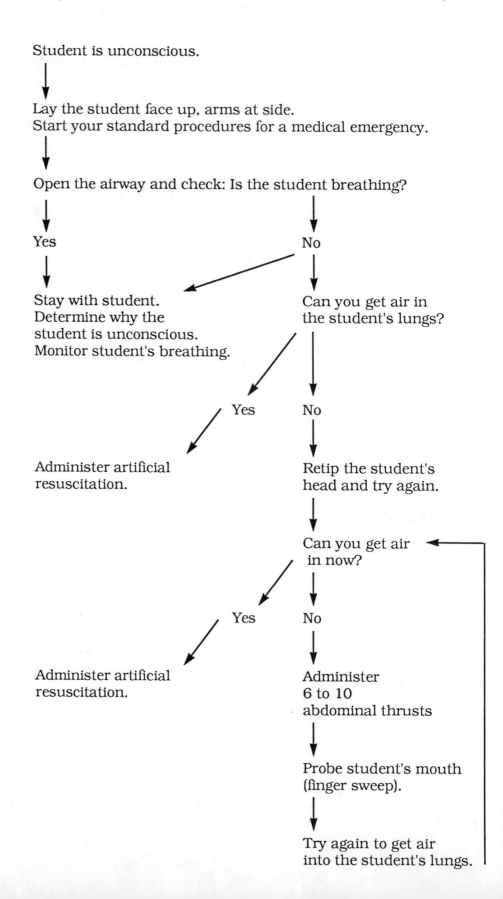

Student is unconscious.

Lay the student face up, arms at side.
Start your standard procedures for a medical emergency.

Open the airway and check: Is the student breathing?

Yes

No

Stay with student.
Determine why the
student is unconscious.
Monitor student's breathing.

Can you get air in
the student's lungs?

Yes

No

Administer artificial
resuscitation.

Retip the student's
head and try again.

Can you get air
in now?

Yes

No

Administer artificial
resuscitation.

Administer
6 to 10
abdominal thrusts

Probe student's mouth
(finger sweep).

Try again to get air
into the student's lungs.

Step 2   *Determine if the student's heart is beating.* If it is not, administer CPR—if you have proper training.

Step 3   *Document the incident in writing.* Include information about predisposing factors in the obstructed airway and the student's activity at the time of the incident. List the events that occurred, in chronological order. Note any emergency procedures done and the time that parents were notified. Finally, note where the student was sent: to class, the physician, the hospital, etc.

This information should be documented in the daily log, the incident report and the Pupil Health Record.

Step 4   *Follow up.* Note medical interventions the student received, prescribed medication and activity restrictions. A student may have a health condition that can cause an airway obstruction; if so, develop an individual health plan to prevent and manage obstructions.

Step 5   Help the staff and other students deal with any incident of an obstructed airway. Talk about what an obstructed airway is and how the incident happened. Explain how an obstructed airway incident can be prevented and what to do if someone has an obstructed airway. Methods for doing all this include health education, health counseling and small group discussion.

Summary

An obstructed airway is partial or complete blockage of the air passage. The blockage may be caused by a number of conditions.

Schools need an established procedure for handling airway and breathing problems. An obstructed airway is a medical emergency that requires immediate action.

Take steps to prevent airway obstructions. Every member of the school staff should be trained in emergency procedures. Identify students with alterations in their ability to swallow or conditions that compromise their respiratory system. Tell appropriate staff members about students with an increased risk for airway obstruction. Finally, encourage safety practices that prevent airway obstructions.

Develop and learn a standard procedure for managing an obstructed airway. Use the instructions in this chapter as a guide.

References

American Red Cross. *Cardiopulmonary Resuscitation (CPR)*. May 1987.

Bleck, E. and D. Nagel, eds. *Physically Handicapped Children: A Medical Atlas for Teachers*, 2nd edition. New York: Grune & Stratton, 1982.

Chapter 36

Managing an Asthma Episode

Cyndy Schuster Silkworth, M.P.H., R.N., C.S.N.P.
Diane Jones, B.S., R.N.

In This Chapter
Information on how to judge the severity of an asthma episode.

Procedures to follow when a student has an asthma episode.

It's essential for your school, working with a health professional, to establish a standard procedure for dealing with an asthma episode. All staff members should be trained in that procedure.

This chapter focuses on guidelines for such a procedure. For more general information on asthma—what it is, why it occurs, and how to prevent it—see Chapter 7.

Judging the Severity of an Episode

In these instructions you will be asked to judge the severity of an asthma episode. Three indicators are used in making this judgement: the intake and output (I:O) ratio, the presence of wheezing and signs of retraction.

The I:O ratio. This indicator is the best way to tell how the student is doing. The I:O ratio is a measure of how long an inhalation lasts, as compared to an exhalation. To get the feel of the I:O ratio, breathe in and out with the student. In a normal breathing pattern, inhalation lasts 50 percent longer than exhalation—an I:O ration of 1.5:1.

When an asthma episode occurs, it takes longer to exhale. In a mild episode, this increase is hardly noticeable. In a moderate episode, inhalation and exhalation become about equal, an I:O ratio of 1:1. In a severe asthma episode, however, the exhalation takes longer than the inhalation. (Plaut, 1983)

Retractions. Retractions are the sucking-in of the soft tissues in the chest; they occur with breathing difficulty. These are first seen below the rib cage, in the soft part of the neck above the breast bone, in the soft tissue over the collarbone, and in the area at the bottom of the breast bone. In more severe episodes, the tissue between the ribs may be sucked in. These changes are a measure of the difficulty of breathing—a good guide to the severity of the episode. (Plaut, 1983)

Wheezing. The high-pitched whistling sound that occurs when air flows through the narrowed bronchial tubes is called wheezing. When an episode starts, the wheezing only occurs on exhalation. In mild episodes, wheezing occurs at the end of the exhalation phase. As the episode gets worse, wheezing lasts through all of the exhalation; finally it occurs with inhalation.

Wheezing does not take place in a bronchial tube that is totally blocked. The absence of wheezing in a student who has severe retractions and a reversed I:O ratio (1:2) is a sign of serious trouble. When this student improves through the reopening of some windpipes, the wheezing will reappear. (Plaut, 1983)

The following table summarizes these signs as they relate to the severity of an asthma episode.

Table 36-1

Severity of an Asthma Episode

	Mild	Moderate	Severe
I:O Ratio	About 1.5:1	About 1:1	Less than 1:1
Wheezing	Mild, on inhalation	Full	On inhalation and marked on exhalation
Retractions	None	Mild	Marked
(Plaut, 1983)			

Keep the information in Table 36-1 in mind for step 2 of managing an asthma episode, described in the procedure that follows.

The major steps in handling an asthma episode are listed on next page.

Handling an Asthma Episode

Procedure:

1. *Determine if the student is having an asthma episode.*
   Watch for these symptoms:

- Wheezing.

- Coughing.

- Difficulty in breathing or breathlessness.

- A feeling of tightness in the student's chest.

- A bluish color in the lips and nail beds.

- A decrease in peak flow. (See "Use of the Peak Flow Meter," page 90.)

2. *Judge the severity of the episode.* Take into account wheezing, retractions and the I:O ratio. (See Table 34-1.)

3. *Find out if the student has been exposed to any asthma triggers.*

   The most common triggers are: colds and other viral infections, irritants, exercise and over-exertion, air pollution and strong emotion.

4. *Help the student sit up,* with the shoulders relaxed.

   As you speak, be calm and reassuring. The student's anxiety can be lessened if you show you understand and know how to help.

5. *Encourage the student to drink fluids.* This helps to thin mucus.

6. *Help the student take the prescribed amount of the prescribed medication.*

   Medications should be given or directed by the school nurse or other qualified health professional. For help on using inhaled medication, see "How to Use Your Inhaler," page 91.

7. *If the medication doesn't seem to work, notify the student's parents and health care provider.*

   Only in rare cases do students with asthma need emergency medical care.

8. *Document the asthma episode.*

   Note it in the the daily log and student health record.

9. *Follow up.* Let the student's parents know about any medical intervention.

Try to identify what triggered the episode. Remove it or plan to help the student avoid it.

Check the supply of prescribed medication, and notify the student and parent if more is needed.

10. *Help other staff members and students understand what asthma is and why it occurs.*

Explore their attitudes and feelings about asthma, and explain what to do if a student has an asthma episode. This can be done through health education, counseling and small group discussion.

Summary

Asthma is a chronic condition in which the air passages become temporarily narrowed or blocked. Asthma episodes can be triggered by a variety of causes, including colds and other viral infections, common irritants, physical activity and strong emotions.

Make sure each student with asthma has a plan for managing asthma at school. The instructions given in this chapter can be a guide. Then make sure staff members are trained to manage an asthma episode.

References

Plaut, Thomas F. *Children with Asthma.* Amherst, MA: Pedipress, 1983.

For Further Reading

American Lung Association. Asthma Alert Series (For Administrators, Teachers, School Nurses and Physical Education Teachers), 1983.

Pfuetze, Bruce L. *Asthma: A Matter of Control.* American Lung Association of Kansas, 1983.

Chapter 37

Dealing with Hypoglycemia and Hyperglycemia

Barbara Balik, R.N., M.S.
Broatch Haig, R.D., C.D.E.

In This Chapter You'll Find: Information on what hyperglycemia and hypoglycemia are—and how to treat them.

Hypoglycemia (low blood sugar) and hyperglycemia (low blood sugar) are two physical reactions associated with diabetes. Because diabetes is one of the most chronic conditions seen in students—and one of the least "visible"—school personnel should know what to when hypoglycemia or hyperglycemia occurs.

This chapter concentrates on actions for you to take when either of these reactions takes place in a student. For more information on hyperglycemia and hypoglycemia—and diabetes in general—turn to Chapter 8.

Dealing With Hypoglycemia

What is hypoglycemia? Insulin reaction, insulin shock and hypoglycemia are different names for the same thing—low blood glucose (sugar). The symptoms are the body's way of telling a person that the amount of glucose in the blood is dropping or has dropped. Reactions usually come quickly. They occur most frequently before meals, during or after exercise and at peak action time of the insulin.

Symptoms of hypoglycemia. When the blood glucose drops, the brain does not receive enough glucose and sends out warning signals. These signals may include:

Symptoms of Hypoglycemia

- Shaking
- Sweating
- Hunger
- Dizziness
- Paleness
- Numbness tingling of the lips

- Irritability
- Confusion
- Poor coordination
- Headaches
- Double or blurred vision

The signals of hypoglycemia may vary from one episode to another with the same student. Parents or students are usually able to identify two to three consistent signals.

Students are able to recognize their own signals and treat their reactions at different ages. Students in lower elementary grades will usually need help in recognizing the signals and treatment. Older students may not be able to handle their own reactions when signals such as confusion, irritability and poor coordination are present.

Treating hypoglycemia. What follows are general suggestions. Work with the health professional in your school to establish a standard procedure for dealing with hypoglycemia.

Some students use a "buddy system" with vigorous sports or activities. A friend who recognizes early signals can help the young person treat hypoglycemia promptly.

Treating Hypoglycemia

Procedure:

1. *Verify that the student is having the symptoms of hypoglycemia.*

2. *Have the student eat a food containing ten grams of fast-acting glucose.*

   Some suitable foods and amounts are:

   - 1 small box (2 Tbsp.) raisins
   - 1 Fruit Roll-up
   - 1/2 cup regular pop or soda (not diet)
   - 6 or 7 Lifesavers
   - 4-5 dried fruit pieces

- 1/2 cup of any fruit juice

- 5 small or 2 large sugar cubes

- 1/3 bottle Glutose

- 2 or 3 BD Glucose Tablets

- Monoject® Insulin Reaction Gel

If a meal or snack time is not due for one hour or more, follow up this treatment with a glass of milk or three or four crackers.

The reaction should begin to resolve in ten to fifteen minutes.

3. *If this brings no results, send the student to the health professional in your school.*

   This person should check the student's blood glucose level and, if necessary, have him or her eat the same amount of food.

4. *When symptoms persist,* call the parent or health care provider.

Dealing With Hyperglycemia

Hyperglycemia is another word for high blood sugar, which is present in undetected, untreated or poorly regulated diabetes. This condition occurs more slowly and less frequently than hypoglycemia.

Hyperglycemia and ketoacidosis. Hyperglycemia can lead to ketoacidosis. This is a dangerous condition—one that can cause unconsciousness and death if not treated immediately.

Hyperglycemia develops when there is not enough insulin in the blood to allow glucose to be used for energy. Excessive blood glucose over a period of time can lead to ketoacidosis. (See page 98 for a more detailed explanation.)

Symptoms of hyperglycemia. If high blood sugar levels persist, the student may experience these symptoms:

- Abdominal pain

- Nausea

- Vomiting

- Blurred vision

Treating hyperglycemia. What follows are brief guidelines for treating hyperglycemia. Work with the health professional in your school to identify students at risk for hyperglycemia. Then adopt a standard procedure to follow in treating this condition during the school day.

Treating Hyperglycemia

Procedure:

1. *Check to see if the student is wearing a diabetes I.D. bracelet, or if the student has a history of diabetes.*

   These symptoms occur in undiagnosed or poorly controlled diabetes.

2. *Verify that the student is having the symptoms of hyperglycemia.*

   The student may appear confused and unable to respond to your questions.

3. *If the student has the symptoms of hyperglycemia and appears confused, send the student to the health professional in your school immediately.* If you cannot do this, contact the student's parents or physician for instructions.

   A health professional can test the student's urine for substances called ketones—a sign of ketoacidosis. A blood sugar level will give the health professional additional information on the student's condition.

Summary

Diabetes is a chronic illness resulting from the body's decreased ability to use insulin.

Hypoglycemia refers to low blood sugar levels. It can result from a variety of factors, including stress, too much insulin, too little food or strenuous or planned exercise. Symptoms can include sweating, hunger, dizziness, headaches and poor coordination.
The student with symptoms of an insulin reaction should eat a food containing 10 grams of fast-acting glucose.

Hyperglycemia is another word for high blood sugar, which is present in poorly regulated diabetes. It can lead to ketoacidosis, a dangerous condition that can result in diabetic coma or death if not treated promptly.

Using the instructions in this chapter as a guide, work with a health professional to establish a procedure for treating these conditions.

Chapter 38

Dealing with Seizures

Carolyn Jones-Saete, R.N.

In This Chapter You'll Find:

Guidelines on how to plan ahead for seizure management.

Instructions on what to do when a student has a seizure.

Seizures can occur with several types of chronic illness or disability, including epilepsy. One point is crucial for school personnel and parents: methods of managing seizures should be consistent between home and school. It is the responsibility of the school to contact parents for information and develop a plan for handling in-school seizures.

Seizures are sudden, brief attacks of altered consciousness, motor activity, sensory phenomena or inappropriate behavior. They are associated with abnormal electrical discharges within the brain.

Planning for Effective Seizure Management

The first step is training. That training should cover the appropriate procedures for helping a student undergoing a seizure. It should also help staff members become aware of their attitudes toward people with seizure disorders.

Next, take steps to prevent seizures from occurring:

- Identify students with a history of seizures. Obtain information from them, their parents and physicians about: the type of seizures the student has had, including a description of the seizure; medications the student is receiving (drug, dose, time and side effects); the most recent assessment by the physician or neurologist; and past and current seizure patterns.

- Tell appropriate staff members about children with known seizure disorders.

- Encourage students with known seizure disorders to wear identification (a medical alert bracelet or necklace).

Work with the health professional. School staff members need to cooperate with designated health personnel in performing the appropriate emergency procedures. Moreover, anti-seizure medications need to be administered or directly supervised by the school nurse or other qualified health professional.

Procedures to follow. Develop a standard procedure for responding to a student experiencing a seizure. These are the essential points to include:

Managing a Seizure

Procedure:

1. *Determine if the student is having a seizure.* Seizures may be expressed as any one or combination of the following:

   - An abrupt change in consciousness or responsiveness, including no response, inappropriate response.

   - An alteration in perception of the environment. Any of the senses may be altered.

   - An involuntary alteration of the individual's movement, such as rigidity or loss of muscle control.

2. *Try to remain calm.* This will help others around you remain calm.

3. *Gently protect the student from injury.*

   If there is a possibility of the student falling, help him or her to a lying position. This is especially important if altered movements are present. Clear the area of hard or sharp objects.

   Do not try to stop or restrain the student or insert anything into the student's mouth. Likewise, don't offer food or drink until the student is fully awake. Do not agitate the student.

4. *If the student does not start breathing after the seizure, begin mouth-to-mouth resuscitation and activate your school's system for handling an emergency.*

This condition is known as status epilepticus, and it require immediate action.

If a student's seizure lasts longer than 5 minutes and the student does not regain consciousness, call the student's physician and parents. If you can't reach the physician at once, take the student to the nearest emergency room.

5. *Also activate the emergency system under any of these conditions:*

   • The student has one seizure immediately after another.

   • The student's seizure lasts longer than five minutes.

   • The student has been injured seriously.

6. *After the seizure is over, stay with the student until full recovery has occurred.* Allow the student to rest if he or she chooses or needs to.

   Offer reassurance and reorient the student, providing any needed information about what happened. Disorientation can last for several minutes following a seizure.

7. *Document the seizure*, making notes in three areas: what happened before, during and after the seizure.

8. *As soon as possible, report the seizure* to the student's parent or guardian, teacher and physician. If it is the student's first seizure, or if there has been a change in the type of seizure, send a copy of the seizure record home. Or send a copy to the student's physician.

9. *Follow up.* Note any medical diagnostic testing that was done and the results. Indicate what medications were prescribed or changed. If appropriate, get an authorization to administer medication at school. Also note any activity restrictions for the student.

   As a further step, schedule a conference with the student, parents and any teachers who work with the student. Share new information on student, as well as concerns, questions, reactions and attitudes.

10. *Help staff members and other students dealing with the seizure.* Talk about what seizures are and why they happen. Explain what to do if a seizure occurs. Beyond this,

explore attitudes and feelings about the seizure. Methods for doing this include health education, health counseling small group discussion.

Using Rectal Valium® for Prolonged Seizures

A prolonged seizure is frightening to anyone. Seizures lasting five to ten minutes or serial seizures call for immediate intervention. Valium® injected in the rectum has given parents and health professionals a way to respond to this type of emergency anywhere.

Note: **Rectal Valium® must be administered by trained personnel, and only when prescribed by a physician for a particular student.**

Administering rectal Valium®. Procedures for this treatment are explained in the following paragraphs. As the first step, however, get a phone number you can call for help for a student with a seizure disorder: an emergency number or physician number.

Before you can inject the Valium®, you must draw it into a syringe—either from a vial or a Tubex®. In either case, you will need the following supplies:

- Syringe

- Needle

- Valium® (Diazepam)

- Alcohol and Cotton

- A lubricant—for example, K-Y Jelly® or Lubra®

- Adhesive tape (optional)

In the procedures below, instructions for this preliminary step come first, followed by instructions for rectal injection. After these are steps to take if the treatment doesn't work.

Drawing Valium® (Using a Vial)

Procedure:

1. *Put the needle on the syringe.*

2. *Remove the vial cover* (it snaps off) and wipe off the rubber top with alcohol and cotton.

3. *Pull back the syringe plunger* to the line that marks the dosage of Valium you will be giving.

4. *Remove the needle cap.*

5. *Put the needle into the vial and push air into the vial.*

6. *Turn the vial upside down and pull the needle* down so it is just above rubber cap. This will allow you to withdraw the medication without getting air into the syringe.

7. *Pull back on the plunger* until the correct amount of medication is in the syringe.

8. *Remove the needle from the vial.* Push out any excess air. Then replace the needle cover.

Drawing Valium® Using a Tubex® or Syringe with Needle Attached

Procedure:

Note: The needles on these do not detach from the syringe.

1. *Pull the plunger on the syringe back* to the line marking the dosage of Valium you will be giving.

2. *Remove the cap of the needle.*

3. *Place the needle into the top hole of the plastic syringe.*

4. *Fill the syringe with Valium®.*

Administering Valium® Rectally

Procedure:

1. *Take the needle off the syringe.*

2. *Lubricate the end of the syringe with K-Y Jelly®.*

3. *Insert the syringe gently* about 1 1/2 or 2 inches into the rectum.

4. *Inject or push the Valium® in.* Squeeze the buttocks together and remove the syringe.

5. *Apply tape or continue to hold the buttocks* together for 10 to 15 minutes. If you choose, you can use the tape and hold the buttocks at the same time.

6. *Stay with the student* until the seizure has stopped. If the seizure has not stopped in 10 minutes, call for help.

7. *Watch the student's respirations and color.* If the skin turns dusky or bluish, be prepared to give mouth-to-mouth respiration; this is done only if breathing has completely stopped.

What to do if Valium® doesn't work. First call the emergency or physician number you have for the student. Then care for the student until help arrives, remembering these points:

- Remain calm. Talk gently to the student. This will help you, too.

- Stay with the student.

- Protect the student from injury: remove objects that might be knocked or hit during seizure.

- Do not restrain the student.

- Do not force anything into the student's mouth.

- Help breathing: keep the student on his or her side.

- Observe breathing and color. If breathing stops completely, start CPR.

Other things to remember. Store all supplies, instructions, Valium®, needles, syringes and lubricant together in a make-up type bag. Periodically check the Valium® expiration date, and keep it from extreme heat or cold. In addition, remember that Valium®, once drawn up, is good for only 45 minutes.

Finally, keep records. Note how often Valium® is used and how long it took to stop the seizure.

Summary

Methods of managing seizures should be consistent between home and school.

Plan ahead for effective seizure management. Train staff members in appropriate procedures. Get a medical history from each student with a seizure disorder. Tell appropriate staff members about these students, and encourage the students to wear some form of identification.

Working with a health professional, develop a clear and consistent procedure for managing seizures. Use the instructions in this chapter as a guide.

Note: A wallet-sized card that summarizes first aid for epilepsy is available from the MINCEP Epilepsy Centers, 27101 University Avenue Southeast, Suite 106, Minneapolis, Minnesota 55414.

References

Dhillon, S., Oxley, J., Richens, A. "Bioavailability of Diazepam After Intravenous, Oral and Rectal Administration in Adult Epileptic Patients."

Dulac, O., Aicardi, J., Ray, E., Olive, G. "Blood Levels of Diazepam After Single Rectal Administration in Infants and Children." *Journal of Pediatrics*, Vol. 93 (1978) 1039-41.

Graves, N. M., Kriel, R. L. "Rectal Administration of Antiepileptic Drugs in Children." *Pediatric Neurology*, Vol. 3 (1987) 321-6.

Hoppuk, K., Santavuari, P. "Diazepam Rectal Solution for Home Treatment of Acute Seizures in Children." *Acta Paediatrica Scandinavica*, Vol. 70 (1981) 369-72.

Kanto J., Iisalo, E., Kangas, L., Valovirta, E. A. "Comparative Study on the Clinical Effects of Rectal Diazepman and Pentobarbital on Small Children: Relationship Between Plasma Level and Effect." *International Journal of Clinical Pharmacology, Therapy and Toxicology*, Vol. 18 (1980) 348-51.

Knudsen, F. U. "Plasma Diazepam in Infants After Rectal Administration in Solution and By Suppository." *Acta Paediatrica Scandinavica*, Vol. 66 (1977) 563-7.

Knudsen, F. U. "Rectal Administration of Diazepam in Solution in the Acute Treatment of Convulsions in Infants and Children." *Archives of Disease in Childhood*, Vol. 54 (1979) 885-7.

Knudsen, F. U., Vestermark, S. "Prophylactic Diazepam or Phenobarbitone in Febrile Convulsions: A Prospective, Controlled Study." *Archives of Disease in Childhood*, Vol. 53 (1978) 660-3.

Lindahl, S., Olsson, A. K., Thompson, D. "Rectal Premedication in Children: Use of Diazepam, Morphine, and Hyocine." *Anaesthesia*, Vol. 36 (1981) 376-9.

Magnussen, I., Oxlund, H. R., Alsbich, K. E., Arnold, E. "Absorption of Diazepam in Man Following Rectal and Parental Administration." *Acta Pharmacologica et Toxicologica*, Vol. 45 (1979) 87-90.

Moolenaar, F., Bakker, S., Visser, J., Juizinga, T. "Biopharmaceutics of Rectal Administration of Drugs in Man. IX: Comparative Biopharmaceutics of Diazepam after Single Rectal, Oral, Intramuscular and Intravenous Administration in Man." *International Journal of Pharmaceuticals*, Vol.5 (1980) 127-137.

Glossary

Allergic reactions result from abnormal sensitivity to foreign material—for example, dust, pollen, insect stings and certain foods. In severe allergic reactions, symptoms may include: swelling, flushing and itching skin; irritability; tightness of the throat; rash; breathing difficulty; seizures; and loss of consciousness.

Allergens are materials that, for certain people, cause asthma attacks or allergic reactions. Dust, pollen, pollens, house dust, animal hair, medications, molds and food can all be allergens.

Ambulatory is a term referring to the ability to walk.

Anaphylactic reactions—See allergic reactions.

Artificial respiration is a means of inducing breathing when it has stopped. A common technique for artificial respiration is "mouth to mouth" resuscitation, where air is breathed into the mouth and lungs and then allowed to escape.

An **audiometer** is an instrument for testing hearing; the test itself is called audiometry.

Autonomic hyperreflexia is a sudden increase in blood pressure associated with certain kinds of spinal cord injury.

The **bladder** is the organ that acts as a receptacle for urine.

Body alignment refers to placing the body in correct anatomical position.

Bronchitis is an inflammation of bronchial membranes.

Cardiac arrest (also known as cardiopulmonary arrest) occurs when the heart suddenly stops beating.

Cardiopulmonary resuscitation (CPR) refers to the rapid sequence of actions performed in an emergency to stimulate breathing and blood circulation.

A **catheter** is a tube for draining or injecting fluids.

Cerebral palsy is composed of a group of disorders resulting from central nervous system damage before, during and after birth. Although nonprogressive, these disorders may become more obvious as the infant grows older.

Clean technique refers to procedures that reduce the number of disease-causing agents, such as bacteria, viruses and other micro-organisms. In contrast, sterile technique destroys all these agents.

A **colostomy** is an incision of the colon that makes a permanent opening (stoma) in the abdomen wall. This opening is used for eliminating body waste. In this surgical procedure, part of the colon is removed or disconnected and all or part of the rectum may be removed.

Conductive hearing loss is an interference with sound transmission in the outer part of the ear. Causes include wax accumulation and chronic ear infections.

Congenital hip dysplasia is an abnormality of the hip joint present from birth. It is the most common disorder that affects hip joints of children under age 3. Congenital hip dislocation can cause abnormal joint development and permanent disability.

CPR—See cardiopulmonary resuscitation.

Cystic fibrosis is a hereditary disease of infants, children and young adults that causes abnormal gland secretions. This condition can be associated with lung disease, malnutrition and diseases of the liver.

Digital stimulation is done to relax the sphincter and stimulate a bowel movement. It is done by inserting a gloved finger about 1 inch into the rectum.

Distal movement indicates movement farther from the center of the body.

Duchenne's muscular dystrophy is progressive muscle deterioration that usually starts between ages 3 and 5. It begins with leg weakness and progresses to generalized muscle weakness.

Emphysema is a disorder of the lung that causes breathing problems and destruction of lung tissue.

Encopresis is the voluntary or involuntary withholding of feces (bowel movements).

Etiology refers to the causes of a specific condition.

An **external cannula**, used in metal tracheostomy tubes, holds the airway open when the inner cannula is removed for cleaning.

Hearing impairment is any condition that interferes with the transmission or perception of sound waves.

In an **ileostomy**, the entire colon is removed, and a portion of the ileum or small intestine is brought through the abdominal wall for elimination of body waste.

An **inner cannula** is used in metal tracheostomy tubes. It fits inside a larger tube (called the external cannula). The inner cannula acts as a lining that can be removed for cleaning while the external cannula holds the airway open.

The **intake and output ratio (I:O ratio)** is a measure of how long an inhalation lasts, as compared to an exhalation. To get the feel of the another person's I:O ratio, breathe in and out with the person. In a normal breathing pattern, inhalation lasts 50 percent longer than exhalation—an I:O ratio of 1.5:1.

Labia minora are two folds of tissue lying on either side of the vaginal opening and forming the borders of the vulva.

To **lavage** is to irrigate or wash out an organ or body cavity.

Legg Perthes disease is a usually one-sided condition in which changes take place in bone at the head of the thigh bone. It occurs most frequently in boys aged 4 to 10 and tends to occur in families.

Manual evacuation, performed by inserting a gloved finger into the rectum, is done to remove feces.

The **meatus** is the external opening of the urethra.

Mucus is secreted by membranes that line certain body passages: those that lead from inside the body to the outside. (Examples are the nasal passages.) Mucus is rich in proteins that moisten and protect the passages.

Myelomeningocele is another name for spina bifida, a defect in the walls of the spinal canal.

An **obturator** is a tube that guides the insertion of a tracheostomy tube. The obturator fits inside the tracheostomy tube. Once the tracheostomy tube is in place, the obturator is removed.

Orthopedics is the branch of medicine that aims to correct or prevent irregularities in bone and skeleton structure.

An **orthosis** is a mechanical appliance used to provide support or stability to a limb or joint.

An **ostomy** is a surgical procedure that creates an opening (stoma) in the gastrointestinal or urinary systems. It allows for the elimination of body wastes.

Otitis media is an inflammation of the middle ear (acute otitis media). Prolonged inflammation (chronic otitis media) can cause prolonged fluid accumulation in the middle ear, leading to scarring, ear damage or hearing loss.

An **otoscope** is an instrument used to visualize the ear canal and ear drum.

Paraplegia is paralysis of the lower part of the body and both legs.

Percussion is a technique used in respiratory therapy to loosen secretions from the lungs. It is done by clapping with cupped hands on the rib cage.

The **perineum** is the mass of skin and muscle located between the vagina and rectum in the female and between the meatus and rectum in the male.

Postural drainage involves putting a person in certain positions that use gravity to drain secretions from the lungs.

Pressure sores are the breakdown of skin caused by pressure from the body itself when it has remained immobile for an extended period of time.

A **prosthesis** is an artificial replacement for a missing body part.

Retractions are the sucking-in of the soft tissues in the chest that occur with breathing difficulty. These are first seen below the rib cage and in the soft part of the neck above the breast bone, as well as in the soft tissue over the collarbone.

Sensorineural hearing loss is a loss of function in the inner ear or the path from the ear to the brain. Causes include birth defects, drugs and prolonged exposure to noise.

Spasticity is increased tension of muscles causing stiff and awkward movements.

Sterile technique refers to procedures that destroy all disease-causing agents, such as bacteria, viruses and other micro-organisms. In contrast, clean technique reduces the number of these agents.

A **stoma** is an artificially created opening between two passages or between a passage and the body's surface.

Suctioning is a procedure done to loosen secretions that accumulate in the airway or in a tracheostomy tube. It consists of inserting a small catheter in the airway or tube. The catheter, in turn, is connected to a machine that helps drain the secretions.

Supportive sitting devices are used by people with physical disabilities that make sitting difficult.

Supportive standing devices are used by people with physical disabilities that make standing difficult. Examples include standers, parapodiums and crutchless standing orthoses.

Syntax is the way in which words are put together to form phrases and sentences.

Tactile deficit refers to any condition that interferes with the sense of touch. Examples are hyperesthesia (exaggerated sensitivity to touch), and hypoesthesia (reduced sensitivity to touch).

Trachea is another name for the windpipe, the passageway that carries air from the nose and mouth into the lungs.

A **tracheostomy** keeps a person breathing when a chronic health condition makes breathing through the nose, mouth and airway difficult. In this surgical procedure, an incision is made through the neck into the windpipe (trachea). A tube is then inserted into the incision.

A **tympanometer** is an instrument for testing ear drum mobility.

The **urethra** is a canal for discharge of urine, extending from the bladder to the outside of the body. (See meatus.)

A **urostomy** is a surgical procedure where the bladder is removed or bypassed and urine is directed to an external pouch.

Vibration is a technique used in respiratory therapy to help loosen secretions. It is done by firmly pressing your hands against the wall of another person's chest, then tensing your arms and shoulders to send fine vibrations through the chest.

Wheezing is the high-pitched whistling sound that occurs when air flows through narrowed bronchial tubes.

Index